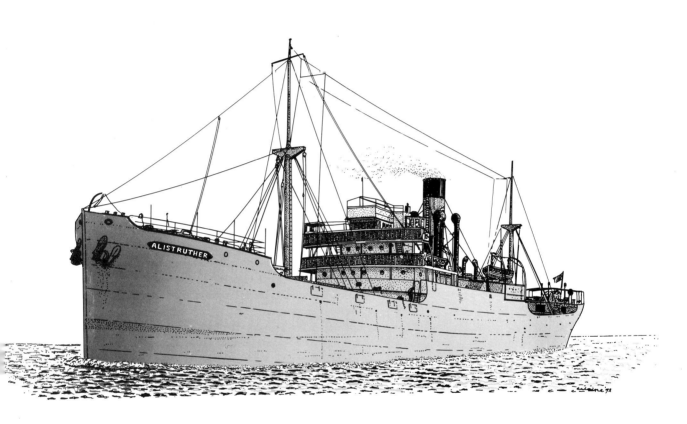

The single deck steamer *Alistruther* 3811/24 was owned by F. Carrick's Medomsley S.S. Co Ltd, Newcastle. She was built by Smith's Dock Co Ltd, Middlesbrough with the registered dimensions 350.0' x 50.5' x 24.5'.

ALSO IN THIS SERIES:

British Ocean Tramps, Volume 2. Owners & Their Ships.
by P.N. Thomas. ISBN 0 905184 14 9. 182 pages.
The second volume...*eagerly awaited by ship enthusiasts and modelmakers alike*...MODEL SHIPWRIGHT. Owners and crews. Histories of the major and minor owners, some 1,300 companies in all, including the early 19th century companies, with notes on some 2,400 ships and typical voyage patterns. A key to the characteristic naming patterns used by companies is included. Illustrated with 56 photos from the 1890s to the 1950s plus 22 colour profiles and 34 plans.

British Steam Tugs
by P.N. Thomas. ISBN 0 905184 07 6. 222 pages. 1997 Reprint
This book is beautifully produced and a must for anyone at all interested in these fascinating craft. MODEL BOATS. A full history covering early tugs, wood iron and steel paddle tugs; harbour, seeking and coastal screw tugs, and ocean tugs. Thames craft tugs, tenders and passenger carrying tugs, naval and wartime tugs. Tug owners and builders. Tug construction, engines and deck gear. Over 1000 steam tugs and 400 owners are covered. The tug plans range from 1833 to 1956 and 29 colour profiles will be of interest to modellers. More than 90 photographs (some colour), sketches, and colour diagram of 88 funnel colours.

Steam Coasters & Short Sea Traders   3rd Edition, 1994
by C.V. Waine & R.S. Fenton   ISBN 0 905184 15 7. 182 pages.
The history of the British steam coaster covering building, repairing, machinery, early designs. Clyde 'puffers' and the various engines-aft types, including the big east coast colliers. Also covered are those with engines amidships and coastal tankers. This new edition has a much expanded text with 25 extra pages concentrating on the smaller coasting shipowners, as those owners mainly in the coal trade are covered in the companion volume, **The Steam Collier Fleets**. Illustrated with 76 plans and 29 colour profiles, selected with the modelmaker in mind plus 97 black and white sketches and photos.

The Steam Collier Fleets.
by J.A. MacRae & C.V. Waine. ISBN 0 905 184 12 2. 226 pages. 1995 Reprint.
This book was begun by Captain Jim MacRae aboard the Thames up-river collier HACKNEY and with Dr. Charles Waine produced this companion volume to **Steam Coasters & Short Sea Traders**. *A book to delight the coaster enthusiast, model-maker or just about anyone who likes pictures of ships...The result must surely deserve the accolade of a definitive work, something which will be referred to time and again*...SEA BREEZES. A full history of the colliers and coasters in the coal trade of the British Isles and near Continent covering over 800 owners, 1200 ships and the harbours built to serve them, illustrated with 93 ship plans and coloured profiles, 55 photos, some in colour and 53 sketches, harbour maps and charts.

British Figurehead & Ship Carvers
by P.N. Thomas   ISBN 0 905184 16 5. 116 pages.
Books about figureheads and decorative work on ships usually state little is known about their carvers. Here Phil Thomas puts the record straight and after extensive research, writes about over 200 merchant ship carvers and around 60 master carvers who worked in the Naval Dockyards beginning around 1600 up to the 20th century. Illustrated with 75 photos, (some in colour and many not previously published), plus 47 drawings, some by the carvers themselves.

Old Time Steam Coasting
by O.G. Spargo & T.H. Thomason. ISBN 0 905184 05 X. 138 pages
An eye witness account of life in Liverpool steam coasters in the 1920s and 1930s. *Between them the authors have made a tremendous contribution to the field of both maritime and social history, for their sharp and detailed accounts provide us with a wealth of important information of the kind which is far too often omitted from shipping histories*...SHIPS MONTHLY. The operation of the coasting trade, vessels, crews and cargoes are fully described. Six colour plates, 5 plans and numerous sketches, photos and voyage charts.

Estuary & River Ferries of South West England.
by Martin Langley & Edwina Small. ISBN 0 905184 08 4. 148 pages.
The many creeks and rivers of the area had rowing and sailing ferries, which were later replaced by paddle and screw steamers or steam chain ferries in a number of cases. Full histories of some 139 ferries and over 300 boats are supported by sketch maps, plans (some in colour) and photographs from the River Severn in the north around the coast to the River Stour, Christchurch and Poole in the south.

For latest list and prices write to WAINE Research Publications, Mount Pleasant, Beamish Lane, Albrighton, Wolverhampton WV7 3JJ, ENGLAND.

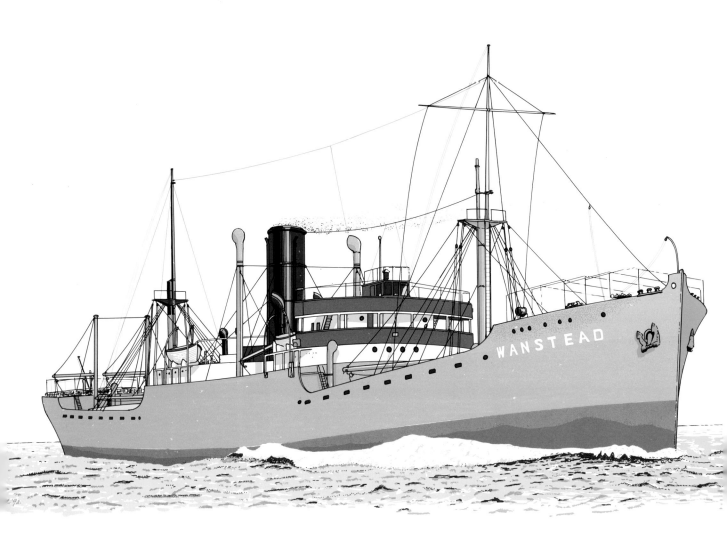

2. *Wanstead* of 5,423 gross was one of three sisters built in 1928 for the Britain S.S. Co Ltd (Watts, Watts & Co Ltd, managers), London by the Caledon Shipbuilding and Engineering Co Ltd, Dundee. They were single deckers designed for bulk cargo.

BRITISH OCEAN TRAMPS

Volume 1. Builders & Cargoes

P. N. THOMAS

3. Enfield 2124/97

Illustrated by C. V. Waine

  **WAINE** Research Publications

This book is dedicated to Dr. William Lind, T.D., LL.D., whose influence and exertions have helped preserve a great many valuable shipbuilding records.

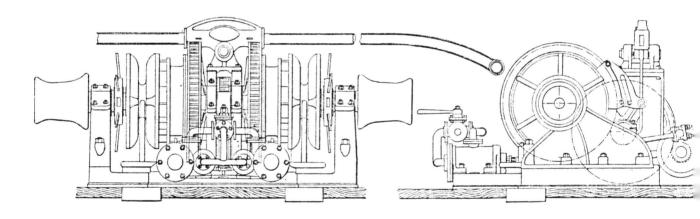

4. Emerson, Walker steam and hand anchor windlass of the 1880s.

By the same author: British Steam Tugs.

Published by:
Waine Research,
Mount Pleasant,
Beamish Lane,
Albrighton,
Wolverhampton
England WV7 3JJ.

First Published 1992
Reprinted 1998

ISBN 0 905184 13 0

Printed and bound in England.

CONTENTS

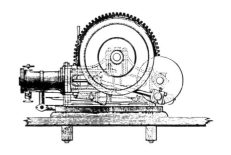

NOTES: Figure numbers indicated thus (5), correspond with page numbers. Ships' names are followed by gross tonnage and the last two digits of the year of build. The registered dimensions are given in feet and tenths. Other dimensions in feet and inches thus 4'9". All plans are from the original scale shipyard drawings unless otherwise stated.

5. Steam cargo winch by Taylor of Birkenhead used higher pressure steam available in vessels with compound engines, see page 151.

Engineering, 1882

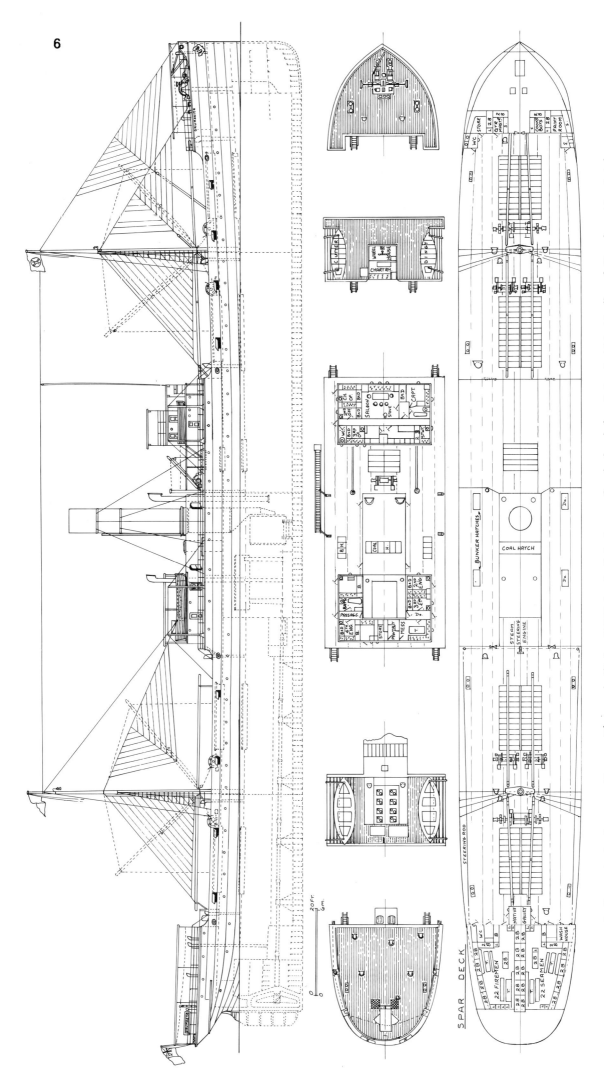

6. Spar deck steamer *Drumgeith* was built in 1905 by J. Priestman, Sunderland for R.A. & J.H. Mudie of Dundee. Her total cubic capacity including the spar and bridge decks was 288,875 cubic feet (bale). This included 12,065 in the br dge deck and 10,930 cubic feet if the peaks and forecastle were used. Three scotch boilers 14'3" diameter and 10' long supplied steam at 180 lbs pressure to a triple expansion engine with cylinders 25", 42" and 68" diameter with a stroke of 48" made by the

SPAR DECK

Foreword

7. Improved horizontal steam winch introduced by Robert Roger & Co, Stockton-on-Tees in the 1880s.

Turnbull's Shipping Register, 1884

When I was first asked in 1984 if I would tackle a book on tramp steamers I was doubtful if such a subject would provide much 'meat' for a book. However, always ready to accept a challenge, I made a start in the Reference Library. It soon became obvious that the steamers themselves were only part of the business of Tramp Shipping. The picture which emerged was one of a smallish number of ships and men whose existence provided employment for a vast worldwide network of other people in shipping offices, docks and harbours, not to mention the producers of the goods which they moved round the globe. The legal profession too, was glad of their existence as there was a continuous stream of lawsuits to settle; disputes over loss, damage, breach of contract and a host of other matters.

The ships themselves, on closer examination, proved not to be just the gaunt three island tramps of popular fancy. All the time the shipyards were working to improve vessels, cut building costs and increase deadweight carrying capacity against the register tonnage on which dues were charged. However, tramp steamer owners did tend to be conservative and the three island vessels remained the mainstay of most fleets.

The chapters in this book contain a number of graphs, tables and statistics because figures were the very essence of the industry, for everyone involved had to be aware of prices, costs and 'going rates' in order to provide reliable estimates before accepting contracts.

The tramp shipping industry was so complex that it proved impossible to cover in a single volume. Even so it has only been possible to cover each aspect in general terms. For any reader who wants to go into the subject more deeply a short bibliography is provided in Volume 2.

Acknowledgements

My thanks are due to the assistants in the libraries and archives who have so patiently assisted me in locating and copying material for this book and to the publishers and holders of records who have given me permission to reproduce plans and photographs:

Scottish Records Office
Glasgow University Archives
Strathclyde Regional Archives
Royal Statistical Society
The Transport Museum, Glasgow.
The Institution of Engineers and Shipbuilders in Scotland
Marine Publications International: ("Shipping World" and "The Shipbuilder")
"Shipbuilding and Shipping Record". (no longer in existence)
"Engineering"
H.M. Stationery Office
Lloyds Register of Shipping.
Dr. W. Lind

Last but not least my thanks are also due to David Burrell for reading the final manuscript, Ivor Rooke for additional photographs and finally to the young ladies in my place of work who have copied so much reference material for me.

P.N.Thomas,
Thornliebank, 1992

SINGLE-SCREW CARGO STEAMER "BANGALORE."

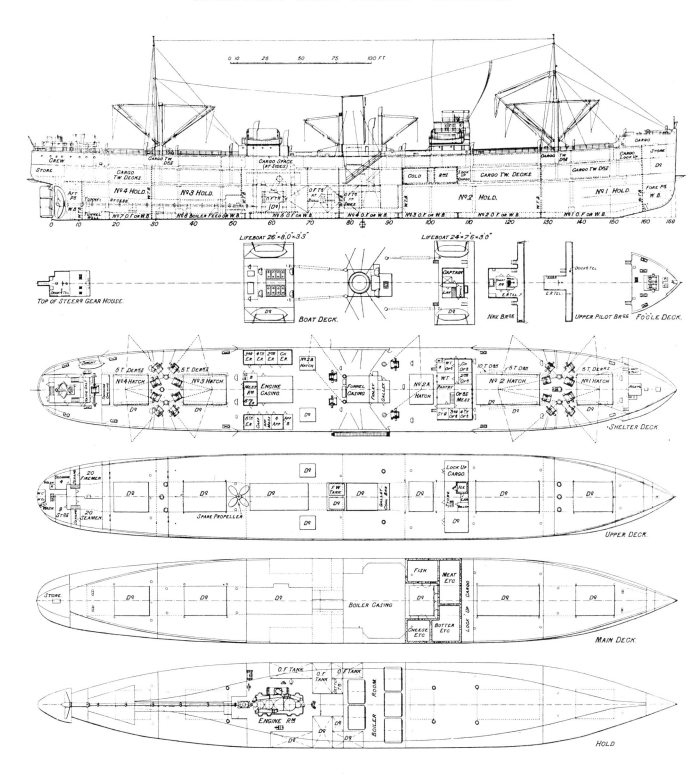

8. *Bangalore* 6067/28 was built for P. & O's liner services but owned and crewed by the Hain S.S. Co Ltd (part of the P. & O. group). Note that she has two decks and a shelter deck designed to stow small parcels of cargo requiring separation. Refrigeration machinery was also fitted to handle perishables. Machinery consisted of a quadruple expansion engine plus a low pressure exhaust turbine giving her more than three times the horsepower common in tramps.   Shipbuilding & Shipping Record, 1928

1.

9. Patent hand and steam steering gear manufactured by Bow, McLachlan & Co, Thistle Works Paisley.

Introduction

From Turnbulls' Shipping Register, 1884

To define the term 'Tramp Steamer' it is probably best to make clear what it was not. In maritime commerce there were three basic types of vessel:

1. The 'passenger liner' whose function was to transport large numbers of people, usually with space for a small quantity of cargo.

2. The 'liner trader' was a cargo vessel primarily, but often had cabins for a small number of passengers. They traded on scheduled routes and sailed at advertised times.

The liner trader was commonly used by shippers who were dealing in 'parcels', i.e. small quantities of goods each of which formed only part of the total cargo. To separate the 'parcels' many liner traders had one or more decks extending through the holds (8). The term general cargo was applied to this type of shipment. The liner trader was not subject to the whims of the market to the same extent as the tramp, as the freight charges were partly protected by Conferences which organised a regular service, limited competition, and set minimum rates. The first Conference was formed in 1875 between companies trading to Calcutta. This was followed quickly by Conferences on routes to China (1875), Australia (1884), South Africa (1895), West Africa (1895), North Brazil (1895), and the River Plate (1890).

3. The 'tramp steamer' was designed to carry bulk goods, i.e. each cargo consisted of only one type of material, the quantity generally being sufficient to load the vessel either to her load line or to her cubic capacity. The tramp steamer sailed only when the owner had obtained a cargo or, if necessary, she would sail in ballast to pick up a cargo at a distant port. Nevertheless the tramp steamer often did carry general cargo. The shipowner in the liner trade had to assess the trade routes carefully in deciding the size of his fleet. Too many ships and they sailed half empty if trade slackened. Too few ships and he could charter a suitable tramp steamer to fill the gap for a single voyage. Should a ship be damaged the liner operator could charter the tramp for as long as it took to replace the loss or to repair the casualty.

This reflected on to the tramp steamer owner who would keep his eye on both types of trade, bulk and general. This is where his problem arose; a steamer designed for a bulk cargo was not very suitable for general cargo, either from the stowage point of view or from the fact that in general cargoes there were often goods which had to be stowed separately from other items. If his vessel was designed for general cargo work the handling of bulk cargo was difficult and loading and unloading times were extended.

In choosing the type of steamer to order, the tramp steamer owner had to compromise as no design was entirely suitable for all the cargoes which she would be called on to carry. For her outward charter she would mainly be concerned with deadweight cargo; coal, iron, steel, phosphates, salt and other 'rough' merchandise. On the homeward run the variety would be greater, usually what was called 'produce', wheat and flour from Australia, beans and rice from the Philippines, grain, lumber and cotton from America, nitrate from Chile, grain and seed from the River Plate and the Black Sea. Her propelling machinery had to be completely reliable as the tramp steamer could be away from the United Kingdom for considerable periods, 12, 18 and 24 month time charters were not unusual, indeed the official agreement and crew list allowed for a voyage of up to three years before a new agreement was required.

Generally speaking the larger the steamer the lower the unit running costs per ton per mile carried, but consideration had to be taken of the ports that she would frequent. The River Plate had a bar which limited a vessel's draught to 22'6"; there were also bars at the mouth of the Danube and at the iron-ore port of Bilbao. Then there were the ports themselves which, unless they were modernised and enlarged to handle the ever increasing size of a vessel, placed a restriction on size. The cargo itself could impose limits; it was no use sending a 7,000 dwt. steamer for cargoes of which only small quantities were being ordered. True, several 'parcels' could be taken if they offered at the same time but this created difficulties of separation for which the open hold tramp was not designed. Some cargoes limited the height to which they could be stacked before damage could occur from the pressure above; sugar, rice and case oil were three which fell into this category. The choice was up to the individual owner. Some went for the smaller handy-sized single decker aimed at the smaller ports and the small quantities, while others took the 'tween-decker' with their sights on time charter to the liner trades, while the owners of large fleets maintained a variety of types and sizes in their fleets.

Owners in different ports had their own ideas as to which type suited them best, and a survey of 3 of the larger fleets shows this for the years 1904, 1921 and 1939:

Evan Thomas, Radcliffe & Co, Cardiff.

Year	Type of Vessel	Age Range	Gross Tonnage Range
1904	6 well-deck	1882–1890	1,058–3,847
	13 three island	1882–1902	1,208–4,074
	2 trunk deck	1897–1898	3,903–4,064
	2 part awning deck	1893–1894	2,866–2,894
1921	9 three island	1897–1915	2,728–6,079
1939	11 flush deck with well-deck aft	1915–1928	4,674–5,754
	4 shelter deck	1929–1937	4,835–5,053

Hugh Hogarth & Sons, Ardrossan

1904	5 sail		
	10 two deck steamers	1892–1903	1,398–4,236
1921	7 three island	1903–1919	1,860–2,508
	1 two deck steamer	1910	1,597
	2 shelter deck	1912–1917	4,418–7,005
	8 three island, two deck	1905–1917	4,319–5,868
1939	26 three island	1924–1933	3,081–3,942
	2 flush, single deck	1927	3,404
	12 two deck	1915–1939	3,061–7,005

Sir R. Ropner & Co Ltd, West Hartlepool

1904	10 well-deck	1888–1901	1,630–2,826
	10 three island	1896–1903	2,639–3,968
	15 part spar deck	1891–1900	1,947–3,703
	5 trunk deck	1896–1904	2,635–4,409
1921	13 three island	1903–1918	3,276–5,552
	4 part awning deck	1894–1896	2,104–2,606
	6 trunk deck	1898–1907	3,089–4,625
1939	41 three island	1909–1937	3,683–5,692
	4 two deck steamers	1929–1936	4,640–4,992

The *Drumgeith* shows the type of tramp common in the fleets at the turn of the century (6). Externally she is the same type of vessel as *Maplegrove* (12), apart from the fact that she has a 'spar deck', there is little difference in her appearance. The drawing is based on the rigging plan and a simple general arrangement drawing used as part of a "capacity plan". The bunkers of *Drumgeith* were 552 tons (allowing 44 cu.ft. per ton) which would limit her range without bunkering to around 5,000 miles, equivalent to the Mediterranean or Canada. Most of the bunker capacity was in the bridge and spar deck on either side of the machinery space. She was built in 1905 by J. Priestman of Sunderland with the registered dimensions 355' x 48' x 17.7', 3,883 grt. for R.A. & J.H. Mudie of Dundee. As with many tramp steamers she changed hands many times, becoming T.& J. Brocklebank's *Matra* in 1915, J. Ridley, Sons & Tully's *Newton Hall* in 1921, passing to the Byron S.S. Co Ltd, London during 1927 as *Maid of Lemnos* and then moved East to become Moller's *Therese Moller* in 1931. Now owned in Shanghai she became the Chinese owned *Chi Hing* in 1946 and *Tien Ping* two years later before being broken up in 1954. She was capable of 12½ kts, which was good for a tramp and in her 'tween decks she could carry a large number of cattle.

TRAMPING

Tramping as such existed in the days of the sailing ship, where, once the vessel had left this country, the captain was on his own with the responsibility for arranging a return cargo after he had unloaded. Some trades did exist where a fairly settled routine eased his burden, coal to Chile, nitrate or guano home. Coal to Australia, wool or grain home. On routes where general cargo and passengers were the order of the day steamers quickly displaced the sailing ship for here customers demanded fast passages. As long as bulk goods were moved cheaply the time spent on the way, in the early days, was of no great importance. Sail gave way to steam as operating costs fell and merchants found higher costs of steam were offset by the need to hold lower stocks of goods as deliveries were now regular and capital was not tied up for long periods financing cargoes in transit, as could happen with sailing vessels.

Some authors quote the opening of the Suez Canal in 1869 as being the event which started the growth of the steam tramp fleets, though the growth for the next ten years was largely in the Black Sea, Mediterranean, Baltic and Bay trades. To be successful the tramp owner needed more than a shortened route to the Far East. If a sailing ship failed to find a cargo on arrival at a foreign port some delay was acceptable as running costs for sail were fairly low. With a higher initial cost and higher running costs the steamer had to find a cargo quickly. The laying of the trans-ocean telegraph cables revolutionised the trading patterns. Now brokers could do business by cable, fixing return cargoes for steamers while they were still on the high seas. To operate the system, a network of reliable local agents was essential. The other requirement was efficient steam machinery. The early steamers with their single cylinder engine and low pressure boiler suffered from high coal consumption which limited their range and their competitiveness. Only the fliers carrying passengers and mails could afford to coal at intervals along their route. John Elder of Glasgow is credited with the introduction of the compound engine with its higher working pressure in the mid-1850s. The consumption of coal was halved, dropping from around 6 lb. per IHP/hour to around 3 lb. This reduced the running costs and meant that more volume was available for cargo on short voyages or double the mileage could be covered for a given bunker capacity. In 1881 *Aberdeen* was launched by Napier's in Glasgow, the first steamer with a commercially viable triple expansion engine. From that time on the sailing ship was pushed out of the major ocean trade routes. By 1900, with improvements in engines and in hull design steamers benefited in a reduction in coal consumption from 10 lb. per ton of cargo per 100 miles to a figure of 4 lbs.

A further aspect was that of cargo; without cargo there was no raison d'etre for the tramp steamer and fleets could only expand as fast as markets became available. As the countries of the world built railways and created industries, the demand for coal grew. As steam shipping increased in volume the demand for bunkers rose. As the population of Europe increased the demand for grain soared and so it went on until, as far as the British tramp shipping was concerned, the carrying trade reached its climax in 1913.

A study of imports of grain and iron ore and exports of coal, indicates an acceleration in demand for these commodities during 1870s, and it would be reasonable to say that these years marked the turning point for the British tramp shipping industry and the expansion of fleets and carrying power began (14). The graph of the number of steamers

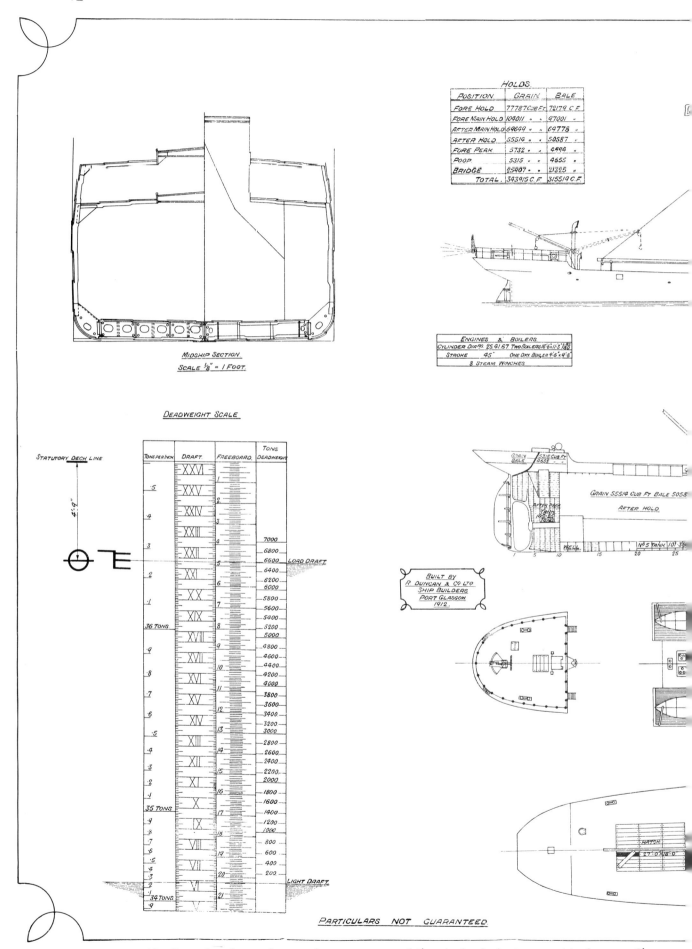

MIDSHIP SECTION
SCALE ⅛" = I FOOT.

HOLDS.		
POSITION	GRAIN	BALE
FORE HOLD	77787 CUB FT	72179 C.F.
FORE MAIN HOLD	104011 "	97001 "
AFTER MAIN HOLD	69699 "	69778 "
AFTER HOLD	55514 "	50587 "
FORE PEAK	5732 "	4994 "
POOP.	5315 "	4655 "
BRIDGE	25407 "	21325 "
TOTAL.	343915 C.F.	315519 C.F.

ENGINES & BOILERS.	
CYLINDER DIARS. 25.41.67	Two Boilers 16.6·11·3
STROKE 45"	ONE DRY BOILER 9·6"×9·6
8 STEAM WINCHES.	

DEADWEIGHT SCALE

STATUTORY DECK LINE
4'·9"

TONS PER INCH	DRAFT	FREEBOARD.	TONS DEADWEIGHT.
·5	XXVI	1	
	XXV	2.	
·4	XXIV	3	
·3	XXIII	4	7000
	XXII	5	6800 / 6600 LOAD DRAFT
·2	XXI	6	6400 / 6200 / 6000
·1	XX	7	5800 / 5600 / 5400
36 TONS	XIX	8	5200 / 5000
·9	XVIII	9	4800 / 4600 / 4400
·8	XVII	10	4200 / 4000
·7	XVI	11	3800 / 3600
·6	XV	12	3400 / 3200 / 3000
·5	XIV	13	2800
·4	XIII	14	2600 / 2400
·3	XII	15	2200 / 2000
·2	XI	16	1800 / 1600
·1			1400
35 TONS	X	17	1200 / 1000
·9	IX	18	
·8			800
·7	VIII	19	600 / 400
·6	VII	20	200
·5			
·4			
·3	VI		LIGHT DRAFT
·2		21	
·1 / 34 TONS	V		
·9			

GRAIN / BALE 5315 CUB FT / 4655 "

GRAIN 55514 CUB FT BALE 5058
AFTER HOLD
AFTER PEAK WELL

No 5 TANK (10) 3
1 5 10 15 20 25

BUILT BY
R. DUNCAN & CO LTD
SHIP BUILDERS
PORT GLASGOW
1912.

HATCH
27·0"×18·0"

12. Capacity plan and general arrangement of the single deck steamer *Maplegrove*. She had been built in 1912 by R. Duncan & Co Ltd, Port Glasgow for W.S. Miller of

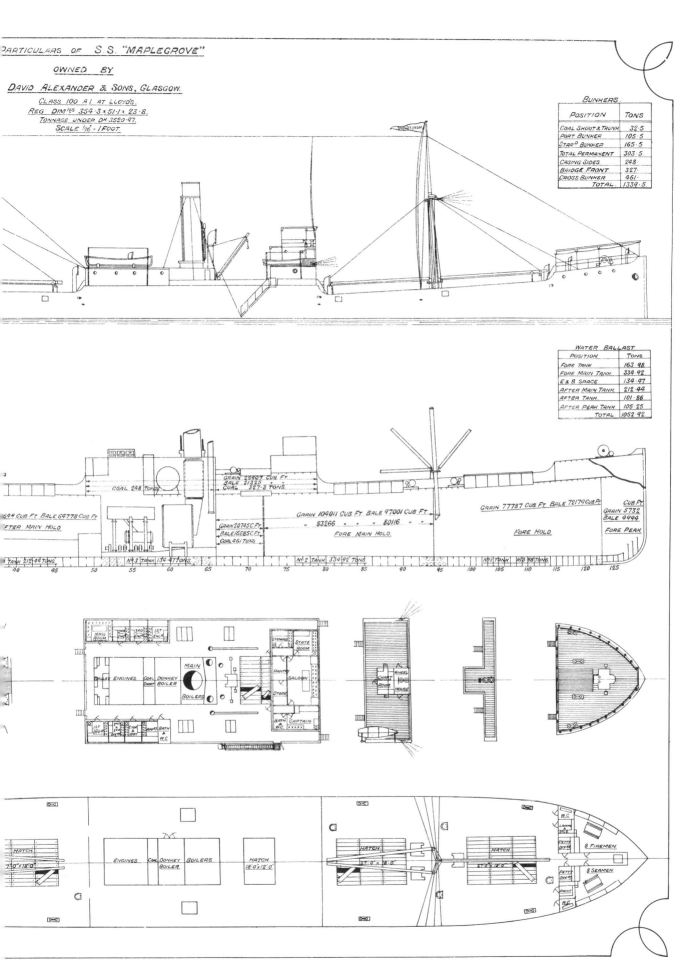

PARTICULARS OF S.S. "MAPLEGROVE"

OWNED BY

DAVID ALEXANDER & SONS, GLASGOW.

CLASS 100 A I AT LLOYD'S.
REG DIM⁹ᴿ 354·3 × 51·1 × 23·8.
TONNAGE UNDER DK 3520·97.
SCALE ¹⁄₁₆ = 1 FOOT.

BUNKERS.	
POSITION	TONS
COAL SHOOT & TRUNK	32·5
PORT BUNKER	105·5
STARᴰ BUNKER	165·5
TOTAL PERMANENT	303·5
CASING SIDES	248·
BRIDGE FRONT	327·
CROSS BUNKER	461·
TOTAL	1339·5

WATER BALLAST	
POSITION	TONS
FORE TANK	163·98
FORE MAIN TANK	334·92
E & B SPACE	134·97
AFTER MAIN TANK	212·44
AFTER TANK	101·86
AFTER PEAK TANK	105·25
TOTAL	1052·92

Glasgow as *Iriston*, eventually passing to D. Alexander of Glasgow in 1924 who renamed her *Maplegrove*.

P.N.Thomas

in service shows a similar upward trend in the same period.

Plenty of official statistics are available regarding Britain's merchant marine but when the researcher comes to study them, he finds many can be of doubtful value. Often the basic elements change every few years, usually the picture is an overall one even when a specific subject is being studied. However, one survey did give some idea of the growth of the steamship trade, and, literally, in which direction. In the table were listed the numbers and total tonnages of steamers arriving in British ports from overseas, broken down into the countries from which they were carrying goods. The original table has been condensed into areas rather than countries and gives average net tonnage rather than totals:

	1854		1870	
Arriving from	No. of steamers	Average net tonnage	No. of steamers	Average net tonnage
Holland/France	2,754	238	6,575	279
Norway/Germany	722	357	1,206	475
Baltic	83	352	1,211	615
Spain/Portugal	66	337	526	428
Mid. Mediterranean	77	402	294	722
Eastern Med/Black Sea	96	765	377	988
West Coast Africa	3	304	69	862
USA/Canada	124	1,166	656	1,545
East Coast S.America	24	958	98	959
Far East	14	1,129	101	1,037
West Coast S.America	0	0	14	1,706

The above figures cover all steamers including tramps, but bearing in mind that in 1870 the average net tonnage of the tramp steamer was estimated to be 600 tons it is apparent that on some routes many steamers were passenger liners and liner traders.

From the above we can deduce general trends:

1)   On routes which were exensively used for passenger trade the average tonnage of steamers increased but little, e.g. U.S.A./Canada and Far East.

2)   Steamers were pushing into the domain of the sailing ship in the Baltic, Spain/Portugal and the Black Sea, and the steamers in these trades had increased in size by around 50%

14. Below: Graphs showing the export of coal and imports of grain and iron-ore.

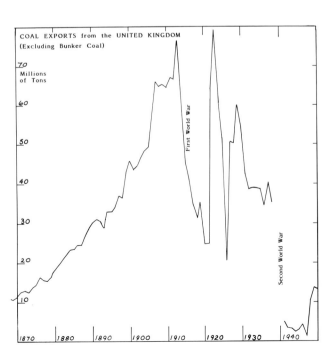

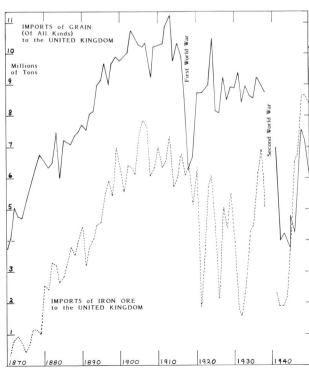

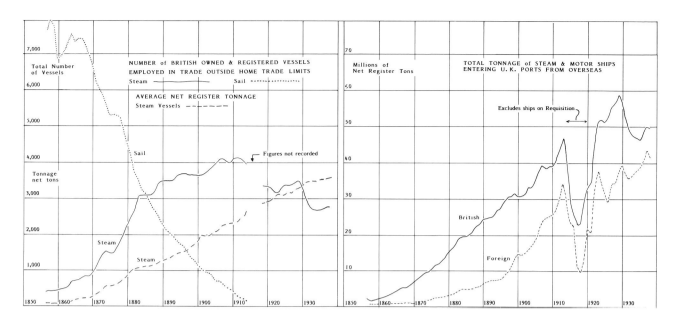

15. Left: Graph showing the number and size of British foreign–going steamers.
Right: Graph of the total tonnage of ships entering U.K. ports from overseas.

Another statistical table broke the number of steamers in the British merchant fleet into those trading regularly in the home trades, the home trades and foreign and those engaged solely in deep sea carrying. The figures in the last group have been plotted in the form of a graph from 1856 to 1938 which shows the rapid growth in numbers and total tonnage of the British foreign–going steamers which levelled off after the first world war, (15). Shown also are the numbers of sailing ships in the same trade and how they declined dramatically. Another figure which levels off is average net tonnage.

What the graph does not show is that after world war one, while the total net tonnage of the British merchant marine levelled off, the total tonnage of the world's fleet continued to rise. This is shown clearly by the following:

Year:	1901	1914	1925	1939	1950	1955	1960
Percentage of world tonnage under British flag:	45	39	32	26	26	19	16

While the liner traders had the Conferences to protect them the tramp steamer owner was subject to the fluctuations of the market created in the atmosphere of the policy of free trade. On the other hand the British tramp steamer owner received no bounties, subsidies, or preferential tariffs and faced discrimination on all sides, whereas owners in other countries received some or all of these. The U.S.A. for years operated a 50–50 rule which ensured that 50% of certain cargoes exported from the U.S.A. were carried on U.S. bottoms although shippers had to pay freights as much as 2½ times that offered by 'foreign' vessels. Not only that, but U.S. coastal trade was restricted to nationally owned vessels. As the trade barriers went up all round the world, politicians and some shipowners resisted change and insisted in sticking to the principle of 'free trade'. In 1934 a long list was published of all countries which protected their national shipping (40 names) and a very short list of those who supported free trade (12 names). With these latter Britain carried on little business.

As the various colonial territories achieved independence one of their first actions was to create national shipping fleets and to pass laws restricting trade to the nationally owned ships. Even if the restriction was only in the coastal trade the cumulative effect on British shipping was severe. After all, before the second world war nearly 25% of the receipts from shipping came from cross-trading, i.e. voyages outside the U.K.

It is common today to complain about 'flags of convenience' but this is not a new problem. As early as 1875 the nautical press reported "Many British owners are trans-ferring to foreign flags because of the safety regulations which foreigners do not have to observe. It is estimated that since January 1873 nearly 900 ships have been reregistered under foreign flags."

Over the years the trading pattern of the tramp steamer changed. During the early days owners could rely on finding cargoes both out and home but gradually they found themselves compelled to send vessels on ballast voyages to find profitable cargo. As other nations became industrialised they reserved more raw material for their own use and new sources had to be found. The most obvious example was metallic ores which had come from Norway, Spain and North Africa and now had to be brought from the Gold Coast, India and Australia. With more time spent on the high seas, more ship capacity was required to move the same quantities of material. Before 1939 a tramp steamer might spend 25% of her time at sea, but after 1945 this percentage rose to around 33%.

TONNAGE

To the layman 'tonnage' is a confusing term because it is prefixed by numerous words such as 'gross' or gross registered tons (grt.), 'net' or nett registered tons (nrt.), 'under-deck' and others. It should first be understood that the 'tonnage' often referred to is actually a volume equal to 100 cubic feet per ton. This practice goes back over 500 years to a time when a 'tun' (barrel) of wine was standardised to hold 252 gallons of wine (old measure), the 'tun' occupying approximately 100 cubic feet, which figure has been traditionally used for centuries.

Under-deck tonnage

This is a measure taken below the TONNAGE DECK, i.e. the uppermost deck in single and two decked vessels and in the case of other vessels up to the second continuous deck. Where the vessel has a double bottom for water ballast this is excluded from the measurement. The calculation is quite a complicated one; the length of the tonnage deck is divided into equal parts: 120 to 180 feet (eight parts), 180 to 225 feet (ten parts), 225 feet upwards (twelve parts). The area of each section is computed from the depth and breadth inside the vessel, taking into account any curvature or sudden change of breadth. The length and the various areas are used in Simpson's Rule and the internal volume of the hull is obtained.

'Tween Deck Tonnage

Where a vessel has three or more continuous decks, this represents the volume of the additional enclosed space.

Gross Tonnage

This is the sum of under-deck tonnage, 'tween deck tonnage and various permanently enclosed spaces on the upper deck including in some cases forecastles, bridge and poop. There are a number of enclosed spaces which are exempted from the gross tonnage calculations, spaces such as winch houses and wheelhouses. In the latter case they were exempt so that owners were not discouraged from fitting them to the detriment of the crew. Gross tonnage gives some idea of the size of a steamship, but it is not much good to the shipper. He wants to know how much the vessel will carry.

Net Tonnage

The approximate volumetric carrying capacity is shown by the Register or Net Tonnage. From the gross tonnage is deducted all the spaces not suitable for cargo carrying, spaces such as engine room, boiler room, shaft tunnel, crew space, store rooms, and some of the water tanks.

Deadweight Tonnage

In fact very few cargoes weigh one ton per 100 cubic feet and so another figure has to be available to give an accurate representation of the vessel's carrying capacity. The deadweight tonnage is the weight of cargo, stores, fuel, water ballast etc. which will take the vessel from its light draught to its loaded draught. Among the drawings provided by the shipbuilder is a deadweight scale which shows how the draught will increase as the steamer is loaded (17). The deadweight capacity has been shown in Lloyd's Register since the 1920s.

Displacement Tonnage

This is another tonnage figure, but it is not used for merchant steamers being the common figure quoted for naval vessels. It is the actual physical weight of the vessel when floating at its normal waterline. Although restricted to naval vessels, it is usual for a shipbuilder to include a displacement scale among his drawings.

This is only the start of the tonnage question, since charges were usually levied on the net register tonnage figure. There was a constant battle between the ship designer and the bodies who were making the charges, so the people concerned with running shipping businesses had their tax avoidance methods. The commonest was the use of *'tonnage openings'*. If an opening could be provided leading into an otherwise enclosed

17

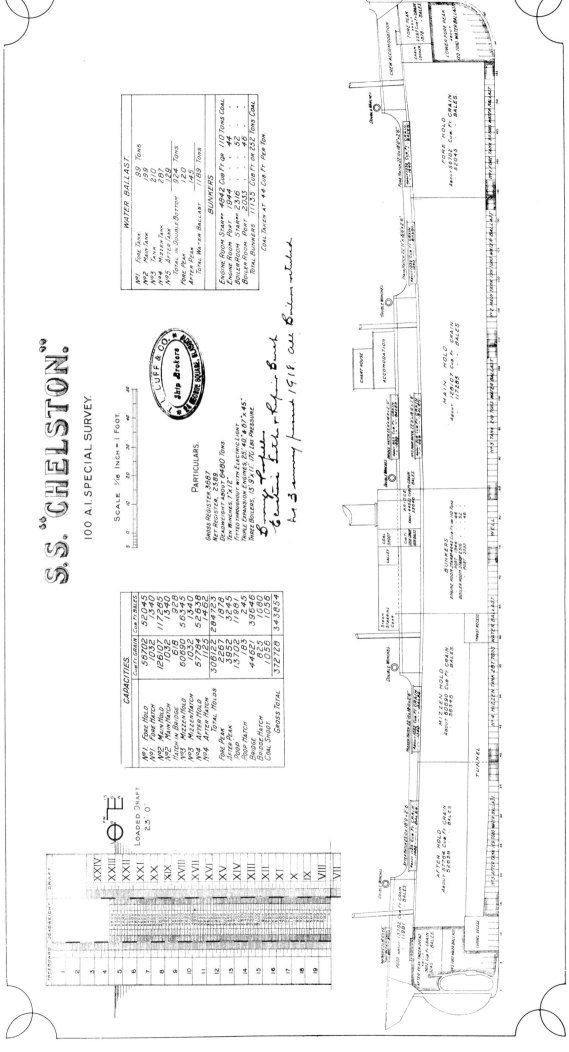

17. Capacity plan of the *Chelston* built in 1904 by A. Roger & Co, Port Glasgow (347.4' x 51.0' x 24.2') for the Chelston S.S. Co, (T.L. Duff & Co, managers), Glasgow.

P.N.Thomas

space, provided that certain strict rules were observed, then that space would be excluded from the tonnage calculations. The basic rule was that no permanent watertight cover could be fitted. The danger was that as soon as the tonnage opening was approved, the owner erected temporary covers over it so that additional cargo could be carried, and these temporary covers might not withstand heavy seas. As a precaution the cargo carried below a tonnage opening was usually of a nature not affected by seawater and freeing ports were fitted to drain away any water entering.

Two other tonnage figures crop up; Suez Canal and Panama Canal Tonnages. The transit dues on the Suez Canal and the Panama Canal were calculated on the net tonnage, but the basis for the calculation differed from that of Lloyd's Register, in both cases being higher. Just before the first world war the Suez Canal authorities changed their method of calculation, reducing the difference. The following are some typical figures.

Nonsuch, 1906. (turret), Bowles Bros,
                          London (42).

Gross	3,826
Net	2,443
Under-deck	3,133
Suez	2,701+10.6% above net

Needles, 1908. Clyde Shipping Co, Glasgow

Gross	4,697
Net	2,996
Suez	3,500+16.9% above net

Empire Mordred, 1942. Min. of Transport

Gross	7,024 London, (98).
Net	4,928
Under-deck	6,571
Suez	5,195+5.4% above net
Panama	4,968+0.8%

Huntsclyde, 1904. Shipping Controller,
                          London.

Gross	2,736
Net	2,000.56
Suez	+4.7% (Calculated 1919)

Hurst, 1910. Clyde Shipping Co, Glasgow

Gross	4,718
Net	2,998
Suez	3,770+25.8% above net

Homer City, 1914. W.Reardon Smith,

Gross	4,533 Cardiff. (see Vol.2).
Net	3,051
Suez	4,030+32%
Panama	3,949+29.4%

There was one point on which the Suez Canal Authorities were very strict; as long as

18. Histograms showing size and age distribution in British tramp fleets.

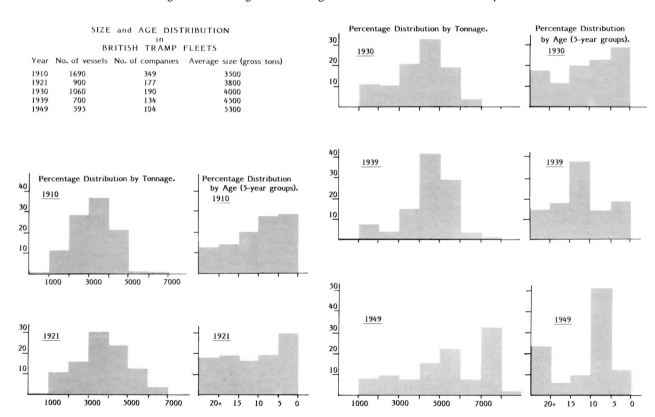

no cargo was carried in a space adjacent to a tonnage opening, that space would be excluded from their calculation, but should the vessel even once carry cargo in that space, that space would be included from then on, whether carrying cargo or not. The above list shows the advantage gained by the turret steamer with an increase above register tonnage for the Suez Canal of only 10.6% against 16.9% and up to 32% for some of the other vessels.

Shipping Ton

The 'Shipping Ton' was set out as 40 cubic feet. Where a cargo occupied 40 cubic feet or over per ton it was termed a 'measurement cargo' as its volume determined what could be stowed. Where it was below 40 cubic feet per ton it was termed a 'deadweight cargo' as its weight decided just how much could be carried. All cargoes had a 'stowage factor' which was a figure expressing how many cubic feet could be stowed per ton weight of the substance. For instance cork had a stowage factor of 300 to 420 depending how it was baled (a measurement cargo), while pig iron would stow at 10 to 12 cubic feet per ton (a deadweight cargo).

To assist the shipper it was customary to issue a capacity plan of the steamer which showed the distribution of the carrying spaces: sometimes it appeared as though every nook and cranny was filled, especially if grain was to be the cargo. In the *Nonsuch* the grain capacity was quoted as 347,330 cubic feet, and the bale capacity as 327,830 cubic feet (less because of the loss of space with frames, stringers etc.) which prevented bales from being stowed in 100% of the available space (42). Usually a much simpler plan was submitted as for example that of *Chelston* (17). In the absence of a capacity plan the shipper had to fall back on the rule of thumb 1:1.6:2.4. This was the approximate ratios of gross to net and deadweight to net tonnage. It varied from ship to ship but on the whole it was not too far out.

Name	Built	Net	Gross	Ratio	Dwt.	Ratio
NETO	1882	1,073	1,696	1.58	2,280	2.12
SAMARA	1889	1,053	1,623	1.54	2,585	2.45
PERSIS (Vol.2)	1890	1,203	1,850	1.54	3,004	2.50
TURRET (33)	1892	1,265	1,970	1.56	3,200	2.53
CHELSTON (17)	1904	2,389	3,687	1.54	6,480	2.74
USSA	1917	1,077	2,066	1.92	3,700	3.44
WAR CREEK (59)	1919	1,885	3,080	1.63	5,050	2.73
WAR RAMPART	1919	3,570	5,666	1.59	8,900	2.49
BRYNMOR (96)	1922	1,545	2,582	1.67	4,175	2.70
ESKDENE (Vol.2)	1935	2,281	3,829	1.68	6,680	2.93
Liberty Ship	1942	4,380	7,176	1.64	10,865	2.48
EMPIRE MIGHT	1942	4,990	9,184	1.84	10,145	2.03

It is said that a picture is worth a thousand words. With this in mind the following histograms were prepared out of a curiosity to see what changes occurred in the tramp shipping world regarding age and tonnage. The figures for 1949 were available from official sources and the others were taken from Lloyd's Register's owners lists. The investigation finished up with five graphs because as each one was drawn it seemed that something was affecting the shape, particularly wars and depressions (18):

Age

1910: There is a common idea that the tramp steamers were always old and battered. The first histogram shows that, on the contrary, the tramp fleets were generally kept up-to-date; 29% were less than five years old and only 12% were more than 20 years old. This was the general trend until the 1930s.

1921: The second histogram shows the effect of the first world war where the losses which had hit the tramp fleets were replaced from the intensive wartime building programme.

1930: Despite the ups and downs of the 1920s the tramp fleets were still being modernised though the number of vessels over 20 years old was up to 18%.

1939: During the slump of the 1930s shipbuilding was badly hit and relatively few new ships were built, but the size had continued to increase.

1949: Here again the tramp fleets were reduced by wartime losses and replaced from the wartime shipbuilding programme. The shortage of tonnage meant that older vessels were kept in service so that 22% were more than 20 years old and also reflected the surge in new building which had occurred. After the war shipbuilding was affected by the flood of Liberties, Empires, Forts, Parks and other types which came on the market.

Size

The diagrams show how the size of tramp steamers (and motor ships) increased. Each histogram shows what mathematicians call a normal distribution except for the last one.

In the 1949 figures it is surprising how flat the distribution is, apart from the peaks at 5,000 to 6,000 tons, and 7,000 to 8,000 tons. The 5,000 to 6,000 tons represents the gradual increase in size seen in earlier normal distributions while the peak at 7,000 to 8,000 tons represents the Liberty which was a similar size, but a closed shelter decker, and other similar war built ships which were mostly a little over 7,000 tons gross.

Another point which emerged from the investigation was that British tramp steamers were not numbered in thousands, the totals dropping from about 1700 in 1910 to about 600 by 1949. Secondly the distribution of the ships changed little between these years and 70% of the fleets consisted of 5 ships or less.

Statistics regarding British shipping had been published since the middle of the last century but they had always been very general in nature. The theme seems to have been to boost the British ego by dwelling on total figures and, when dealing with tonnage of ships entering British ports to include everything which floated. The problem of total figures was illustrated in 1916/17 when arrivals and sailings at ports was a total figure, i.e. anything that moved. The large numbers were used as a reason for the impossibility of convoying ships. It was only after the figures were broken down and 'true' deep sea figures extracted, that the possibility of convoys became evident. It was not until 1935 that any really serious effort was made to study the tramp shipping industry of Great Britain. During that year special record cards were sent to all shipowners and on them they were requested to note a whole series of details of voyages, cargo, freight costs, port of departure and port of termination of the voyage. From the mass of figures supplied, the author, Dr. L. Isserlis, was able to prepare a paper which was read before the Royal Statistical Society on 21st December 1937 which gave a clearer picture of tramp steamer activity than had previously been possible. One of the main tables of statistics provided in the paper was one which detailed the cargoes carried during the year, the volume of goods and the number of steamers involved. Using this as a basis the following table has been prepared but the results have been interpreted in a slightly different fashion, less emphasis being placed on the financial aspect.

Some interesting facts may be gleaned from the table opposite:

1. Nearly two-thirds of the tramp steamers were employed in carrying coal and grain.
2. The average of the cargoes in the first group is 6,960 tons (approx. 4,640 grt.), which suggests that most of the tramp steamers were of a fair size.
3. The average of the second group is 1,695 tons, but the spread of average cargo sizes is from 511 to 3,594 tons, which indicates a wide variation in the size of vessels employed. (This ignores the figure of 180 tons for paper, which is extremely low.)
4. The number of tramps carrying general cargo is surprisingly low, considering the amount of chartering usually done by the liner trades.

CARGOES CARRIED BY TRAMPS in 1935.

Based on information gathered by Dr. L. Isserlis and published by the Royal Statistical Society in 1937.

Cargo	Vessels of 3,000 gross registered tons and over.					Vessels of less than 3,000 gross registered tons.				
	No. of cargoes	Percentage of total cargoes	Total weight of cargo	Percentage of total	Average tons per cargo	No. of cargoes	Percentage of total cargoes	Total weight of cargo	Percentage of total	Average tons per cargo
Coal & Coke	1873	38.9	12,590,477	37.6	6720	4299	61.8	8,013,955	68.0	1864
Grain	1200	24.9	8,977,951	26.8	7481	416	6.0	301,056	2.6	723
Grain & Timber*	105	2.2	892,500	2.7	8500					
Timber	196	4.1	1,346,533	4.0	6870	377	5.4	1,120,271	9.5	2971
Timber & other	19	0.4	110,484	0.3	5815					
Ore	398	8.3	2,829,055	8.4	7108	323	4.6	839,482	7.1	2600
Sulphur & Zinc concentrates	7	0.1	44,100	0.1	6300					
Fertilizer	207	4.3	1,533,419	4.6	7408	227	3.3	287,290	2.4	1266
Sugar	204	4.2	1,424,969	4.3	6985	18	0.3	9,198	0.8	511
Scrap metal	99	2.1	748,272	2.2	7558	262	3.8	212,666	1.8	812
Salt	86	1.8	695,740	2.1	8090					
Paper	30	0.6	140,455	0.4	4682	5	0.1	900		180
Strawboard						40	0.6	32,000	0.3	800
Esparto grass	7	0.1	16,555		2365	87	1.3	148,248	1.3	1704
Bauxite	17	0.3	88,672	0.3	5216	18	0.3	64,692	0.5	3594
Sand and cement						299	4.3	218,270	1.8	730
China clay	10	0.2	48,390	0.1	4839	55	0.8	29,700	0.3	540
Pitch & asphalt						144	2.1	169,200	1.4	1175
Cork						16	0.2	12,768	0.1	798
W. African produce	40	0.8	245,120	0.7	6128					
General & mixed	314	6.5	1,759,206	5.3	5603	368	5.3	330,488	2.8	898
Ballast voyages	114					7				
Average (tons per cargo)					6960					1695

*Shipments from British Columbia

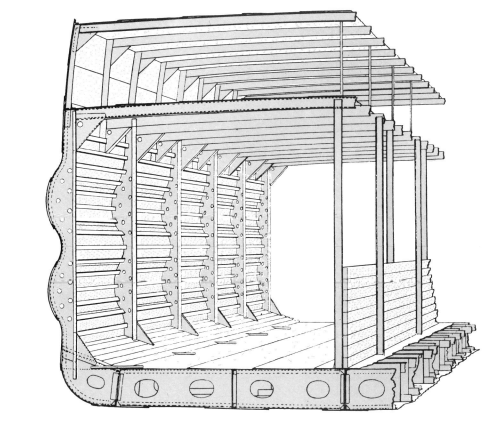

2.

22. Perspective section of the left-hand side of the hold of a Monitor corrugated ship showing the corrugated side plates and special framing needed. Note the staggered arrangement of the centre-line pillars (right), arranged so that shifting boards can be slotted into them to form a wooden centre-line bulkhead when carrying loose cargoes such as grain.

Design & Construction

The wooden cargo carrying sailing ship of around 200 feet in length was massively built with wooden frames spaced apart by the width of the frames themselves, covered outside with thick wooden planks and lined inside with planking only slightly thinner. Frequently a thicker plank or two was worked in for additional strength. When iron construction was included in Lloyd's rules in 1855, the frame spacing and the distribution of material was influenced by wooden shipbuilding practice. In 1863, as the result of experience with iron, the rules were revised, and were further revised in 1870, each time reducing weight of sections and allowing wider spacing of frames, to take advantage of the stronger material. By this time steel was already being used for ship construction but it was not until 1877 that rules were formulated to cover the reduced scantlings which this stronger material allowed. Thus the weight of metal in a ship of a given size was progressively reduced. Iron construction reached its peak in 1883, though in 1899 iron steamers were still being built:

Steamships built and registered in the United Kingdom - nett tons

	Number of Ships		Average size-Nett tons	
	Steel	*Iron*	*Steel*	*Iron*
1860	–	149	–	343
1870	–	382	–	583
1880	26	362	1,519	1,235
1883	92	548	1,539	1,355
1890	432	110	1,891	365
1899	534	64	2,159	190

From Transactions of the Institution of Naval Architects, (1900)

After 1883 iron was used only for the construction of small vessels such as tugs and trawlers.

In the construction of a ship's hull account had to be taken of the stresses to which the structure would be subjected during its normal working and also under the extreme conditions due to storm, stranding or even careless loading. When supported at bow and

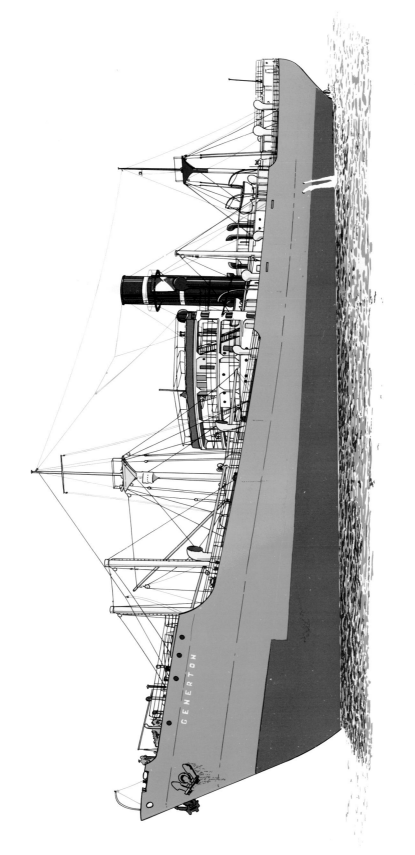

23. Shelter deck steamer *Generton* built 1936 by Short Bros Ltd, Sunderland, 4,801 gross, 8,100 deadweight, for the Carlton S.S. Co Ltd, Newcastle (R. Chapman & Son, Newcastle, managers). The Maierform bow and hull lines proved advantageous in smooth water, but in heavy weather the spoon bow tended to stop the vessel. This kept the decks drier, but proved a particular disadvantage when trying to maintain position in North Atlantic convoys during world war two. Her registered dimensions were 426.5' x 54.0' x 23.7' and she had a triple expansion engine running on superheated steam at 220 pounds per square inch.

stern on wave crests the vessel 'sagged'. Should the crest of a wave support the vessel amidships, she 'hogged'. Similar stresses were induced to a lesser extent when heavy cargo was distributed unevenly along her length. The hull was also exposed to twisting stresses as waves supported the hull unevenly. To bond the hull sides, bottom and deck to resist the stresses, hold beams spanned the breadth, and hold pillars tied and supported the bottom, the beams and the deck. These were of course of great inconvenience when loading and unloading cargo, and changes in design were introduced to get rid of them. These will be referred to later.

When sail gave way to steam the layout of the ships did not alter. The designer produced a sailing ship with a steam engine and boiler squeezed in aft, together with the coal bunkers, generally all positioned just forward of the mizzen mast. Cargo steamers had, from the outset, to be screw propelled. Not only were the engines of the paddle steamers large and inefficient in proportion to the size of the vessel, but the paddles had to be immersed to a constant depth, as far as was practicable, and this was not possible with cargo steamers which sailed on different draughts between fully loaded and in ballast.

The early cargo steamer was constructed on the lines of the sailing ship and she carried extensive sails, sometimes as a full rigged ship, but more usually reduced to a brigantine or barquentine rig which still carried square sails on the foremast. This arrangement could still be seen on steamers built in the late 1890s. The sailing ship was long and narrow and there was a belief that to cut down the resistance of a steamer's hull and so obtain greater speed from a given power of engine, the hull had to be narrow. To provide a reasonable cargo capacity the hull was deepened and as a result the vessel became very 'tender'. A large number of this type of cargo steamer were built but after many of them went missing or were lost by foundering it was realised that the design was not suitable for commercial applications and it was abandoned, new vessels having less extreme proportions. Most of the vessels lost were carrying cargoes of grain, coal or iron ore, all liable to shifting, at a time when regulations had not been formulated for the prevention of movement of these 'fluid' materials by fitting shifting boards. The following table of casualties gives some idea of the extreme proportions in use at that time:

Name	L.(ft).	B.(ft).	D.(ft).	L/B	D/B	Voyage	Cargo	Lost
Lord Jeffrey	270	35	24.4	7.71	.70	Tyne-Port Said	coal	13.10.1886
Hylton Castle	251	32.4	19.2	7.75	.59	New York-Rouen	corn	11.1.1886
Swiftsure	275	34.5	24.5	7.97	.71	Odessa-Portishead	barley	15.10.1886
Tom Morton	260	31.9	23.7	8.15	.74	Cardiff-Odessa	coal	4.12.1886
Castleton	279.5	34	23	8.22	.68	Cardiff-St.Lucia	coal	14.10.1886
Domingo	249.5	35.4	18.1	7.05	.51	Cuba-Philadelphia	iron ore	17.11.1888

A few years later the depth to breadth ratio had come down although the length/breadth ratio had changed little:

Name	Built	Dimensions (feet).	L/D	D/B
Orestes	1888	260.0 x 36.0 x 20.2	7.22	.56
Highland Lassie	1891	296.0 x 40.3 x 22.2	7.34	.55
Clydesdale	1895	351.5 x 44.7 x 26.4	7.86	.59

Another factor which contributed to these losses was the fact that the early steam vessels were in general flush decked and heavy seas could sweep the decks. The engine room skylight was exactly that, a glass skylight, very vulnerable and frequently the contributory cause of a casualty. Not only that but there was a continuous loss of life as waves swept men overboard and created havoc on the unprotected deck, as these reports show:

18 Nov.1880 *Dudley* 825/65. T.W. Smith, Newcastle. Susa, Tunis to London. Esparto and lead. Two boats smashed, hatch stove in, one man lost. 46º20'N.8ºW. Wind WSW force 9.

12 Feb.1881 *Birkhall* 1447/79. H.A. Davidson, Aberdeen. Newcastle to Alexandria, coal. Wheel, charthouse, carried away, two lives lost, 70m. SSW of Start Point. Wind NW, force 11.

2 Mar.1881 *England* 1068/77. Short & Dunn, Cardiff. Rio Marina to Newport, iron ore.

Bridge, wheel, lifeboat etc. carried away. One man killed. 41º28'N. 8º20'E.Wind WNW force 10. (Even in the Mediterranean ships were subjected to heavy seas).

These were vessels which survived. Between 1880 and 1882 no less than 337 British steamers were lost and a survey was carried out to see if the cause could be highlighted. What it did show was that 59% of the losses were due to the vessels stranding, not due to any weakness in their design or structure. Most of the other losses were blamed on the shifting of the cargo of coal or grain.

The *Knight Templar* had a very slim hull and had the low engineroom skylight and boiler casing which caused losses among the early steamers (26). There was only a simple bridge of a few planks above the wheel amidships, which was unprotected. The Captain however had the use of a small chart house at the aft end of the casing. She was provided with steam winches for working the cargo but the crew had to raise the anchor by hand with an Armstrong Patent windlass.The ship's complement was spread out; crew in the forecastle, officers amidships and the captain aft with a few passengers. *Knight Templar* was fully rigged as a topsail schooner. She was built in 1872 by J.G. Lawrie of Whiteinch, Glasgow. Registered dimensions were 241.3' x 30.4' x 25.55', 1,380 gross registered tons for Baird & Brown of Glasgow and she was lost in January 1873 on a voyage to India.

The first move towards a safer ship was to raise the engineroom skylight on a six foot high casing. Through time this casing was carried to the side of the deck and extended to carry the wheel, thus forming the bridge deck and providing some protection for the captain and helmsman. A raised forecastle on the bow helped to break the seas coming over the bow and a raised poop aft completed the design of what became known as the 'three-island type', which became synonymous with the tramp steamer. See *Maplegrove* (12) and the numerous examples in Volume 2. Another common type which could sometimes look like a three-islander was the 'well deck steamer'. As can be seen from the drawings (27), when the machinery was positioned amidships as it generally was in larger vessels, a considerable volume was lost in the after hold because the shaft tunnel ran through it. Allied to this, to ensure a good flow of water to the propellor, it was necessary to keep the lines of the hull aft fairly fine. When the fore and aft holds were filled to capacity the vessel was found to 'trim by the head', i.e. she was deeper in the water at the bow than at the stern. This was overcome by raising the after deck by up to 4 feet to create a raised quarterdeck which increased the capacity of the after hold. It was at first feared that the well formed between the forecastle and the raised quarterdeck would be a hazard due to the seas which broke over the vessel filling the well and making the ship bow heavy. However the volume left between the hatch coaming and the rails and the superstructure was quite small and water was cleared by the freeing ports. Later, by keeping the top of the hatches above rail level there was no possibility of water lying on the top of the hatch itself to any extent. The well deck design was much favoured for coastal work and indeed many were to be found in the deep-sea and intermediate trades. It was estimated that by 1890 just under 40% of the ships built for overseas trading were of the well-deck type.

One point about the well-deck steamer regarding strength was that the break in the deck constituted a weakness in the longitudinal structure, which had to be countered by the inclusion of special stiffening brackets. In the later three-island vessel the main deck ran right through with the superstructure superimposed and stiffening was only required either side of the engine and boiler rooms.

The well-decked vessel *Waterloo* shows all the characteristics of the early steamer – narrow hull and deep compared to her beam. The engineroom skylight was still low and she was fully rigged. The accommodation was reminiscent of the old sailing ships, crew forward, officers aft, and the 'idlers' amidships; to these had been added the engineers. *Waterloo* was built in 1879 by the London & Glasgow Shipbuilding and Engineering Co Ltd. 254.4' x 33.1' x 18.7', 1,283 grt., for A.C. Gow of Glasgow. Her bunker capacity would allow her to carry out voyages to North America or to Italy, using the space below the bridge. She shows several advances compared with the *Knight Templar*, particularly the forecastle containing a steam windlass placed there to avoid the extra weight of strengthening the deck above. Though there is still a steering position aft, a substantial enclosed wheelhouse and chart room is provided below the bridge. Note the cargo doors in the bulwarks allowing bagged cargoes to be carried to and from the well deck. The arrangement of the ladders from the well deck to the boat deck was

26

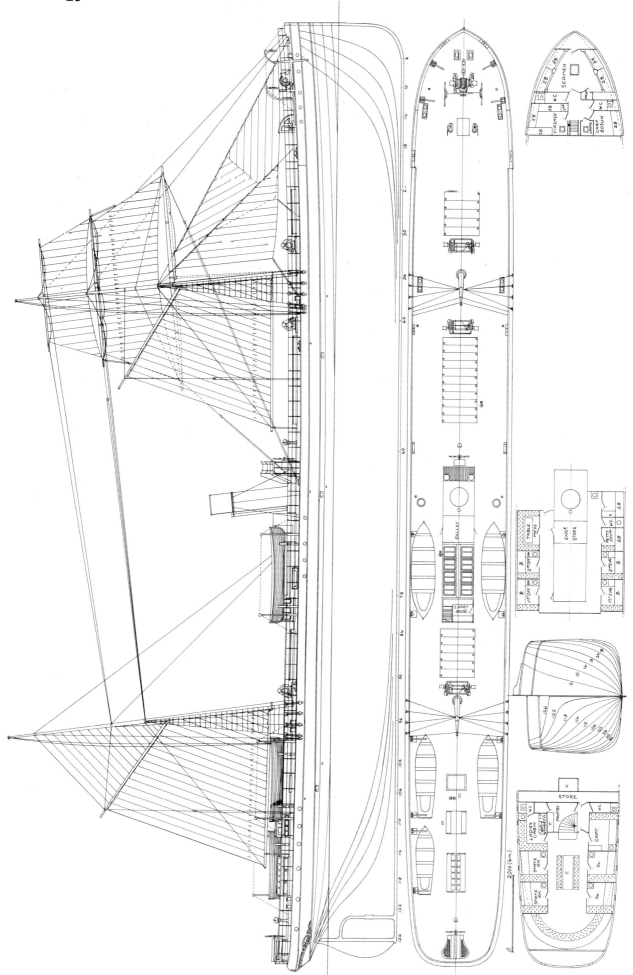

26. The two deck steamer *Knight Templar* 1380/72 was built by J.G. Lawrie, Glasgow for Baird & Brown, Glasgow. See page 25.

Strathclyde Regional Council

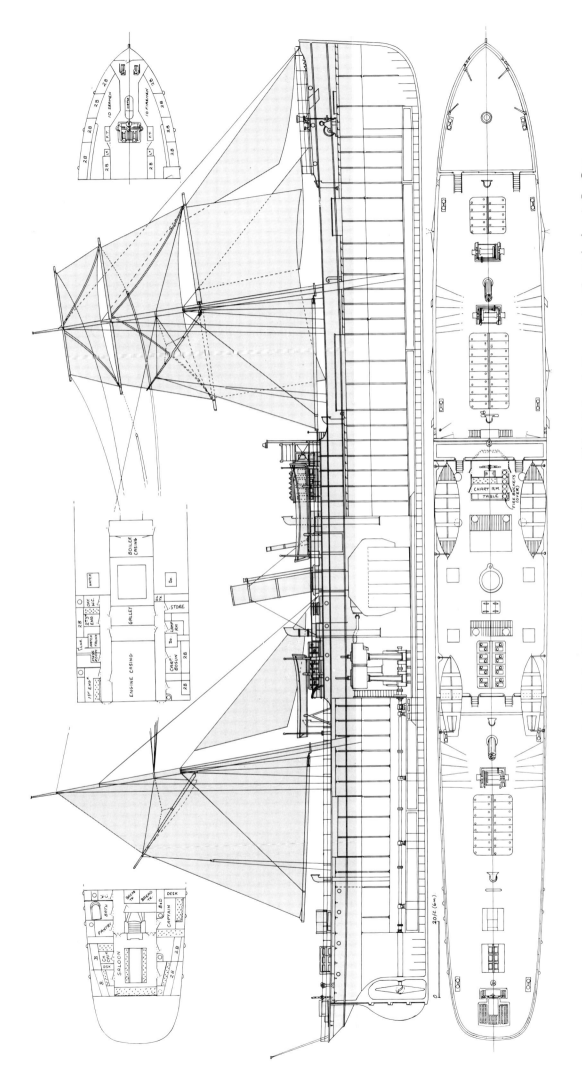

27. Well–deck steamer *Waterloo*, built in 1879 by the London & Glasgow Shipbuilding & Engineering Co Ltd, for A.C. Gow, Glasgow. Her registered dimensions were 254.4' x 33.1' x 18.7', 1,283 gross registered tons. See page 25 and volume 2 for colour profile.

P.N.Thomas

unusual, generally they were fitted facing fore and aft. The profile is well detailed so the omission of the cargo winches at least in outline is surprising. She passed to Norwegian owners in 1895.

In 1889, William Gray of West Hartlepool launched the steamer *Iona* for the local tramp steamer company of Herskind & Woods. During the first 4 voyages her chief engineer kept a record of her performance.

Voyage 1.	Loaded or Ballast	Days on Voyage	Average Speed	Percentage of Voyage in ballast	Distance miles
Nov. 1889 to Feb.1890					
Tees–Bombay	L.	34.79	7.55 kts.		6,610
Bombay–Karachi	B.	2.29			517
Karachi–Bristol	L.	34.52	9.17 kts.		5,964
Bristol–Cardiff	B.	0.14		4.25	18
Voyage 2					
March 1890 to June 1890					
Cardiff–Colombo	L.	33.33	8.07 kts		6,448
Colombo–Cuddalore	B.	2.45			648
Cuddalore–Marseilles	L.	29.77	9.42 kts.		5,721
Marseilles–Carthagena	B.	2.08			377
Carthagena–Tees	L.	9.20		7.30	1,845
Voyage 3.					
June 1890 to Sept.1890					
Tees–Tyne	B.	0.16			16
Tyne–Savona	L.	11.75	8.72 kts		2,365
Savona–Serpho	B.	3.89			860
Serpho–Rotterdam	L.	13.58	10.27 kts		2,940
Rotterdam–Cardiff	B.	2.31		29.0	692
Voyage 4					
Sept.1890 to Nov.1890					
Cardiff–Leghorn	L.	10.06	7.61 kts		1,890
Legorn–Ibrail	B.	7.22			1,458
Ibrail–Rotterdam	L.	20.47	9.04 kts		3,689
Rotterdam–Cardiff	B.	2.68		38.5	692

The *Iona* had the dimensions 275.1 x 37.3 x 19.0 feet, 2,094 grt, 1,348 nrt, loaded draught 20'8". She was powered by a triple expansion engine 22",34",57" with a stroke of 39" supplied by twin scotch boilers working at 165 lbs per square inch assisted by a forced draught fan. In addition there was a donkey boiler working at 80 lbs for driving the cargo winches in port. The chief engineer calculated that his engine had developed 640 to 677 indicated horsepower. He calculated the coal consumption as follows:

	Bunkers taken onboard (tons).		Tons/day
	At home	Abroad	(at sea).
Voyage 1	296	544	9.75
Voyage 2	390	498	9.71
Voyage 3	370	15	10.21
Voyage 4	295	165	9.33

When early steamers were in ballast, i.e. without cargo, to retain stability they had to take aboard a considerable quantity of ballast in the form of gravel or stone. On arrival at their destination this had to be unloaded at a ballast bank before the steamer was taken alongside the wharf, all at additional expense, but one which could not be avoided until the idea of water ballast was put forward. At first water was carried in tanks or even rubber bags placed on top of the floors. These were found to be unsatisfactory and inconvenient and it was left to John McIntyre, manager of Palmer's Shipbuilding on the Tyne to design a permanent system. Girders were riveted to the floors and plated across the top to form another floor in the holds. This design was superseded by the structurally more efficient double bottom. At first ballast tanks were included in the tonnage measurement and owners were unwilling to fit them as they could not be used for cargo space. However, common sense prevailed, ballast tanks were excluded from the ship's register tonnage and they became standard on all types of steamer.

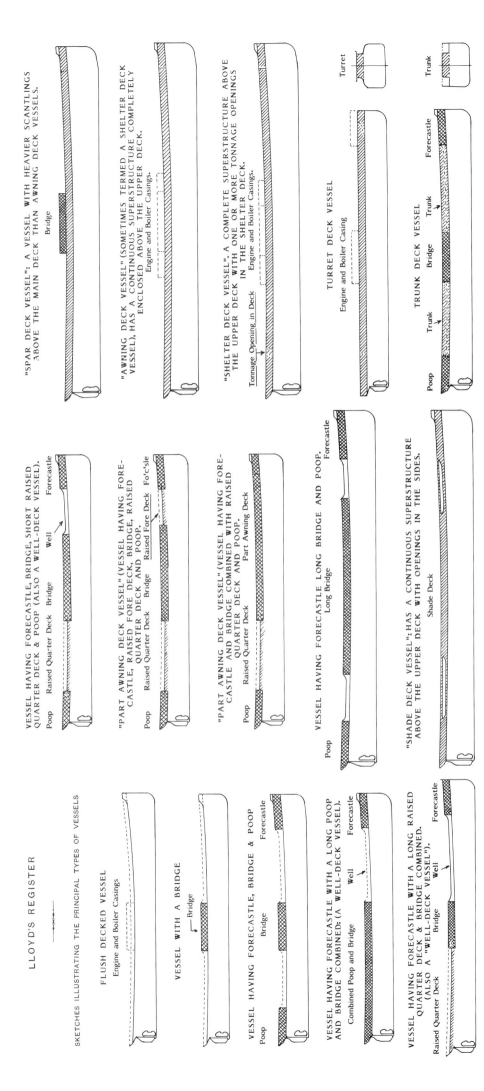

LLOYD'S REGISTER

SKETCHES ILLUSTRATING THE PRINCIPAL TYPES OF VESSELS

FLUSH DECKED VESSEL
Engine and Boiler Casings

VESSEL WITH A BRIDGE
Bridge

VESSEL HAVING FORECASTLE, BRIDGE & POOP
Poop   Bridge   Forecastle

VESSEL HAVING FORECASTLE WITH A LONG POOP AND BRIDGE COMBINED: (A WELL-DECK VESSEL).
Well   Forecastle
Combined Poop and Bridge

VESSEL HAVING FORECASTLE WITH A LONG RAISED QUARTER DECK & BRIDGE COMBINED. (ALSO A "WELL-DECK VESSEL").
Well   Forecastle
Raised Quarter Deck   Bridge

VESSEL HAVING FORECASTLE, BRIDGE, SHORT RAISED QUARTER DECK & POOP (ALSO A WELL-DECK VESSEL).
Poop   Raised Quarter Deck   Bridge   Well   Forecastle

"PART AWNING DECK VESSEL" (VESSEL HAVING FORE-CASTLE, RAISED FORE DECK, BRIDGE, RAISED QUARTER DECK AND POOP.
Poop   Raised Quarter Deck   Bridge   Raised Fore Deck   Fo'c'sle

"PART AWNING DECK VESSEL" (VESSEL HAVING FORE-CASTLE AND BRIDGE COMBINED WITH RAISED QUARTER DECK AND POOP.
Part Awning Deck
Poop   Raised Quarter Deck

VESSEL HAVING FORECASTLE LONG BRIDGE AND POOP.
Forecastle
Long Bridge
Poop

"SHADE DECK VESSEL": HAS A CONTINUOUS SUPERSTRUCTURE ABOVE THE UPPER DECK WITH OPENINGS IN THE SIDES.
Shade Deck

"SPAR DECK VESSEL": A VESSEL WITH HEAVIER SCANTLINGS ABOVE THE MAIN DECK THAN AWNING DECK VESSELS.
Bridge

"AWNING DECK VESSEL" (SOMETIMES TERMED A SHELTER DECK VESSEL), HAS A CONTINUOUS SUPERSTRUCTURE COMPLETELY ENCLOSED ABOVE THE UPPER DECK.
Engine and Boiler Casings

"SHELTER DECK VESSEL". A COMPLETE SUPERSTRUCTURE ABOVE THE UPPER DECK WITH ONE OR MORE TONNAGE OPENINGS IN THE SHELTER DECK.
Tonnage Opening in Deck   Engine and Boiler Casings.

TURRET DECK VESSEL
Engine and Boiler Casing
Turret

TRUNK DECK VESSEL
Trunk
Trunk   Bridge
Poop   Forecastle
Trunk

29. Diagrams published by Lloyd's Register at the turn of the century showing the various types of ship and the description used. Lloyd's came about through a loose association of merchants underwriters and brokers who regularly met at Lloyd's coffee house and eventually moved to rented rooms at the Royal Exchange in 1774. Lloyd's Register became a separate organisation responsible for laying down rules for the construction, classification and survey of ships. Included in the work was the supervision of the manufacture of iron and steel used in construction and the testing of anchor chains and other equipment. Originally there were various classes, but it became usual to construct vessels to the highest class (100A1) and vessels intended for arduous trades were often built to exceed the class requirements. They were also responsible for assigning a freeboard (or load line) when this became mandatory.

Lloyd's Register/P.N.Thomas

Three terms are regularly encountered in the older Lloyd's Registers for steamers with two decks – 'spar decked', 'awning decked' and 'shelter decked', see (29). Flush decked vessels were often built with full scantlings, i.e. the dimensions of the angles, channels and plates as laid down by the Lloyd's Rules as appropriate to the size of the steamer, up to the main deck. In spar decked vessels the upper deck was of lighter construction and there was no heavy superstructure placed above it. Generally the enclosed space was used for the carriage of passengers or light cargo. They were not allowed to load as deeply as two deck ships. Sometimes even lighter construction was employed; the 'awning decker', and as such were required to have even more freeboard than the spar decked ships. As the well-decked vessels developed, the size of the well was reduced as the front of the bridge was pushed forward to increase the space below the weather deck. Cattle were frequently carried in the well-deck and temporary wooden shelters were erected only for the voyage and were not counted for assessment of tonnage. It was a natural step to build light steel permanent covers and to incorporate them in the weather deck. Thus the 'shelter decker' was born. The snag was that the shelter deck came within the tonnage measurement and the charges on the ship increased. This was countered by leaving 'tonnage openings' on the upper deck, which, as long as they were not closed by permanent hatches allowed deduction of the enclosed space when assessing tonnage. Over the years the upper structures have been made stronger making them a part of the stress bearing shell and these terms have tended to change in their meaning and to fall into disuse. The word "tweendecker' tended to replace them. Some of the last steam tramps returned to the use of tonnage openings and were shelter deckers, but only in terms of tonnage measurements.

Up to the 1880s most of the larger steamers were at least two decked in one form or another. This was useful when carrying general cargo as a great deal of separation was required, and, in any case lighter, more fragile goods had to be stowed on the upper deck where they would not be crushed, while the heavy items would go in the lower holds. The two decker was less suitable for the bulk cargoes such as coal, grain, ore and cotton as the numerous deck beams and pillars made stowing and unloading difficult. For bulk cargo carriers open holds were to be preferred. As time went by the size of tramp steamers increased as the following survey shows:

	Average size in service, gross tons	Average size being built, gross tons	Range of tonnage being built, gross tons.
1870	870	1,050	1,100-1,400
1880	1,330	1,580	1,200-1,800
1890	1,500	2,150	2,000-3,000
1900	1,900	3,100	3,000-4,000
1905	2,250	3,300	3,000-4,500

As the size of steamers increased different methods of construction were introduced in an effort to provide the clear holds demanded by the owners. To compensate for the omission of the beams and pillars 'web frames' were used. The web frames were deep in section from 15" to 20" spaced with three to seven ordinary frames between them. In conjunction with the web frames several side stringers, the same depth as the web frames, ran along each side of the hull. At the intersection of these deep sections diamond shaped plates were rivetted to tie them together (34,36). While the web frame system was structurally sound there were too many ledges in which loose cargo gathered, a nuisance with grain cargo where sweeping out loose grain is essential to avoid rotting grain which would contaminate new cargo. To meet this objection deep framing was used where all the frames were deep in section reinforced by bulb section or angle with a single wide stringer plate at mid-depth, and later with shallow stringers.

The owner of the liner trader was content with the two decked vessel as it suited his requirements best. However the progressive tramp steamer owner was always on the lookout for ways of cutting his costs by decreasing the net register tonnage to reduce all the dues which were based on this figure and ways of speeding up loading and unloading. One of the earliest approaches adopted was 'self-trimming'. When a cargo steamer was loaded with a 'fluid' cargo such as coal or grain, trimmers had to be employed to ensure that all spaces were filled as the cargo was loaded. If this were not done, the cargo would settle unevenly and would shift when the vessel rolled in rough seas. Grain settles

GENERAL ARRANGEMENT OF WHALEBACK STEAMER.

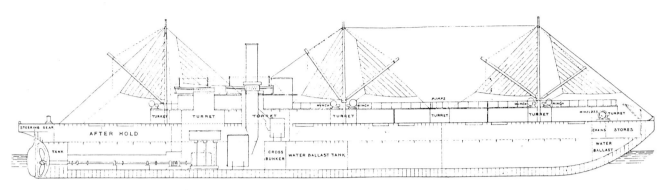

PROFILE.

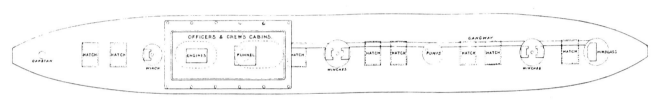

DECK PLAN.

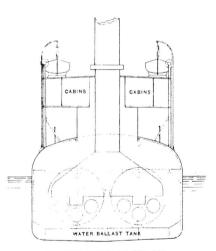

SECTION THROUGH BOILERS.

31. Above; plan of a whale-back steamer and left a photo of the *Sagamore* 2309/93 a whaleback steamer built by Doxford.

about 5% to 6% which could leave a gap of one foot between the deck and the cargo. To counter this possibility the regulations regarding the carriage of grain laid down that either the hold be filled right up to the hatch coamings which then formed a trunk to feed grain as the cargo settled or, that if the hold were not completely filled, at least two layers of grain in bags be laid over the loose grain. In the 'self-trimmer' the corners of the hold at top and bottom were faired off to eliminate the possibility of empty spaces and to ensure that the top of the hold acted as one large feeder trunk. An interesting development in the self-trimmer was the 'turret' steamer, a design which incidentally reduced the net register tonnage for a given deadweight, or put another way, the turret steamer could carry more deadweight for a given net tonnage than a standard vessel. When the Suez Canal tonnage of a turret steamer was calculated the difference was even more marked and this made them very popular with owners who traded regularly to the Far East. It is frequently stated that the turret steamer was designed to reduce the tonnage measured in accordance with the Suez Canal rules. The Doxford patent in fact claimed only qualities regarding self-trimming. Any other advantage was an additional benefit. On the Great Lakes the Americans employed a type of vessel called the 'whaleback steamer' and in 1891 one of these ships, *Charles W. Wetmore* visited this country. The curiosity of the British naval architects was aroused but they were very pessimistic about the suitability of this type for the tramping trade. Their fears were justified, as the steamer was badly knocked about on her return voyage to America as she rounded Cape Horn and was wrecked shortly after on the Oregon coast on the 8th of September 1892. She was, as the name suggests, like a whale with a rounded hull and having no deck as such, only a narrow gangway leading from the forecastle to the rest of the vessel which was aft with the machinery, boilers and bridge. The bow was spoon shaped, and she had no hatch coamings; the hatch covers were plates bolted on to form part of the hull. The machinery casing and deckhouses were on steel cylinders called 'turrets' (31). Because there was no deck, sails could not be easily handled, a fault which was held against her, and this in the early 1890s. She had no bulwarks and the seas could wash over her. Her stability was in question as she lacked the necessary righting moment should she heel excessively.

One shipbuilder, however, decided that the self-trimming aspect was worth pursuing. In 1893 William Doxford built a steamer, almost identical to the American design (31). She was called *Sagamore*, 311.0' x 38.2' x 25.2'. and was registered in the name of the Belgian-American Maritime Trading Company, managed by W. Johnston & Co Ltd of Liverpool who employed her from Liverpool and Cardiff to Antwerp and the Danube. Despite the pessimism of the naval architects the master and the crew of *Sagamore* spoke of her as a good sea boat. Looking at her tonnages she was 1,801 nrt. 2,309 grt. 3,350 dwt. The ratios of grt : nrt = 1.28 and dwt : nrt = 1.86 do not compare favourably with the normal ratios of 1.6 and 2.4, therefore her tonnage charges were expensive. She remained in the Johnston fleet until 1911. In 1893 the second Doxford steamer sailed on her maiden voyage. This time she was a true turret steamer, although many sceptics referred to her also as a 'whaleback'. The *Turret* was similar to the whaleback but in her case the hull was raised in a broad spine formed by connecting the 'turrets' of the 'whaleback' design which ran the length of the hull providing an elevated deck, safer for the crew to work and providing righting buoyancy should she heel in rough seas (33). She was 280.2' x 38.0' x 20.3' with tonnages of 1,265 nrt. 1,970 grt. and 3,200 dwt., giving ratios of 1.56 and 2.53, the latter being better than the normal. As usual there were the 'experts' who stated that she could not survive an Atlantic crossing, as given certain sea conditions she would sail under. Several years later and numerous crossings later the same critics were still prophesying doom and disaster! Her new managers Messrs. Petersen, Tate & Co of Newcastle were very pleased with her performance and Captain Petersen even deliberately put her into the situation described by the sceptics, from which she emerged safely. On her maiden voyage *Turret* encountered storms which caused the loss of several larger vessels and she came through unscathed. For this first voyage Captain Petersen had some difficulty in recruiting a crew as seamen had heard rumours being circulated about the turret design. However, once that first trip was over the same crew remained aboard her for a year and many of those who were paid off went straight to one of the new turret steamers which were now being built in quantity. In 1894 two more steamers followed, *Turret Age* and *Turret Bay*, both 311.0' x 38.2' x 21.6' with an even better dwt:nrt ratio of 2.64. They had a draught of only 19 ft. loaded which gave them access to many of the difficult ports where bars

33.
Turret built
1893.

restricted the draught of vessels using them. In service they had low fuel consumption and were easily loaded and unloaded. They carried deck cargoes of timber lashed either side of the turret without loss even on voyages from Montreal to the River Plate in winter (95). One awkward deck cargo which *Turret* had carried was fifteen iron girders 74 ft. long, each weighing 23 tons, from Baltimore to the West Indies. One captain after another praised the turret steamers. All agreed that they were 'dirty' but not 'wet' vessels, i.e. seas never broke over the decks although they were frequently showered by spray. Other shipowners were impressed by their performance and order followed order. Clan Line had 5 delivered in 1897/8 and by 1907 they had 30 in their fleet. In all 176 turret steamers were built by Doxford, 2 by Vickers, Sons & Maxim, 3 by C.S. Swan & Hunter and one each by R. & W. Hawthorn, Leslie & Co and Fried Krupp of Kiel. Originally in order to prove the 'turret' concept, Doxfords had taken a 50% shareholding in the Belgian–American Maritime Co, the balance being held by Wm. Johnston. The vessels proved so successful that Doxfords sold their share to Johnstons in 1900 at a profit of £70,000. They also helped promote the Turret Steam Shipping Co Ltd in 1892 to own the first turret ships *Turret* and *Turret Age,* Wm. Petersen and his firm subscribing £5,074 and the Doxford family £2,051 out of the £36,426 issued. At the time when the turrets were being built the method of calculating the tonnage on which the Suez Canal charges was based operated in favour of the turret steamer, but after 1912 when the basis of calculation was changed, the advantage was very small and the turret dropped out of favour. The last turret in service was *Nuestra Senora del Carmen,* built in 1895 as *Diciembre* which was wrecked in 1963.

The turret steamer proved to be quite a versatile craft and Doxfords issued several patents for improvements. In 1901 they built *Argyll* for A.M. Sutherland of Sunderland with an enhanced cubic capacity for general cargo work. In 1903 an arrangement was proposed to enable a turret steamer to carry cattle and sheep on the cargo deck. In the layout shown there was a capacity for 250 head of cattle and 1,100 sheep. The idea looks dangerous but in fact the cattle deck was 12' above sea level as against 5' on an ordinary vessel. In 1906 a patent was issued for a design which eliminated hold beams and pillars, a modification of the deep frame principle.

Nonsuch (42) was one of the later designs with a clear hold for stowage of cargo, though the bale capacity was reduced by the deep frames and broad stringer. She was built in 1906 by Doxford, 350.5' x 50.2' x 22.4', 3,826 grt., for Bowles Bros of London. The wife of the owner was a philanthropist and when the vessel was built the crew were provided with two berth cabins, running water, fans and electric light. The crew unfortunately did not appreciate such luxuries and apparently sold everything movable. After a few voyages the owners reverted to the common living space for all deck hands. *Nonsuch* was one of the first tramps to be equipped with wireless telegraphy. With a bunker capacity of 1,372 tons she was capable of round trips in all the deep sea trades. In 1912 she was sold to A. Yule & Co (Anglo-Oriental Navigation Co) and renamed *Clearway*. By 1920 she was in the hands of the Edwards S.S. Co, Calcutta.

In 1907 a 'tweendeck version was built for general cargo work. The largest turrets built were *Queda* and *Querimba* launched in 1905 for the British India S.N. Co, 455.2' x 58.1' x 30.2' with a deadweight of 12,000 tons and a cubic capacity of 690,000 cu. ft. Over 30 British tramp owners ordered turret steamers, among them well known names such as J.P. Bruce, Cairns, Noble, Laing, Ritsons, Runciman and Watts, Watts & Co. Sutherlands were sales agents as well as operators of turret steamers and many steamers were laid down for them and sold prior to launch or completion.

In 1894 Messrs. Ropner of Stockton-on-Tees introduced their 'trunk' steamer which had the self-trimming and tonnage charge advantages of the turret, together with economy of steelwork. Lloyd's regulations demanded that where a cargo carrying vessel had a length which exceeded 13 times its depth, a bridge had to be erected on the weather deck extending at least half the vessel's length. This added strength amidships but also added space which was chargeable under tonnage measurements which did not carry cargo. It was customary to form the bridge so demanded by extending the structure to the sides of the vessel, but Ropners argued that the same strength would be gained by moving the sides in to span only half the breadth of the ship (34). Having done this the obvious thing to do was to extend the trunk so formed forward to the forecastle and aft to the poop. While the side of the hull had a normal sheer the deck of the trunk had none. The effect of the trunk was to stiffen the weather deck and to enable the designer to reduce the number of pillars in the hold. Although some of the self-trimming features of the turret design were lost, the trunk acted as a deep feeder more than sufficient to allow for the settling of the coal during a voyage. However, to restore some self-trimming the camber of the deck was made double that which was standard practice, i.e. 12" as against 6" per 12 feet of beam. *Trunkby* (35) was built in 1895 and the builders claimed a dwt:nrt ratio of 2.53, somewhat less than the turret, but as the trunk steamers were designed on a restricted draught this was to be expected. The close similarity of the turret and trunk deck designs led to a dispute and court action, Doxfords claiming that Ropners had infringed their patents and cited *Clarissa Radcliffe*

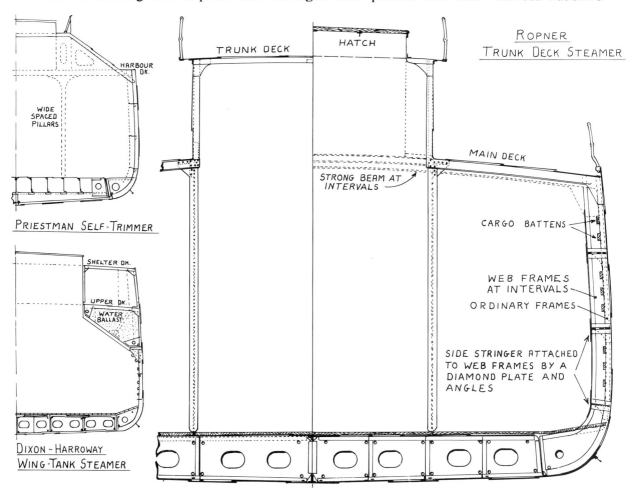

PRIESTMAN SELF-TRIMMER

DIXON-HARROWAY WING-TANK STEAMER

ROPNER TRUNK DECK STEAMER

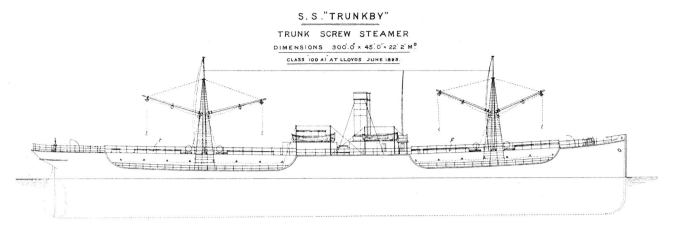

S.S. "TRUNKBY"
TRUNK SCREW STEAMER
DIMENSIONS 300.'0" x 45.'0" x 22' 2" M.º
CLASS 100 A1 AT LLOYDS JUNE 1895.

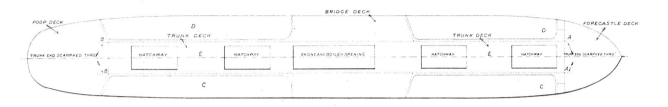

4703/04 which the Board of Trade measured as a turret and not a trunk decker. The trunk steamer proved to be less popular than her predecessor and only 44 were built. In Sweden *Lappland* 2238/06 and *Polarcirkeln* 1920/07 were built by Lindholmen, Gothenburg, for Swedish owners.

The drawing of the trunk steamer is not of any particular vessel (36) but shows the layout of a typical vessel built in the 1890s. In outline they had the appearance of flush deck steamers with a short forecastle, but in the drawing the line of the harbour deck can be seen dotted, with a hand rail running the full length. The hold ventilators projected sideways and upwards clear of the trunk, as can be seen in the photograph of *Teespool* (36). Most of them were destined for the Ropner fleet, while other owners ordered ones and twos and did not repeat the order. Among them were E. Thomas, Radcliff of Cardiff, Watts, Watts of London and Bennetts of Grimsby.

The Priestman shipyard in Sunderland entered the lists with their own self-trimming 'tower deck' design (37) which had a narrow main deck like the turret and the trunk steamers, but on either side the hull sloped down at an angle of about 45º to a walkway which went the full length of the hull (34). It did not prove a popular design and only three vessels of this type were built (3).

Other variations on the self-trimming theme were Henry Burrell's 'straightback' design (37). Two were built *Ocland* 3201/07 and *Ben Earn* 3911/09. The hull had a trunk with a very narrow side deck (44) and no sheer, hence the name. It was a forerunner of the engines-aft bulk carrier and even had deck cranes with grabs for rapid discharge and a hopper shaped bunker which fed the stokehold without the need for trimming.

By the end of the 19th century a greater number of vessels were being compelled to sail in ballast on deep sea voyages and more attention was paid to the stability and performance of steamers in ballast trim. In addition, with more efficient machinery less coal had to be carried and therefore, to ensure sufficient immersion of the propellor, more water ballast was required. With water in the double bottoms only ships tended to be stiff, i.e. when they rolled the righting moment was such that the vessel came upright very quickly imparting great strain on the rigging and masts. One solution which owners found to their liking was the fitting of deep tanks, usually amidships. These gave a higher centre of gravity for the water ballast, but, more important, when the ship was loaded with cargo, the deep tank could be used as a hold, thus wasting no space.

In 1898 Messrs. Wm. Gray & Co of West Hartlepool built *Mancunia* of 3,533 grt. for Sivewright, Bacon of Manchester. In Lloyds she is described as having "cellular side tanks amidships". These were in fact McGlashan tanks. In effect the double bottom was continued up round the bilge and up the side of the hull to form water ballast tanks at

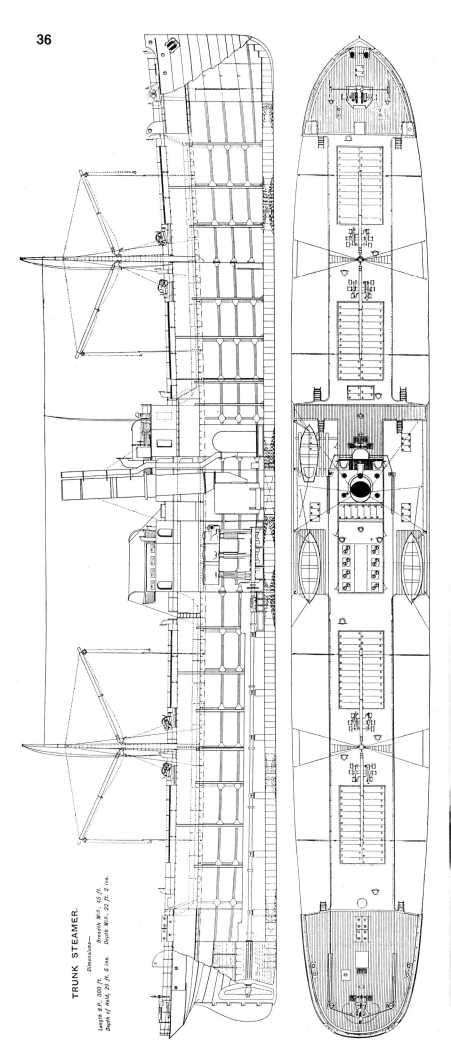

TRUNK STEAMER.

Dimensions—

Length B.P., 300 ft. Breadth Mld, 45 ft.
Depth of Hold, 20 ft. 6 ins. Depth Mld, 22 ft. 2 ins.

36. General Arrangement of a typical trunk deck steamer and left, a photo of Ropner's 'trunk' deck steamer *Teespool* 4577/05 which was scrapped after 30 years service (1935). Her dimensions were 351.5' x 53.0' x 27.6', 7480 dwt.

T.Walton 'Steel Ships', c.1900. Photo: I.W.Rooke collection

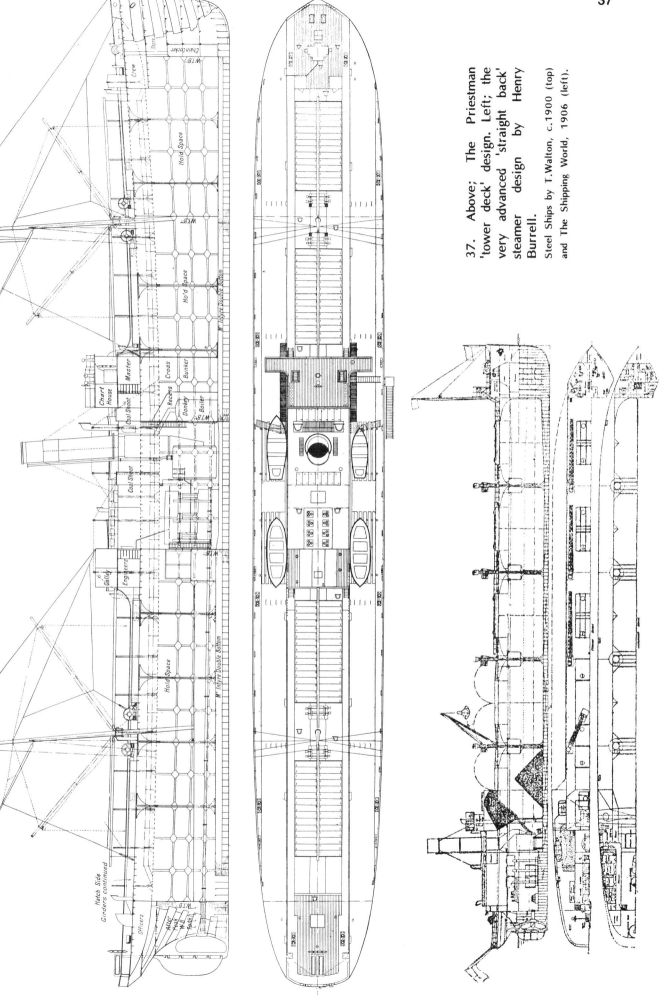

37. Above; The Priestman 'tower deck' design. Left; the very advanced 'straight back' steamer design by Henry Burrell.

Steel Ships by T.Walton, c.1900 (top) and The Shipping World, 1906 (left).

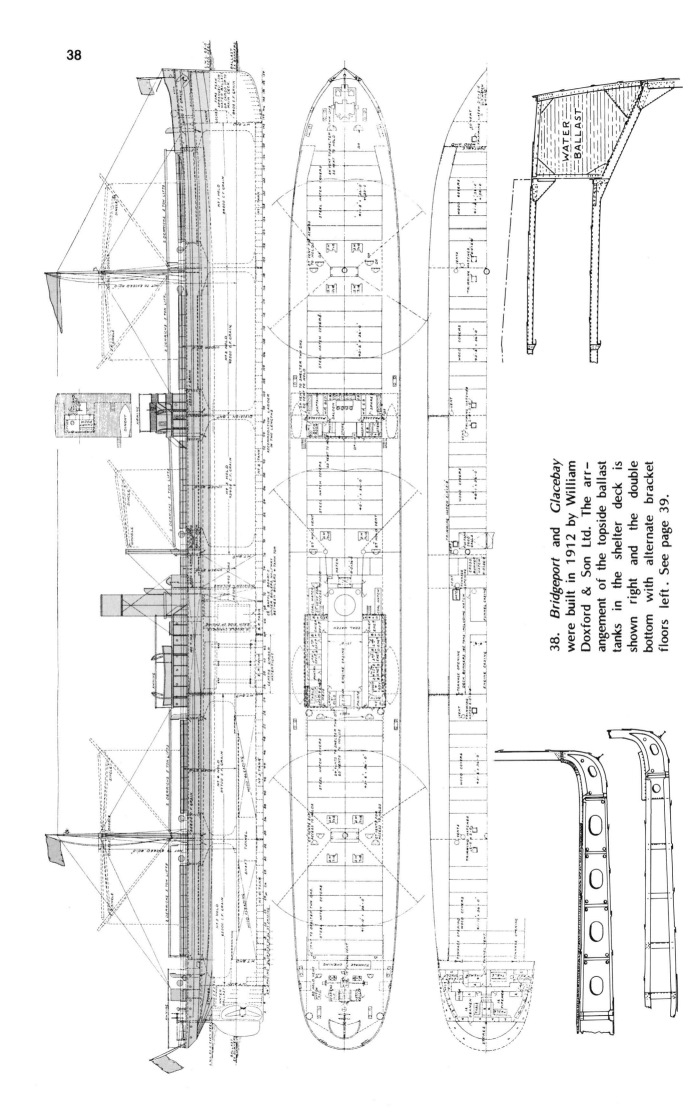

38. *Bridgeport* and *Glacebay* were built in 1912 by William Doxford & Son Ltd. The arr - angement of the topside ballast tanks in the shelter deck is shown right and the double bottom with alternate bracket floors left. See page 39.

higher level. It was not a very popular design and by 1908 only 11 vessels had been built incorporating McGlashan tanks. These were superseded in 1904 by the Harroway-Dixon 'cantilever' design where the ballast tanks were constructed in a triangular form at the junction between the hull and the maindeck. There were three advantages to the design. A smaller water ballast tank at the higher level had the same result as the McGlashan tank. The slope on the inner face of the tank gave a self-trimming effect for coal and grain cargoes. The triangular sections were like a girder, imparting great strength to the hull with an economy of steel, and the builders found it possible to do away with hold beams and pillars, again ideal for bulk cargoes. By 1908 at least 22 vessels had been built to Raylton, Dixon & Co's design which continued to be used well into the 1920s. In 1909 they launched a vessel, *Victor Hugo*, for French owners, 290.0' x 42.9' x 19.1', with ratios for grt:nrt = 1.9 and dwt:nrt = 2.9 both far higher than could be achieved with conventional designs. Like the turrets and the trunk steamer she had a very shallow draught of 18.4'. Two years later *Berwindvale* was launched for J. Esplen of Liverpool for charter in the coal carrying trade between American ports and Cuba. She was a large collier for her day and, with machinery aft, an unusual one. She was fitted with a new design of hatch cover which could be raised and lowered in 90 seconds and needed no tarpaulins. Her tonnages were 2,706 nrt. 5,242 grt., 8,650 dwt. giving ratios of grt:nrt = 1.94 and dwt:nrt = 3.2, the latter being one of the highest ratios to be achieved. She could take on 2,900 tons of water ballast of which 1,130 tons was carried in the topside tanks.

The large steamers *Bridgeport* and *Glacebay* were built in 1912 by Wm. Doxford & Sons Ltd, Sunderland, for Brown, Jenkinson & Co of London, with dimensions 442.8' x 58.0' x 28.9' and were constructed on the 'cantilever principle'. They were designed primarily for the carriage of coal, grain or ore but nevertheless were provided with a shelter deck to reduce tonnage (38). A feature of their construction was the heavy web stiffeners on either side of the watertight bulkheads dividing the holds, two on each side in line with the sides of the very wide hatchways which had steel hatch covers. These webs stiffened the structure and supported the masts and winches. Neither vessel lasted long. *Bridgeport* went missing and *Glacebay* was wrecked, both in 1913.

The builders of tramp steamers were always working on new ideas for reducing building costs and increasing the dwt:nrt ratio to keep down the tonnage charges. As vessels became larger it became more difficult to achieve these goals until in 1908 J.W. Isherwood introduced his system of multiple longitudinal stringers with widely spaced deep frames (39). This construction gave a larger carrying capacity for a given register tonnage by reducing the weight of steel used in construction, exactly what the shipbuilder was looking for.

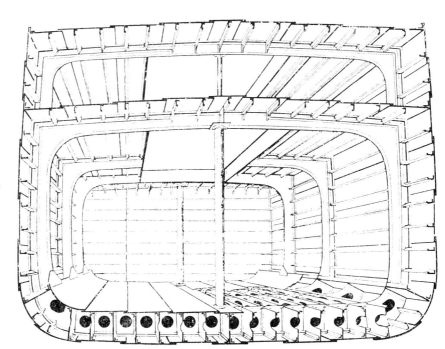

39. Perspective section through the hold of a steamer with Isherwood's longitudinal framing.

Shipping World, 1907

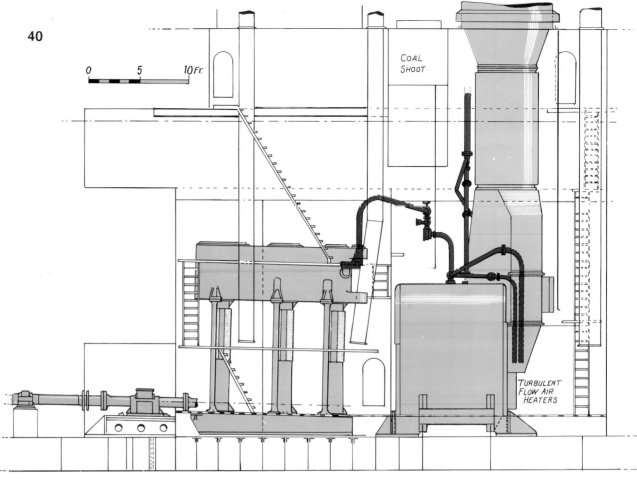

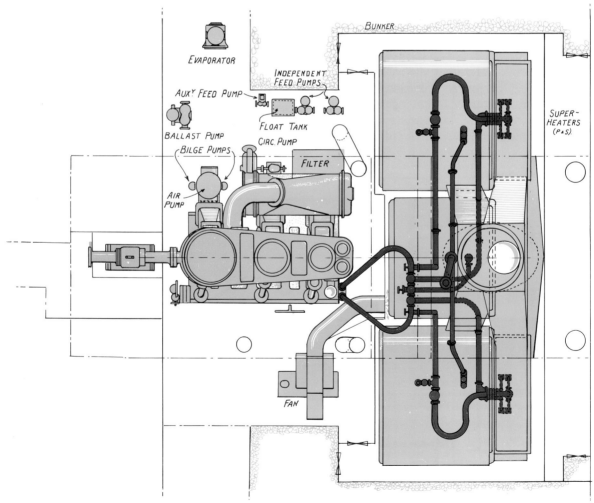

40. Machinery of *Arcwear* 4157/34. Only the main steam lines are shown in red. Numerous other lines, returns and the auxiliary condenser are omitted for clarity.

Shipbuilding & Shipping Record, 1934

R. Craggs & Sons Ltd, Middlesbrough were the first to launch ships to Isherwood's patent, the tanker *Paul Paix* in August 1908 for local owners J.M. Lennard & Sons, followed in November 1908 by the cargo vessel *Gascony* for D. MacIver, Sons & Co, Liverpool. The Isherwood system was suitable for almost every kind of vessel and two years later Richardson, Duck & Co of Stockton had on their stocks a 360' bulk oil carrier, a 360' three decked shelterdecker, a 390' two decked steamer and a single deck steamer. The number of ships using the Isherwood system rose year by year:

Year	No. Built	Total (gross tons)	Average Gross Tonnage
1908	2	7,330	3,665
1909	8	21,934	2,742
1910	25	92,709	3,708
1911	40	154,634	3,866
1912	52	234,615	4,512
1913	79	384,372	4,865

By 1918 a total of 1,050 vessels of 8.7 million tons deadweight had been built on the Isherwood system in Britain and abroad. The advantages and disadvantages of the system were summarised as follows:

Advantages	*Disadvantages*
1. Increased dwt:nrt ratio	1. Reduced capacity for long timber.
2. Increased longitudinal strength	2. A large number of ledges from
3. Increased bale and grain capacity	which loose grain had to be brushed
4. Increased local strength.	
5. Improved ventilation	
6. Less vibration	

Even the success of the Isherwood design did not deter the inventors. In July 1909 *Monitoria* was launched from the yard of Osbourne, Graham & Co, Sunderland, built to the 'monitor' design with a corrugated hull, 279.5' x 42.0' x 18.3', 1,165 nrt., 1,904 grt., 3,300 dwt. The feature which characterised the monitor form of construction was the groove formed by the two corrugations between the load water-line and the light water-line (22), which merged into the hull fore and aft. The advantages claimed for the corrugated hull were:

1. Increased deadweight capacity for a given net tonnage.
2. A steadier vessel at sea with reduced rolling.
3. Greater strength and regidity.
4. Freedom from vibration.
5. More economical on fuel than a plain hull, increasing her earning power.

The extra deadweight came from the capacity of the grooves which were not included in the measurement of net tonnage. The corrugation acted as a kind of bilge keel steadying the vessel. The groove acted as a guide for water, reducing wave-making and producing a smoother flow to the screw which in turn called for less power at a given speed. The original patent was based on the application of the groove to a turret steamer but when *Monitoria* was built a standard hull was employed. The construction used widely spaced web frames and because of the corrugation no longitudinal stringers were fitted, giving holds which were easily cleaned between cargoes. The owners of Monitor steamers were full of praise and quoted figures of 6 to 16% saving on fuel costs. The Ericcson Shipping Co Ltd quoted an advantage of £1,240 for freight on extra cargo carried and savings in bunker coal on one year's operation of *Hyltonia* and £1,130 for *Monitoria*. Owners who did not have monitor steamers were still arguing as late as 1924 that the claims of efficiency were unproven or fallacious. Masters of corrugated steamers were full of praise for their seaworthiness; in a gale which forced *Lusitania* to slow down, the much smaller *Monitoria* behaved admirably and no heavy seas broke over her. The monitor design was not widely accepted and only 30 were built, the last being *Rio Diamante* 4641/28. Problems were reported regarding the steamer *King James* 5122/25 belonging to the King Line which suffered from frequent cracking of hull plates due to the uneven flexing effect between the flat hull and the corrugations. Contrary to the claims of the inventor her master reported that she rolled excessively due to the lack of bilge keels. Probably the ship was too big for the monitor principle to work, she was 400 feet long while the inventor had intended his ideas to be applied to relatively small

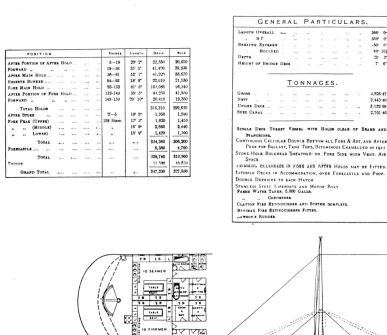

GENERAL ARRANGEMENT

S.S. "NONSUCH."
Launched—March, 1906.

GENERAL PARTICULARS.

Length Overall	366' 0"
„ B.P.	350' 0"
Breadth Extreme	50' 0"
„ Moulded	49' 10½"
Depth	25' 3"
Height of Bridge Deck	7' 6"

TONNAGES.

Gross	3,826·47
Nett	2,443·40
Under Deck	3,132·98
Suez Canal	2,701·40

Single Deck Turret Vessel with Holds clear of Beams and Stanchions.
Continuous Cellular Double Bottom all Fore & Aft, and After Peak for Ballast, Tank Tops, Bituminous Enamelled in 1911
Stoke-Hole Bulkhead Sheathed on Fore Side with Vent. Air Space
Trimming Bulkheads in Fore and After Holds may be Fitted.
Litosilo Decks in Accommodation, over Forecastle and Poop.
Double Derricks to each Hatch.
Seamless Steel Lifeboats and Motor Boat
Fresh Water Tanks, 5,000 Galls.
„ „ Condenser.
Clayton Fire Extinguisher and System complete.
Minimax Fire Extinguishers Fitted.
Lawson's Rudder.

POSITION	FRAMES	LENGTH	GRAIN	BALE
After Portion of After Hold	5—19	29' 2"	22,550	20,650
Forward „	19—36	33' 3"	41,490	39,230
After Main Hold	36—61	52' 1"	61,920	58,670
Reserve Bunker	84—93	18' 9"	22,610	21,530
Fore Main Hold	93—132	81' 3"	103,080	98,340
After Portion of Fore Hold	132—149	35' 3"	44,250	41,850
Forward „	149—159	20' 10"	20,410	19,350
Total Holds			316,310	299,620
After Store	T—5	10' 5"	1,950	1,590
Fore Peak (Upper)	159 Stem	17' 3"	1,820	1,450
„ „ (Middle)	„	16' 9"	2,860	2,440
„ „ (Lower)	„	15' 9"	1,420	1,100
Total			324,360	306,200
Forecastle			5,380	4,760
Total			329,740	310,960
Bridge			17,590	16,870
Grand Total			347,330	327,830

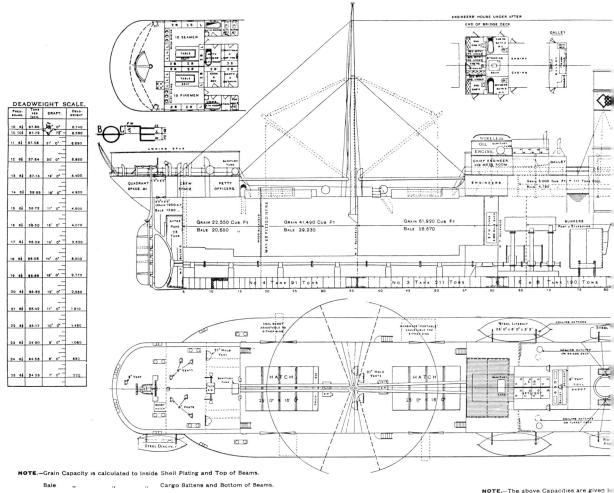

NOTE.—Grain Capacity is calculated to Inside Shell Plating and Top of Beams.
Bale „ „ „ Cargo Battens and Bottom of Beams.

NOTE.—The above Capacities are given in

42. Above: Capacity plan of the 'turret' deck steamer *Nonsuch.* Normally far less detailed plans were used. The photo opposite shows a view looking aft aboard the turret deck steamer *Heathdene* 3541/01 at Hull on the 27th of October 1907. She belonged to the Dene Steam Shipping Co Ltd, Newcastle, managed by J.T. Lunn.

W.Lind/McLaren Collection. Photo: P.N.Thomas collection

BOWLES BROTHERS,
34, Great St. Helens, London, E.C.

Telegraphic Address: "BOWLINES," LONDON.

Telephone No.: 10141 CENTRAL.

Marconi Wireless Telegraphy.
Submarine Signal Apparatus.
Porhydrometer.
Complete Suit of Sails.
Line-Throwing Rocket Gear.
Self-Lubricating Cargo Blocks.
Byres 3½-ton Anchors.
Lacey & Sea Anchor.
Special Outfit of Navigational Instruments and Charts.

MACHINERY PARTICULARS.

Engines—Triple Expansion.
Cylinders—24" × 41" × 68" × 45" Stroke.
Nominal Horse-Power, 349
Effective ... 1,700
Boilers (2) 14' 4" Dia. × 11' 6" Long, 180 Lbs.
Consumption—27 Tons per Day
Speed—10 Knots

AUXILIARY MACHINERY, &C.

New Clarke-Chapman Winches, Fitted throughout in Dec., 1912, Exhausting into Special Condenser (Contraflo).
Steam Windlass—Clark Chapman's Latest Quick-Warping Direct Grip Type
Steam Steering Gear Amidships.
Morison's Patent Contraflo Winch Condenser and Grease Extractor
Morison's Patent Evaporator and Surface Feed-Heater and Oil Extractor
Howden's System of Forced Draft.
New Woodeson's Patent Slow-Speed Feed and Ballast Pumps, with Brass Water Ends, Fitted in Nov., 1912.
Thompson's Patent Couplings.
Geddes Drain Traps
Edward's Air Pump.
Cast Steel Propeller Blades Sheathed with Yellow Metal.
Tail End Shaft of Richardson & Westgarth's Lockfast Iron, 14"

Drysdale Centrifugal Winch-Condenser Circulating Pump.
Tangye Donkey Pump.
Diamond Flue Blowers.
Ramsay's Governor.
MacNabb Revolution Indicator.
500 C.P Acetylene Flares.
Sturrocks' Furnace Bridges.
Salamander Fire Bars.
7" Centre, 10' Gap Lathe, Driven by Starting Engine.
Hand-Drilling Machine.
Portable Shaping Machine.

BUNKER CAPACITIES.

Position	Tons
Port Bunker	167
Starbd.	167
Coal Shoot (to Bridge Deck Level)	27
Total Permanent	361
Bridge (Included in Cargo Capacities)	390
Total	751
Reserve Bunker (Included in Cargo Capacities)	621
Total	1,372

WATER BALLAST CAPACITIES.

Position	Tons
No. 1 Tank	152
„ 2 „	453
F. & B.	190
No. 3 „	211
„ 4 „	91
Total Double Bottom	1,097
After Peak	23
Total	1,120

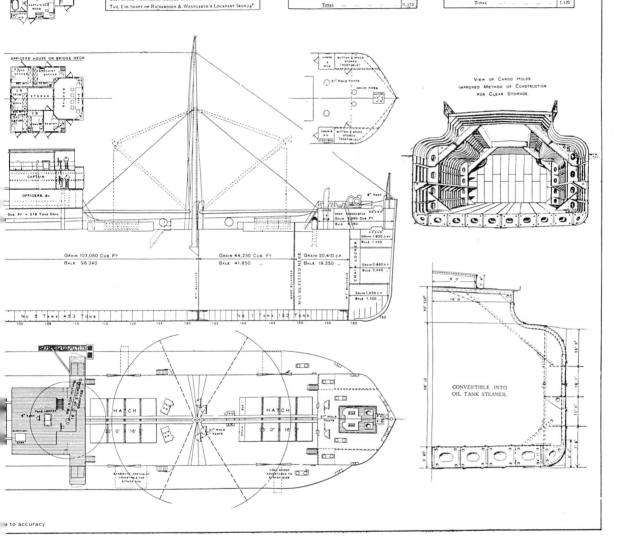

View of Cargo Holds.
Improved Method of Construction for Clear Stowage.

Convertible into Oil Tank Steamer.

to accuracy

steamers. Corrugated steamers saw service in the fleets of Walter Runciman & Co, Common Bros of Newcastle and the Thompson Steam Shipping Co of London.

The drawing (below) shows the 'monitor' corrugated steamer *Elva Seed* built in 1924 for the Seed Shipping Co Ltd, of Newcastle, 290.3' x 44.9' x 19.4', 2,241 grt. She was launched by the New Waterway Shipbuilding Co of Schiedam. There was nothing in her profile to indicate that she was anything but an ordinary tramp steamer, only a closer inspection of her hull would have revealed the groove along her sides. In way of the corrugations the hull was stiffened by deep web frames spaced six feet apart. The Seed Shipping Company kept *Elva Seed* for only a few years and then sold her to Swedish owners in 1929 to be renamed *Stig Gorton*.

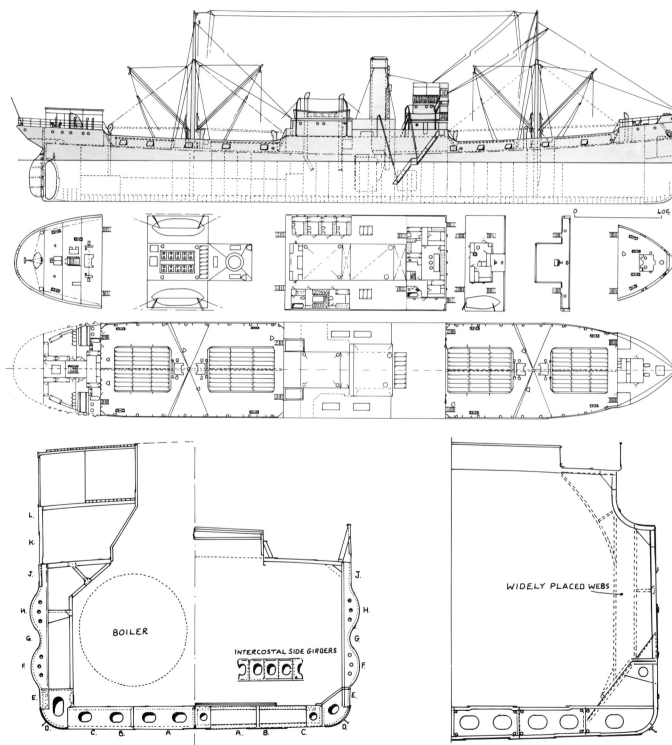

44. General Arrangement and Midship section of the 'corrugated' steamer *Elva Seed,* see above. Right: Midship section of Burrell's 'straight back' steamer, see page 37.

Marine Publications International Ltd and Shipping World, 1906

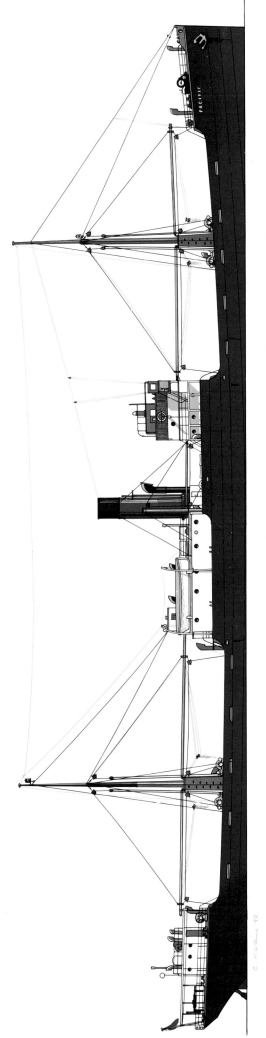

Pacific 2816/23 was built for Sir W.H. Cockerline of Hull. The derricks are placed well up the masts to be clear of deck cargo such as timber which was imported through Hull in large quantities. See page 97 for a General Arrangement plan.

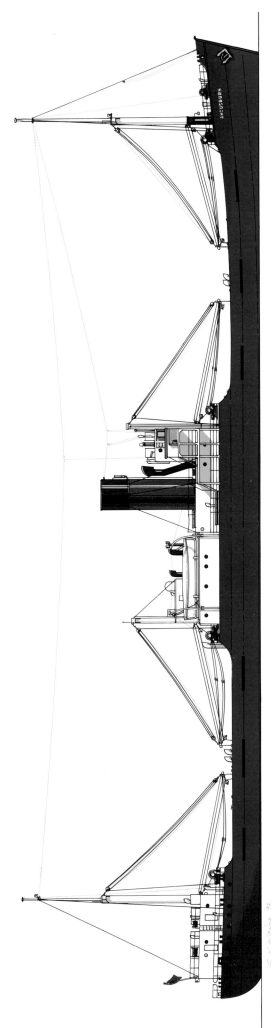

Angusburn 2853/42 was built as the 'Scandinavian' type *Empire Bard* and purchased by the Dundee, Perth & London Shipping Co Ltd, Dundee at the end of the war. With the decline in the company's coastwise liner trade, other trades were being explored and *Angusburn* was used in the iron ore trade for a few years. For General Arrangement, see page 64.

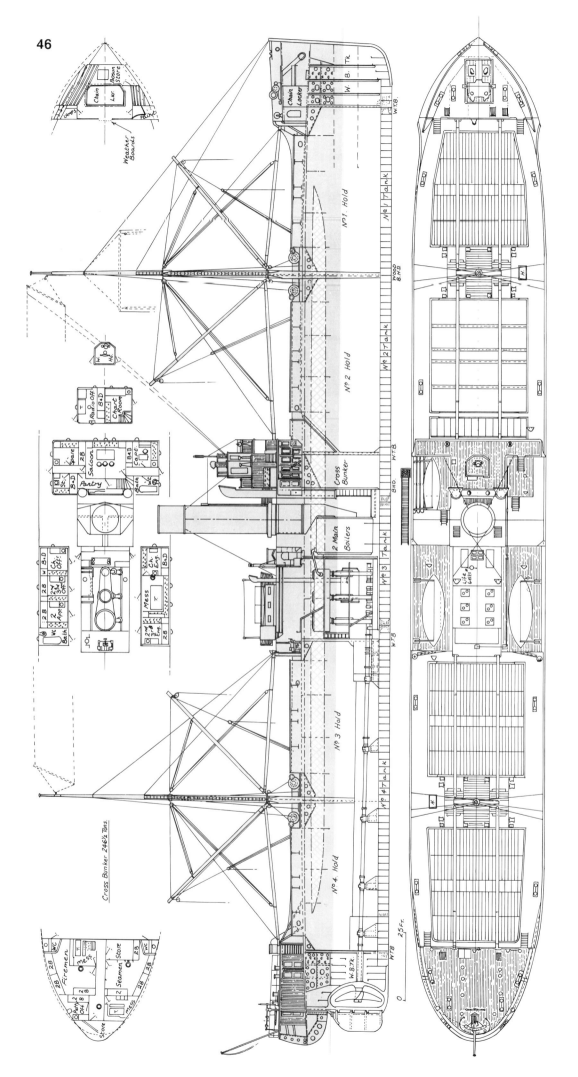

46. The 'arch' deck steamer *Sheaf Don* 2172/17 was an improved version of the *Sheaf Arrow*, built in 1912. Both were owned by the Sheaf Steam Shipping Co Ltd (W.A. Souter & Co), Newcastle and employed in the coastwise and continental coal trade for which they were well suited as they were self-trimmers with unobstructed holds, see opposite.

Shipbuilding & Shipping Record 1917

47.
The 'arch' deck tramp
steamer *Danapris* built as
Tullochmoor in 1924.

Photo: W.H.Brown/
I.W.Rooke collection

On the 2nd of March 1911 Messrs. Osbourne Graham & Co launched the *Edenor* which had been built on the Ayre–Ballard 'arch' principle for use in the Baltic trade. (Her construction was delayed by industrial action, a not infrequent occurrence). The primary object of the design was economy of steel by redistributing it, and a saving in hull weight of 12% was claimed. As it turned out, when measured under the Suez Canal rules, the Ayre–Ballard steamer gave a much lower figure then an equivalent three island vessel:

	Net	Gross	Deadweight	Suez
Three Island	2,463	3,952	6,207	3,317
Arch steamer	2,467	3,962	6,659	2,987

Edenor was 240.2' x 34.2' x 20.1' and she sailed on a loaded draught of 16.1'. Her tonnages were 1,182 nrt., 1,435 grt., 2,141 dwt., giving ratios of 1.77 and 2.64, both quite respectable. Viewed broadside on the Ayre–Ballard steamer apparently had no sheer (above). In fact, although the bulwarks were level, the weather deck had a reverse sheer being higher amidships than at bow and stern giving the arch effect from which the hull gained its strength. In cross section the hull was very unusual as the sides of the vessel curved in at the top to finish inboard of the edge of the deck which overhung them. This curve gave a self-trimming effect which was needed for her collier work (46). There

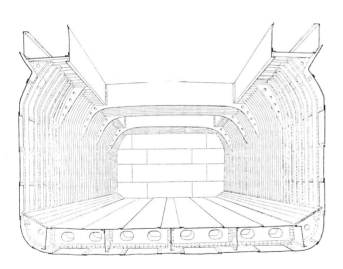

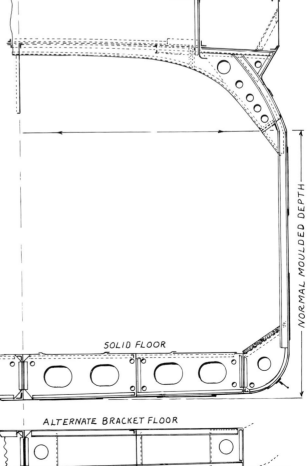

47.
Above: Midship section of *Sheaf Arrow*. Right: Midship section of *Sheaf Don* showing alternate bracket floors.

Shipbuilding & Shipping Record

were no stringers which was an advantage when carrying grain and the frames were relatively shallow, an advantage when carrying bales or timber. Messrs. W.A. Souter of Newcastle added *Sheaf Arrow* to their fleet in 1912, 279.0' x 40.3' x 22.6', 2,049 grt, and appointed to her the captain from *Sheaf Field* 1533/06, a traditional three island steamer of similar size and capacity. He reported several features in favour of his new command: firstly, there was almost a complete absence of vibration, secondly she was much drier in heavy seas, thirdly she handled easily and answered her helm beautifully. However the crew's quarters were rather wet as any water coming on board gravitated down the slope of the deck. In later vessels the crew was accommodated aft in the poop.

Although designed primarily for the carriage of coal, the 'arch' steamer was equally suitable for grain, timber or general cargo because of the open hold with no beams or pillars; and stowed timber well. As can be seen from the plan of *Sheaf Don* (46), the inverse sheer meant that there were no wells to accumulate water in heavy seas and also eliminated climbing up and down ladders to the bridge deck. The hatches were large for easy trimming of coal and two steam winches were provided at each hatch. An unusual feature was the cruiser stern.

Despite the advantages claimed for the 'arch' design it did not prove popular and only a few were built between 1911 and 1928. Among the owners who did buy them were W.A. Souter of Newcastle, the Donald Steamship Co of Bristol, and Furness, Withy of Hartlepool and London. The shipyards which built them were Osbourne, Graham & Co Ltd of Sunderland and Blyth Shipbuilding & Dry Dock Co Ltd.

Over the years little attention was paid to hull form apart from slight alterations to the underwater lines, though the engine builders were making improvements all the time. Propellors were also receiving a lot of time and testing in the tanks around the country in an effort to reduce at least one of the costs of running a tramp steamer. However, in 1933, Sir Joseph Isherwood instituted tests at the ship tank at Teddington of his 'arc-form' hull (below). He had been of the opinion for many years that the traditional box shaped hull was responsible for high drag by preventing a smooth flow of water along the hull surface. His solution was to round off the hull, even taking the rounding above

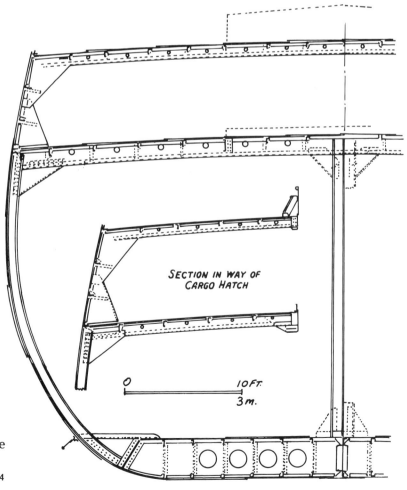

SECTION IN WAY OF
CARGO HATCH

0   10 FT.

3 m.

48. Midship section of the 'arc-form' steamer *Arcwear.*

Shipbuilding & Shipping Record, 1934

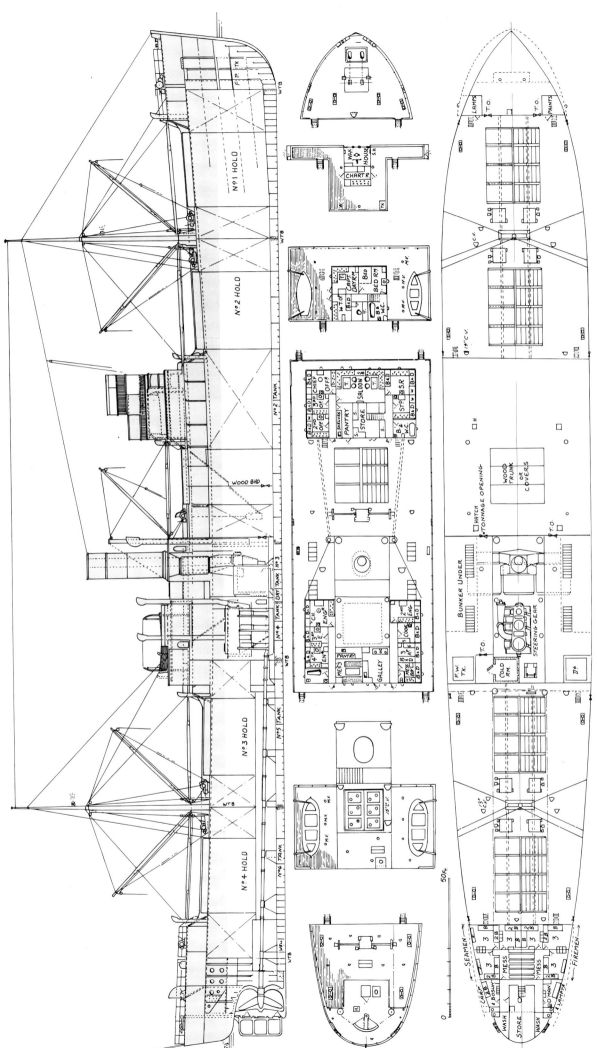

49. Arcwear of 7,068 tons deadweight was completed in 1934 to the order of Sir Joseph Isherwood to his 'arc–form' design and proved very efficient in service, see page 50. The engine room layout is shown on page 40.

Shipbuilding & Shipping Record 1934

the water-line to give considerable tumblehome. The results of the experiments were impressive and three shipbuilding firms laid down keels in 1933. Messrs. Short Bros of Sunderland built *Arcwear* 4157/34, Furness Shipbuilding Co Ltd *Arctees* 3953/34 and Messrs. Lithgow Ltd of Port Glasgow *Arcgow* 4118/34. Sir Joseph formed Isherwood Arc Form Ships Ltd to manage the vessels *Arcwear* (51) was 360'0" b.p. x 57'3" mld. x 26'9" mld. draught 22'7½". Her tonnages were 2,503 nrt., 4,157 grt., 7,068 dwt., giving ratios of 1.66 and 2.82. The results of the voyages of these vessels were very satisfactory giving coal consumptions as much as 50% down on those of a similar sized vessel built 10 years previously. After the first voyage of the three arc-form steamers the following con-sumptions were quoted:

Average coal consupt. per day:	8.6	10.15	12.05	14.40	16.80	19.40	22.30 tons
Average service speed	8	8½	9	9½	10	10½	11 kts.

Arcwear and *Arctees* were fitted with special steel hatch covers made to a patent taken out by Sir Joseph Isherwood. Their strength was tried when *Arcwear* was caught off Finisterre in a severe storm which swept the funnel off the German freighter *Europa* and compelled 17 ships to send out distress signals. One particularly high sea smashed down on the foredeck partly damaging the steel hatch covers. The captain was sure that if the hatch had had the old fashioned wooden hatch boards they would have been stove in and the ship would have been lost. In bad weather the 'arc-form' ships were found to roll but with an easy motion which was not excessive and caused no alarm. In head on seas they shipped a fair amount of water but the captains found that they had to ease off their speed only moderately, say about 20 revs. One captain commented that on one occasion navigating a narrow channel in the River Plate only the fact that *Arcgow* had such a rounded bilge prevented her from running aground. Isherwood ordered two more vessels launched as *Arcscott* and *Arcrown*, but following his death they were sold and completed as *Mount Ida* 4202/38 and *Wray Castle* 4252/38. In all between 1933 and 1954 a total of 19 general cargo vessels and 31 tankers were built to the 'arc-form' design.

In 1938 *Anglo-Indian* was built by Short Bros of Sunderland for the Nitrate Producers Co. Ltd. (Lawther, Latta) of London (426'0" x 61'2" x 36'6"), on the 'arc-form' principle but because of her longer length she incorporated the longitudinal framing of the original Isherwood system. She was 3,341 nrt., 5,609 grt., 9,850 dwt., giving ratios of 1.68 and 2.95. She was modern in design and incorporated a shelter deck as was becoming common with large tramp steamers. *Anglo-Indian* had permanent steel grain divisions clear of the hatches with provision for portable shifting boards below the hatches. At the forward end of No.3 hold there was a deep tank for either grain or water ballast. She passed into the hands of Sir Wm. Reardon Smith during the war and was later renamed *Tacoma City*. In 1954 she was sold on to Hong Kong owners.

The Burntisland 'Economy' steamer: As the 1920s wore on it became evident that the slump would not end for many years and that if the tramp steamer owner wished to survive he would have to cut his costs. Equally the shipbuilder was forced to examine ways of reducing the running costs of the vessels which he was offering. The Burntisland shipyard was one of the pioneers of the 'Economy' type tramp steamer. The first versions had a carrying capacity of 7,950 deadweight. Among the first shipowners to purchase the 'Economy' steamers were Turner, Brightman with *Zitella* 4251/29 and Turnbull, Scott who ordered *Eskdalegate* and *Skeldergate* 372.0' x 52.4' x 25.2', 4250 grt. They were basically three island tramps but the bridge deck was extended fore and aft to leave only small well decks (70). Tonnage openings were cut in the bulkheads excluding the 'tween decks from the tonnage measurement. Permanent steel centerline bulkheads were fitted and between the hatches portable wooden shifting boards were used when carrying coal and grain. The crew were berthed aft and a portable gangway was fitted to avoid them having to descend into the after well when making their way back and forth. Both survived the second world war, *Eskdalegate* (75) passing to German owners while *Skeldergate* was wrecked in 1950. The builders claimed that while the vessels were capable of 11 kts. if required, they would keep going at 9 kts. on less than 19 tons of coal per day as against 24 to 25 tons commonly used by existing tramp steamers. To back up their claim they quoted the results of several voyages undertaken by a Burntisland steamer:

Voyage	Coal consumpt @ 9 kts.	Weather
Sunderland to Genoa	17.90 tons	Moderate
Tyne to Venice	18.47	Moderate
Barry to Barcelona	18.08	Moderate to heavy
Cardiff to Savona	17.62	Moderate to heavy
New York to Monte Video	16.82	Moderate
Ibicuy to Las Palmas	18.28	Variable
Hull to Australia	19.0	Heavy
Iquique to Novorossisk	19.7	Moderate

These savings were achieved by:

(1) Careful design of the propellor for optimum thrust from a given power input.
(2) Streamlining of the rudder post to eliminate drag by eddy disturbance.
(3) Redesign of the engine.
(4) In some cases the steam installation worked on superheated steam reducing consumption to 16.25 tons per day though superheated steam was not too popular with tramp steam engineers.
(5) Improved insulation to cut down heat losses.

A later design of 7,800 dwt. capacity reduced consumption to 18 tons per day. Further modifications to the engine valve system and the application of an exhaust turbine were estimated to reduce consumption to around 11.25 tons per day.

Standard 7,800 dwt. 'Economy' steamer	18 tons of coal per day
Plus balanced slide valves	15.8
Plus superheated steam	13.63
Plus exhaust turbine	11.25

To show the shipowner how he could turn a loss into profit the Burntisland Shipyard produced an estimate to compare an elderly tramp with one of their design on a voyage to the River Plate and back: The average tramp burning 25 tons/day had to carry extra bunkers, so for the same size ship the Burntisland steamers could load 680 tons more coal outwards and 265 tons more grain back which resulted in a gain of £1,210 on the round voyage, a considerable sum in those days.

51. The steam steering gear of the *Arcwear* (larger tramps had permanent steam steering).

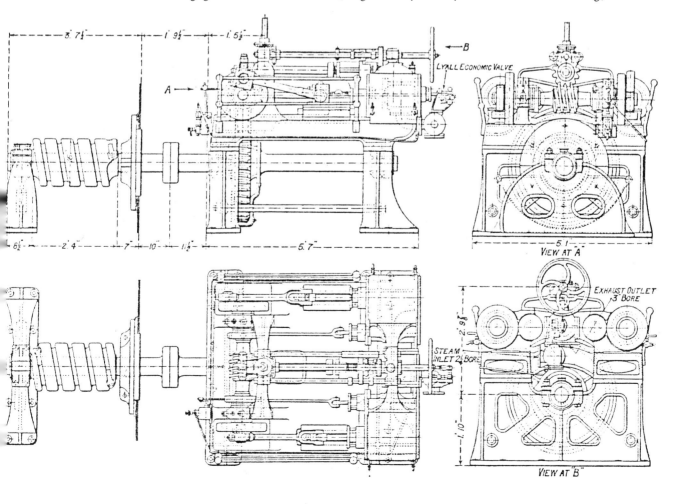

Designers were also attempting to increase carrying capacity within a given set of dimensions. In 1932 a Dane, K.G. Meldahl, patented the idea of placing the boiler on deck instead of low down in the hull. To a layman this may seem ridiculous but from a technical point of view it had many advantages:

(1). Raising the boiler increased the cubic capacity available for cargo where the cross-sectional area of the hull was greatest. An additional advantage for a timber carrier was that wood stowed below deck obtained a higher freight than deck cargo.

(2). Stability loaded was not affected as the cargo stowed below deck usually weighed more than the boilers which would have been there.

(3). Stability light loaded, was improved as the weight of the boilers and bunkers counteracted the 'stiffness' encountered with water ballast along the bottom of the hull.

(4). The temperature in the stokehold was below that of a conventional boiler room.

(5). The thickness of the tank tops was less as no allowance had to be made for corrosion below the boilers.

(6). There was a 6-10% increase in cubic capacity for a given deadweight.

The advantages for a timber carrier are illustrated by the following figures (measurement in standards).

	Conventional steamer	Boilers on Deck steamer
Stowed below deck	511	562
Deck cargo	309	283
Total	820	845

The British shipping industry did not seem too keen on this new idea and it was not until 1939 that Wm. Gray of West Hartlepool built *Elmdene* for the Dene Management Co of London, followed in 1940 by *Industria* for Metcalfe, Sons & Co of Hartlepool. *Elmdene* was 416'0 x 56'1" x 23'9" and had a gross tonnage of 4,853. After the war, between 1947 and 1953 a further 9 boilers on deck steamers were built, all by Wm. Gray. They were employed most profitably in trades involving measurement cargoes such as coke out to South America with low density grain as a return cargo.

Many of the new ships ordered at the end of the second world war were shelter deckers, improved versions of those built in the 1930s with better accommodation. The design was not very suitable for bulk cargoes such as coal or grain as considerable trimming was required and grab discharge was hindered by the small hatches and second deck, but they were well suited to liner companies chartering extra tonnage.

The British Iron & Steel Corporation initially chartered single deck ships such as *Angusburn* (64), but in 1952 a review of their requirements led to them time chartering specially constructed bulk carriers. This type of vessel was not new as similar vessels had been used in the London coal trade and a few had been built for longer voyges such as *Ben Earn* (37) and *Mercedes* 4315/01, built for J.R. Christie of Cardiff (68). This vessel was specially designed for a charter to carry Australian Coal to the west coast of South America. To give maximum space for the large hatches and unobstructed holds, the machinery was placed aft. For fast discharge, derricks were provided equipped for temperley transporters and grabs which allowed the cargo of almost 7,000 tons to be discharged in 16 hours. For the return voyage across the Pacific, ballast tanks were provided for 2,400 tons of ballast. A similar 6,080 deadweight collier was built by Swan & Hunter for the Pensacola Trading Co Ltd (Watts, Watts & Co, London managers). *August Belmont* 4640/03 was equipped with Dodge discharging gear, essentially simplified grab cranes which allowed discharge in about 11 hours. Because of the higher cost and the trim problems of engines-aft ships on long voyages, few were built for ocean trading. The trim problem was resolved when the cheapness and availability of oil and more efficient machinery reduced the weight of bunkers for distant voyages.

Another company to look at bulk transport after world war two was Tate and Lyle who chartered the conventional tramp *Baron Haig* to carry bulk raw sugar from the Dominican Republic in 1949 and in 1950 they decided to acquire more suitable ships of their own and purchased two, *Empire Malta* Class engines-aft raised quarterdeckers which became *Sugar Transporter* and *Sugar Refiner*. The vessels worked in conjunction with a specially equipped berth in Liverpool.

The Hudson S.S. Co who had traditionally been east coast collier owners observed these trends and the *Hudson Firth* 3117/49 was completed with cargo winches, oil firing and an enlarged fuel bunker to suit her for the West Indies sugar trade. She proved very successful and carried more sugar than coal.

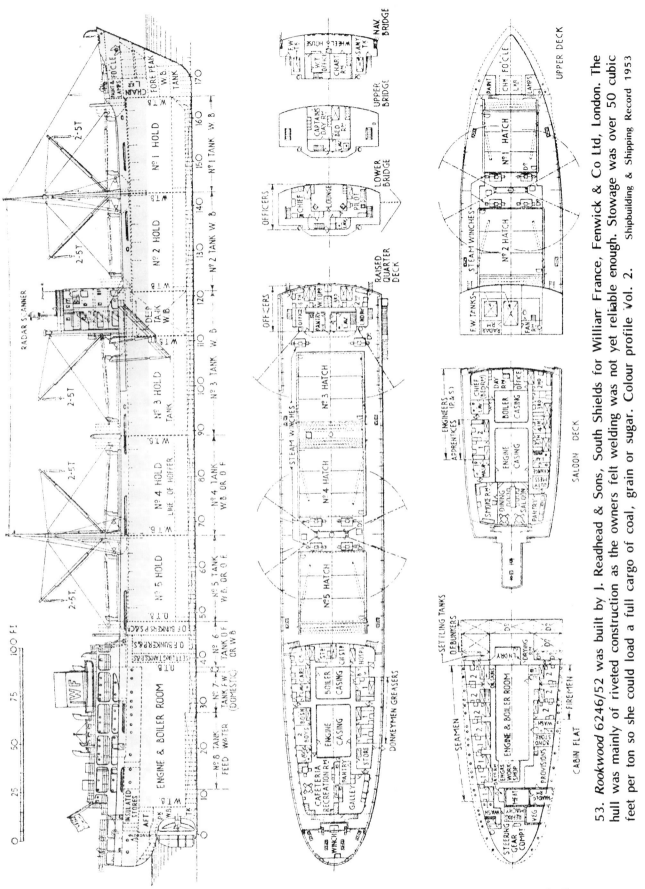

53. *Rookwood* 6246/52 was built by J. Readhead & Sons, South Shields for William France, Fenwick & Co Ltd, London. The hull was mainly of riveted construction as the owners felt welding was not yet reliable enough. Stowage was over 50 cubic feet per ton so she could load a full cargo of coal, grain or sugar. Colour profile Vol. 2. Shipbuilding & Shipping Record 1953

Similarly, collier owners Wm. France, Fenwick moved into the deep sea bulk cargo trades with large raised-quarterdeckers such as *Rookwood* 6246/52 and *Rushwood* 6208/53 (405.0′ x 55.7′ x 33.8′). They had 5 large hatches, two forward of the bridge and three aft (53) They could carry about 7,800 tons on a draft of 23′6½″ at a service speed of 12 knots. A similar vessel, *Cydonia* 6231/55 was completed for Stag Line. They had triple expansion reheat engines with Bauer-Wach exhaust turbines. The holds were self-trimming with hopper sides for grab discharge, features which were incorporated in the bulk carriers which replaced the steam tramps.

WORLD WAR ONE DESIGNS: In 1914 Great Britain possessed nearly 20,000,000 gross tons of shipping; by the end of 1915 some 1,600,000 tons had been lost by enemy action, surface raiders and submarines, and the U-boat campaign was intensifying. In the shipyards production went on as usual with almost 500 merchant vessels totalling 1,800,000 gross tons on the stocks, though slowed down by the withdrawal of skilled labour which was being called up for service with the armed forces or employed on urgent Admiralty work in the shipyards. The full variety of commercial vessels was represented from passenger liners to fishing boats, although priority was being given to the building of naval vessels. It was not until 1916 that any real effort was made to speed up the production of merchant ships when at the end of that year the Merchant Shipbuilding Advisory Committee met. It was agreed that the building of 100 standard cargo steamers should be started at once taking priority over the variety of orders at present in the pipeline. The Committee realised that each shipyard had its own specialist practices and so a number of standard types were permitted, though the yards had to build repeats of the same type. The vessels were to be kept simple with few extras, designed to give maximum carrying capacity with the minimum of material; real 'utility' vessels. For identification each type was given a letter:

A	400' x 52'	5,030 grt.	8,175 dwt.	2,500 ihp.	11 kts.	Single deck
B	400' x 52'	5,030 grt.	8,075 dwt.	2,500 ihp.	11 kts.	Two deck
C	331'x 46'6"	3,000 grt.	5,050 dwt.	2,200 ihp	11½ kts.	Single deck
D	285'x 41'9"	2,300 grt.	2,980 dwt.	1,900 ihp.	11½ kts.	Collier
E	376'x 51'6"	4,400 grt.	7,200 dwt.	2,500 ihp.	11½ kts	Tween deck
F	411'6"x55'6"	6,440 grt.	10,795 dwt.	3,650 ihp.	12 kts.	Tween deck
F 1	400' x 53'	5,680 grt.	9,000 dwt.	3,650 ihp.	12 kts.	Shelter deck
G	450' x 58'	8,000 grt.	10,800 dwt.	5,500 ihp.	13 kts.	Various

(These last ships were mainly refrigerated vessels to replace losses of meat-carrying vessels, some were single screw, some twin screw).

H	303' x 43'	2,800 grt.	3,860 dwt.	1,400 ihp.	10½ kts.	Single deck
N	411'6"x55'5"	6,500 grt.	10,500 dwt.	2,300 ihp.	11 kts.	

This latter group of ships were built to a design well ahead of its time: They were designed for prefabrication on the basis of straight lines and flat plates, the bilges being cut at 45º and the stern having a triangular transom. In all 33 were built to this design but only two were completed before November 1918. The remainder were finished and sold to civilian owners, and 21 of them were still afloat when World War Two began. Specifications for the main types are given opposite. The variations not only reflected intended use but also the lengths of the building berths available.

In an effort to reduce the possibility of ships being sighted by submarines, funnels were restricted in height and masts and derricks were designed to telescope or fold down, leaving only enough to support the wireless aerial as can be seen on *War Thistle*, a Type A standard ship built by John Brown & Co Ltd of Clydebank in 1917 (56). She was armed with two guns aft and carried paravanes for deflecting mines. The crew were berthed aft where they would be safer. *War Thistle* was torpedoed in January 1918, repaired and sold abroad. Many other vessels of this design served British owners, for example *War Aconite* became Hain's *Trefusis* until sunk in 1943. *War Crocus* built by William Gray & Co Ltd had what was the shortest career of any of the war-built ships, she was completed in June 1918, taken over by her crew on the 7th July and sunk by the German U-boat UB 107 off Flamborough Head on 8th July.

The detailed design of each type was entrusted to a builder who was already producing vessels of the type in question. The designing shipyards were instructed to restrict the number of steel sections used in their vessels in order to facilitate the production at the steel rolling mills.

Type	Builder
A and B	D. & W. Henderson & Co Ltd, Glasgow. See *War Thistle* (56).
C	Tyne Iron Shipbuilding Co Ltd, Newcastle. See *War Creek* (59).
D	S.P. Austin & Son Ltd, Sunderland
E	Robert Duncan & Co Ltd, Port Glasgow.
F	Joseph L. Thompson & Sons Ltd, Sunderland
F1	Northumberland Shipbuilding Co Ltd, Howden-on-Tyne, (58).
G	Workman Clark Ltd, Belfast
H	S.P. Austin & Son Ltd, Sunderland.
N	Harland & Wolff, Belfast.

TYPE A.
SINGLE DECKER, WITH POOP BRIDGE AND F'CLE.

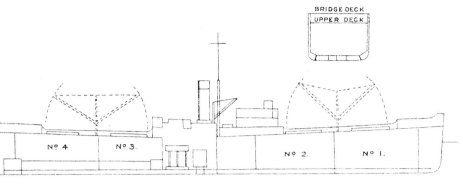

BRIDGE DECK
UPPER DECK

DIMENSIONS	400.0" B.P. × 52.0" MLD. × 31.0" MLD.
DISPLACEMENT	11,375 TONS
DRAFT	25' 1"
BLOCK COEFF.	·762
DEAD WEIGHT	8175 TONS
GROSS TONNAGE	5030 "
HULL (STEEL)	2225 "
W. & O.	405 "
ENGINES WT	570 "
LIGHTSHIP	3200 "
ENGINES	27"×44"×73"×48" STROKE.
BOILERS	THREE 15'.6" DIA. × 11'.6" H.F.D.

No 4   No 3.   No 2.   No 1.

TYPE C.
SINGLE DECKER, WITH POOP, BRIDGE AND F'CLE.

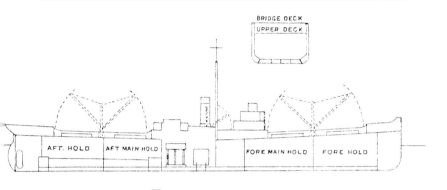

BRIDGE DECK
UPPER DECK

DIMENSIONS	331'.0" B.P. × 46'.6" MLD. × 25'.6" MLD
DISPLACEMENT	7200 TONS
DRAFT	21'.8"
BLOCK COEFF.	·760
DEADWEIGHT	5050 TONS
GROSS TONNAGE	3000 "
HULL (STEEL)	1390 "
W. & O.	300 "
ENGINES WT.	460 "
LIGHTSHIP	2150 "
ENGINES	25'×41"×68"×45" STROKE.
BOILERS	THREE 14'.0" DIA. × 11'.6"

AFT. HOLD   AFT MAIN HOLD   FORE MAIN HOLD   FORE HOLD

TYPE D.
RAISED QUARTER DECK, WITH POOP, BRIDGE AND F'CLE.

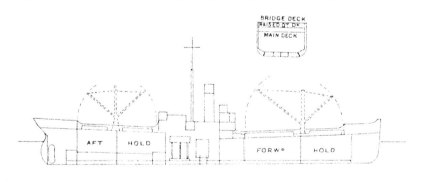

BRIDGE DECK
RAISED QT. DK
MAIN DECK

DIMENSIONS	285'.6" B.P. × 41'.9" MLD. × 21'.2½" MLD.
DISPLACEMENT	4750 TONS
DRAFT	19'.0"
BLOCK COEFF.	·732
DEADWEIGHT	2980 TONS
GROSS TONNAGE	2300 "
HULL (STEEL)	1110 "
W. & O.	240 "
ENGINES WT	420 "
LIGHTSHIP	1770 "
ENGINES	25'×41"×68"×45" STROKE
BOILERS	TWO 16'.6" DIA. × 11'.9"

AFT   HOLD   FORW'D   HOLD

TYPE E.
TWO DECKER WITH POOP, BRIDGE AND F'CLE.

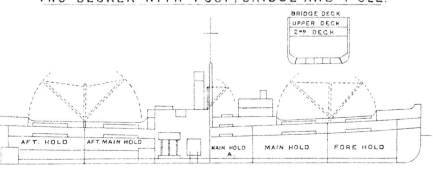

BRIDGE DECK
UPPER DECK
2ND DECK

DIMENSIONS	376'.0" B.P. × 51'.6" MLD. × 29'.0" MLD.
DISPLACEMENT	9910 TONS
DRAFT	23'.9"
BLOCK COEFF.	·749
DEADWEIGHT	7020 TONS
GROSS TONNAGE	4400 "
HULL (STEEL)	1920 "
W. & O.	400 "
ENGINES WT	570 "
LIGHTSHIP	2890 "
ENGINES	27"×44"×73"×48" STROKE
BOILERS	THREE 15'.6" DIA. × 11'.6"

AFT. HOLD   AFT. MAIN HOLD   MAIN HOLD A.   MAIN HOLD   FORE HOLD

55. Specifications of some of the main types of standard tramps built towards the end of world war one from a paper by Sir George Carter read to the Institute of Naval Architects in 1918.   Trans. Inst. Naval Architects, 1918

No 468

S.S. "WAR THISTLE"

GENERAL ARRANGEMENTS.

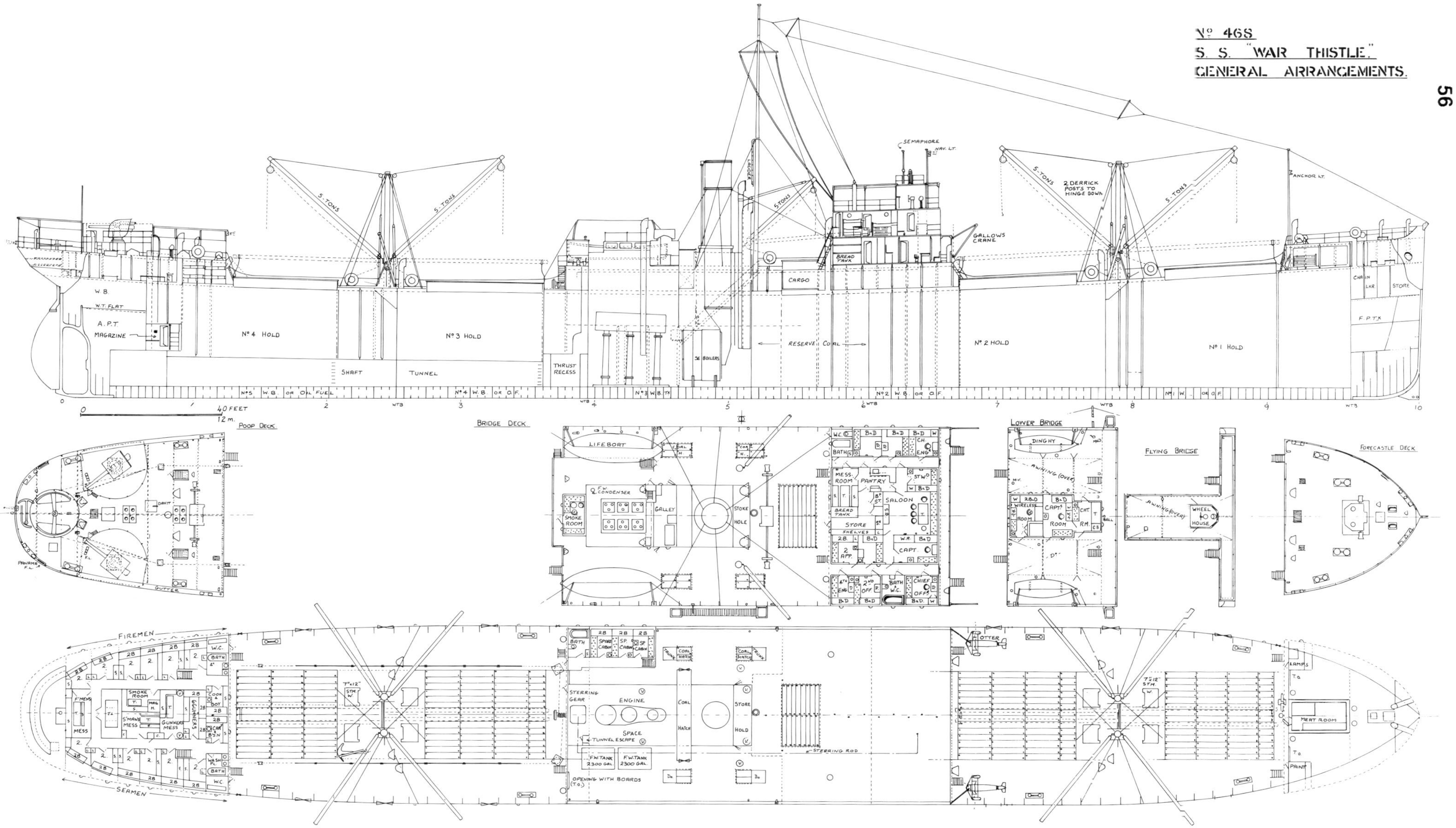

56. *War Thistle* was a single deck 'A' type steamer built by John Brown & Co Ltd of Clydebank in 1917. The plan clearly shows the squat outline produced from the U-boat's viewpoint by keeping the funnel and masts short. As far as possible there was an attempt to create a symmetrical outline to confuse the submarine as to which direction the vessel was heading. This was added to by dazzle painting, see 62

Scottish Record Office

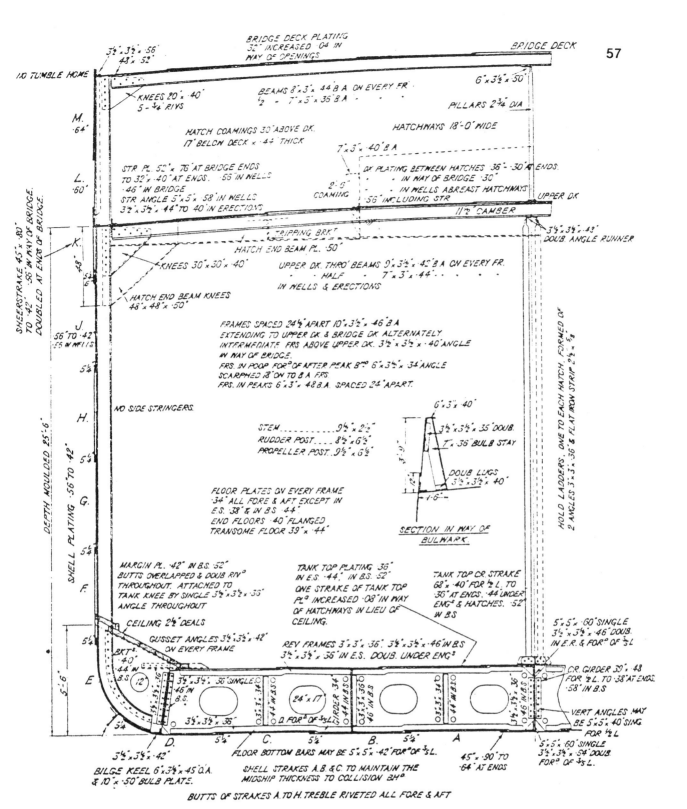

57. Midship section of a 'C' type vessel *War Creek.* For profile see 59.

Some critics claimed that the standard ships should have had higher speeds, but this would have needed a finer hull with a loss of carrying capacity and with larger bunkers causing a further reduction in cargo deadweight. A further complaint was that the vessels were not 'unsinkable', but more steel would have been needed and steel was in short supply. The requirement of the standard ship was the greatest deadweight carrying capability for the minimum steel usage (57). Designs also aimed at reducing the time spent bending the frames, reduction in the number of hold pillars, (achieved by strengthening the decks in way of the hatches). In general the officers and engineers were in the bridge deck with the crew aft in the poop. A lot of shipbuilding records were set during the war. *War Citadel* (an F1 type) was launched by the Northumberland Shipbuilding Co on the 4th of November and handed over on the 7th of November. *War Beetle* (a B type) was completed between launch and hand-over in three and three quarter working days.

SHELTER-DECK CARGO STEAMER

— DIMENSIONS —

LENGTH BETWEEN PERPENDICULARS .... 400' 0"
BREADTH EXTREME .... 55' 0"
DEPTH MOULDED TO UPPER DECK .... 26' 11"

58. *War Keep* was completed as *Saint Dunstan* in 1919 for Rankin & Gilmour of Liverpool (77). She could carry about 9,000 tons on a draught of of 26' 3" and was powered by a triple expansion engine with cylinders 27", 44" and 73" in diameter and a stroke of 48" using steam from three scotch boilers at 180 lbs. pressure which developed 517 nominal horse power. She was a sistership of *Saint Andrew*, see colour profile, volume 2.

Shipbuilding & Shipping Record 1920

59. *War Creek.*

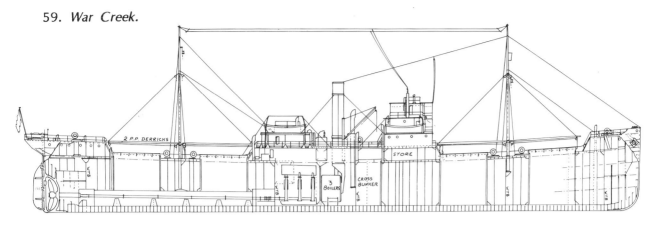

As so often happens it was a case of 'too little too late'. Although orders were placed for over 430 vessels only about 110 were completed before the Armistice. Twenty were cancelled and the remainder were finished and sold to civilian shipowners. Among these was the type 'C' steamer *War Creek*. She was completed in 1919 by the Tyne Iron Shipbuilding Co Ltd and taken up by Charlton, MacAllum & Co of Newcastle under the name *Hallside* (331.2' x 46.8' x 23.1', 3,037 grt). As she was completed after the war ended there was no need for a low profile and the drawing (above) shows the vessel as delivered with full height funnel and masts. The forward holds were divided by a watertight steel bulkhead but in the after holds only a removable wooden division was provided, a feature which permitted the carriage of long items. The holds were not clear, however, as there were numerous hold pillars between the hatches. With bunkers of 1,151 tons she could make round trips to the River Plate and to India without refuelling. *Hallside* was sold to Spain in 1929 and renamed *Delfina*. A considerable number were taken up by British owners at the end of the war.

War Keep (58) was a type 'F1' vessel completed in 1919 by the Northumberland Shipbulding Co Ltd for Rankin & Gilmour of Liverpool. (400.0' x 53.0' x 32.8', 5,662 grt). She was of the shelter deck type making her suitable for the liner trade while still

59. Lines of *War Thistle.*

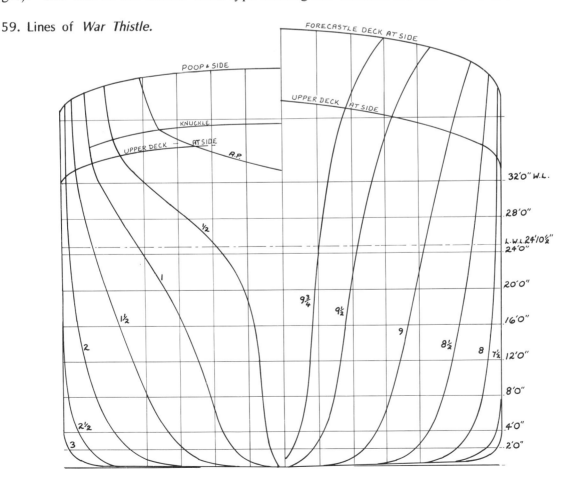

able to handle normal bulk cargo. Instead of the numerous hold pillars which were used in *War Keep* (completed as *Saint Dunstan)* a smaller number of stronger supports were used to reduce obstruction in the holds. There was a saying at sea - "Water and oil don't mix". On *Saint Dunstan* the deck officers were housed below the bridge while the engineers were located further aft on either side of the engine casing. *Saint Dunstan* remained in the Rankin & Gilmour fleet until she was torpedoed in 1940. Another 'F1', *War Turret* was purchased and completed as *Saint Andrew,* later becoming *St.Anselm* when the Saint Line was sold to Mitchell Cotts & Co. She was torpedoed in 1941.

Only 4 standard ships were lost by enemy action, while a further vessel was lost by shipwreck. Another 5 torpedoed were salvaged. In addition to the above, various coasters and tankers were built but these are not considered here. The Shipbuilding Advisory Committee soon realised that the output from British shipyards could not supply the country's needs for cargo vessels and naval vessels, and approaches were made to the U.S.A. and Canada for assistance. Neither of these countries had much of a shipbuilding industry and what there was, was not geared to the construction of large ocean-going dry cargo steamers. In 1914 the U.S.A. launched only 175,000 tons. Because the U.S.A. was neutral the British Government could not place orders direct but had to employ agencies, but by March 1917 orders had been placed for 750,000 tons. However, when America entered the war the U.S. Government requisitioned all ships under construction in the rapidly expanding newly created shipyards. In the end only 11 steel hulled and two wooden hulled vessels were delivered to Britain. The American programme also built up rapidly and in all about 3,500 dry cargo ships were built. In peacetime there was no employment for these vessels and most of this vast armada was laid up in the backwaters around the coast, many still being afloat when world war two broke out. Some of them were purchased by Great Britain to replace the ever-mounting losses of merchant tonnage.

From Canada 87 ships were ordered, of steel and of wood construction. Here again new shipyards had to be created. The ships varied from 1,800 tons dwt to 8,800 tons dwt. In all 48 steel and 47 wooden ships were built (the extra 8 were built to civilian order after the end of the war). Only 18 of the steel ships and less than half of the wooden ships were completed before the Armistice.

WORLD WAR TWO DESIGNS: When war broke out, about 1,000,000 gross tons of shipping was on the stocks in British shipyards, vessels of every shape and size, each being built to a particular owner's requirements and none of them designed for quick construction. World war one had shown the desirability of changing the traditional policy of shipbuilding on a one-off basis to a series of standard vessels. Several shipyards already had standard designs of their own and where these conformed to the requirements of the Ministry of Shipping, later the Ministry of War Transport, the yard was allowed

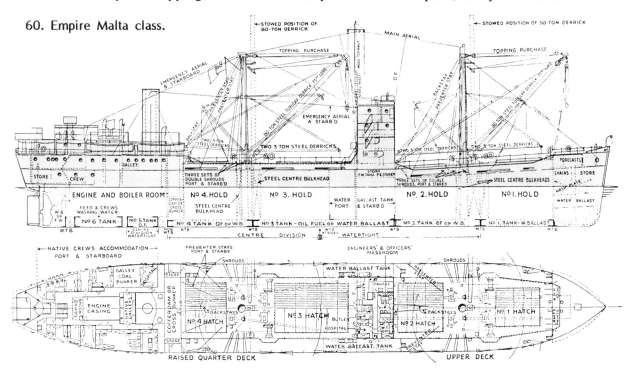

60. Empire Malta class.

to carry on building them. Later, control of shipbuilding was transferred to an Admiralty committee and standard designs were approved and issued to shipyards. The basic requirement for cargo carriers of the tramp type was for vessels of 7,000 tons gross, 10,000 tons deadweight, generally 420 to 430 feet in length and 56 feet beam with a speed of 10 to 12 knots. The plan of *Empire Mordred* (98) shows a type 'B' standard ship of which 11 were built, by far the largest group of this size. She was built in 1942 by Charles Connell & Co Ltd, Glasgow, 431.3' x 56.3' x 35.2', 7,024 grt, and she was allocated to G.Nisbet & Co of Glasgow for management. She did not last long being sunk by a mine in February 1943. She was a two-decked ship with no sheer between the foremast and the poop. The profile was kept to a minimum with a short funnel and sampson posts as masts. Derricks had a capacity of 5 tons, but a 40 ton and 50 ton derrick were fitted to handle heavy loads (63). As she might be called on to carry coal or grain central steel dividers were fitted in the holds between the hatchways. *Empire Mordred* was a coal burner.

Some were fitted with refrigerated hold space. For simplicity most of these vessels were propelled by the traditional triple expansion engines, only a small proportion being diesel engined. The ships built were given names prefixed *Empire* .... Altogether 277 of the tramp type were built, 70 being lost by enemy action. A further 14, damaged by bombs, torpedoes or gunfire, survived to sail again. In the construction of the *Empire* vessels a certain amount of prefabrication was introduced into the designs. As requirements changed during the war and the military cargoes increased in bulk, bigger hatches were fitted and the profiles of the vessels altered slightly.

A further standard design was introduced for the intermediate trades, i.e. for relatively short voyages, known as the 'Scandinavian' type. As the name suggests the masts and derricks were placed at the breaks in the superstructure like some timber carriers, not between the hatches. William Gray's of West Hartlepool built 24 from 1941 onwards while 14 others were built by 5 other builders. Dimensions were generally 315.4' x 46.5' x 23.0', 2,847 grt, 4,700 deadweight. They were of the three-island type with masts and derricks against the breaks in the superstructure as was common to timber carriers for the Scandinavian trade. As standard, 5 ton derricks were fitted, but some vessels were later equipped with 15 ton, 50 ton or 80 ton derricks for convoys to Northern Russia where they were used to unload other vessels without heavy lifting gear. They were heavily armed with a 12-pounder gun, Oerlikons and four machine guns. In all 38 were built and 6 were lost to torpedo or mines. After the war they were sold off: Hugh Hogarth of Glasgow bought three and renamed them *Baron Elibank (ex Empire Ransom), Baron Elcho (ex Empire Lorenzo)* and *Baron Ailsa (ex Empire Harcourt)* The plan shows *Empire Bard* (64) which was built in 1942 by the Caledon Shipbuilding & Engineering Co Ltd, Dundee. She was purchased by the Dundee, Perth & London Shipping Company at the end of the war and converted for peacetime use by her builders. She became *Angusburn* in 1946 and was chartered to the British Iron & Steel Corporation to carry iron ore, and sold in 1954 to the Brebner Shipping Co Ltd, London who renamed her *Brettenham* (105).

One of the more unusual types of standard ship based on a similar hull was *Empire Malta* a large raised quarter deck engines aft vessel, 315.5' x 46.5' x 22.1', 3,539 grt (approximately). In 1944 and 1945, 10 of these ships were built by Wm. Gray & Co Ltd of West Hartlepool to an Admiralty design. The normal derricks were rated for a 5 ton lift, on most vessels additional 50 ton and 80 ton derricks were fitted. The *Empire Malta* class (60) proved to be very versatile and they were used as colliers, cased oil carriers and for the transport of large heavy vehicles. In fact the nickname *'Empire Heinz'* was given to this class of standard steamer. After the war they found ready buyers, among them Tate & Lyle who purchased *Sugar Transporter (ex Empire Calcos)* and *Sugar Refiner (ex Empire Aldgate)* which were managed by R.S. Dalgliesh of Newcastle. *Empire Malta* herself was sold to Hong Kong owners, while *Empire Barbados* became *Tennyson* of the Rodney S.S. Co, London.

The original *Empire* design was developed by J.L. Thompson of Sunderland and the first vessel, *Empire Liberty* was launched at their North Sands yard in 1941. In 1940, while the design was being discussed, the desirability of prefabrication was emphasised, not so much from the speed of construction but rather that stocks of sections should be held in reserve to replace parts damaged in air raids on the shipyards, a situation which, in the event, occurred infrequently. Prefabrication was generally limited to the parallel body which represented about a third of the hull's length. To achieve prefabrication the

62. *War Drake* was an 'A' type standard ship completed by D. & W. Henderson in 1918 and is seen in the dazzle paint scheme devised by marine artist Norman Wilkinson who was a lieutenant-commander in the Royal Naval Volunteer Reserve during the first world war. His method was to try and produce as confusing an outline as possible so that it was difficult, particularly in hazy conditions for an attacking submarine to determine the heading of the vessel or even whether one or more vessels were present. To assist the deception, masts were often offset from the centre line, or made to fold down. The colours used were mainly black, white, greys, greens and blues. The various schemes were applied to models first, using wash colours which could be easily changed until the best results were obtained when the model was observed through a submarine periscope. The combinations of pattern and colour were varied to give the best results for the particular vessel and area where she was expected to operate. The designs were always different on opposite sides of the ship and the junctions between the shades were carefully arranged so they did not correspond with the outline of the ship. The pattern on the starboard side of the ship was carried some distance round on to the port side and the stern was treated similarly. Eventually it was found that simple sloping stripes gave the best results. The *War Drake* had the dimensions 400.6' x 52.3' x 28.5' and was sold in 1919 to the Sefton S.S. Co Ltd (H.E. Moss & Co, managers), London, becoming the *Mount Everest*.

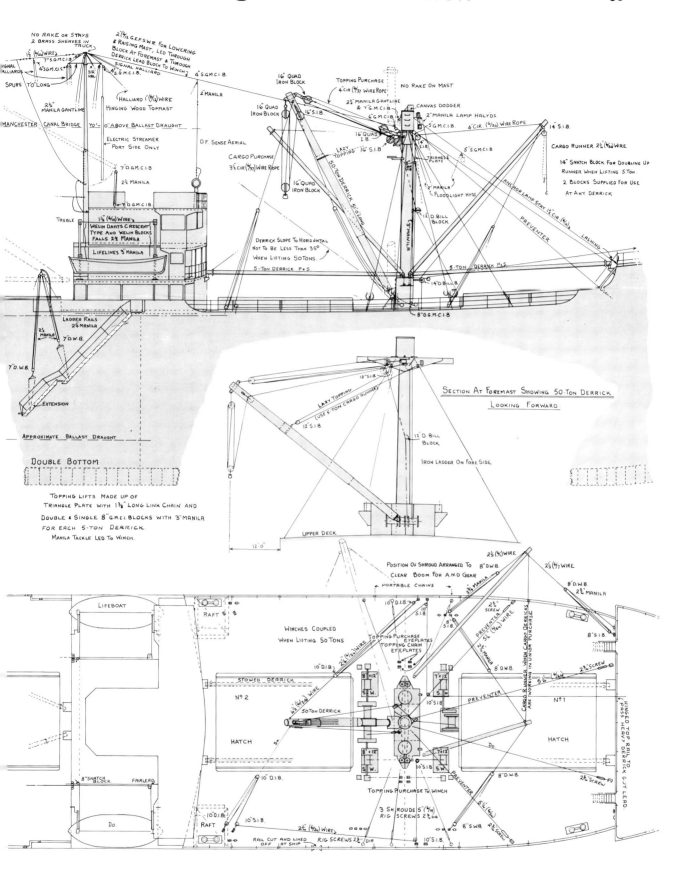

63. Part of the rigging plan of the 'B' type *Empire Mordred* showing the foremast and derricks. The arrangement was similar to that in most tramps though the mast was strengthened to accept the 50-ton derrick essential for lifting military equipment and no topmast was fitted above the crow's nest look-out. The 5-ton derricks were subjected to 6.25 tons on test and the 50-ton derrick to 55 tons as required by the Factory Act. Many tramps had lighter derricks of around 3-tons capacity. See also (98).

Scottish Record Office

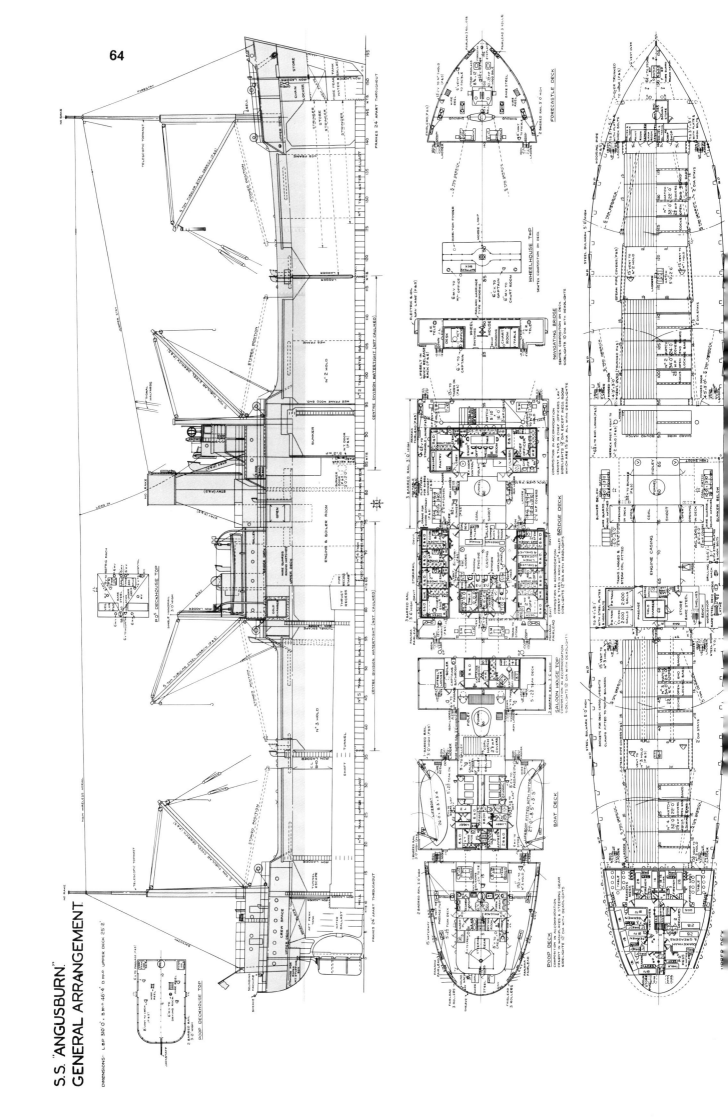

S.S. "ANGUSBURN."
GENERAL ARRANGEMENT.

DIMENSIONS:- L&P 310'0", B.Mld 46'4", D.Mld UPPER DECK 25'2"

radius of the bilge was increased and the ends of the hull were made fuller to counter the reduction in displacement. The design was known as the Partially Fabricated vessel, shortened to P.F. The first design was not used and the modified plans were called the P.F.(B). These were subsequently altered twice and the designations P.F.(C.) and P.F.(D) were applied.The arrangement of the bouble bottom in the P.F.(C) type is shown below. The general arrangement of the *Empire Liberty* is the simplified drawing published in 1942 during war-time and omits such details as the armament (66). The machinery was similar to pre-war designs except the superheaters and the reheater between the high pressure and intermediate pressure cylinders were omitted to speed construction (67).

It was claimed that the *Empire* tramp steamer could carry in one voyage enough flour, cheese, bacon, ham, canned and dried fruits to feed 225,000 people for a week; 2,200 tons of steel; enough Bren gun carriers, trucks and motor cycles to motorise an infantry battallion; enough bombs to load about 1,000 bombers; two complete bombers on the after deck and about four tanks on the forward deck and enough aluminium to build 659 fighter planes.

As they had done in the first world war the British government turned abroad for assistance. Lying in the backwaters of the North American continent were vast numbers of cargo steamers, ships which had been completed too late to take part in the previous conflict. Despite the fact that many of these vessels were in poor condition after twenty one years of neglect a large number were purchased by the Ministry of Shipping and were put into service bearing the familiar *Empire* names. Approaches were made to Canada but as in world war one, Canada's shipping fleet was very small, barely 40 ships were ocean-going, and the shipbuilding industry had only about ten shipyards, all of which had orders for naval vessels. The British Merchant Shipbuilding Mission visited Canada late in 1940 and as a result of their discussions orders were placed for 26 vessels. This was only a start and as time went by existing shipyards were expanded and new ones were opened, and by the end of the war some 450 merchant vessels had been built. There were a number of standard types. The 7,130 gross ton, 10,000 deadweight *Fort....* had a length of 425 feet and a beam of 57 feet constructed in accordance with drawings from the North Sands shipyard of J.L. Thompson & Sons, Sunderland (sometimes called the 'North Sands Type'). As they had been designed in a British

65. Details of the partially fabricated double bottom of the 'C' type standard Empire ship. See page 147 for a side elevation.   Shipbuilding & Shipping Record, 1946

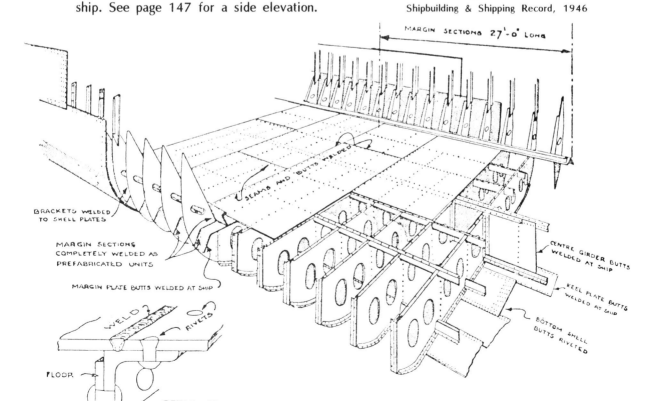

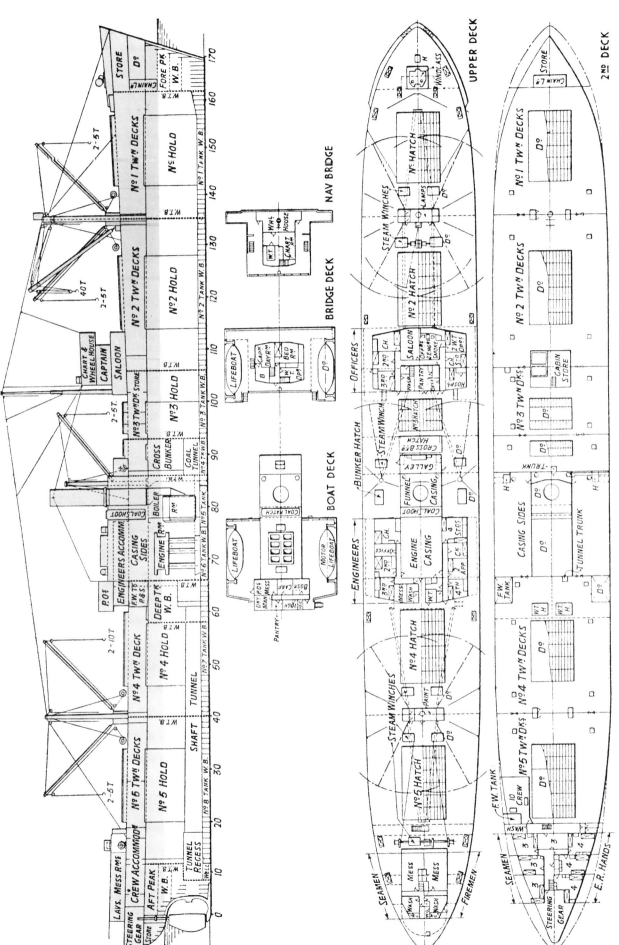

66. *Empire Liberty* of 7,157 gross tons was completed in 1941 for the Ministry of War Transport. The design was used as a prototype for the *Forts, Parks* and *Oceans* ordered from Canada and the U.S.A. The *Empire Liberty* herself was sold to the

shipyard they were intended for riveted construction as opposed to the welded construction commonly used in the United States. The first ship, *Fort St. James*, took 281 days to build and deliver, a figure which over the years dropped to an average of 163 days. In 1941 an agreement was reached between the U.S.A. and Canada under which the Americans bought 90 of the 154 *Forts* from Canada and chartered them to Great Britain under the Lease-Lend agreement. Another group was known as the *Victory* type, the North Sands design again, but fitted to burn oil fuel; 32 were built for dry cargo work with an additional 12 for refrigerated cargo. The North Sands design was used for a third group of ships which were given names ....*Park*, of these 114 were built. A demand arose for smaller vessels and to meet this Wm. Gray's of Hartlepool provided drawings of their timber carrier, a vessel of 2,875 tons gross and 4,700 tons deadweight with a length of 315'6" and a beam of 46'6". These were given names with the *Park* nomenclature and a total of 43 were built. They were not all identical as there were differences in derrick configuration and accommodation.

While the Shipbuilding Mission was in North America they also visited the United States and arranged contracts for a series of *Ocean....* ships, 7,180 tons gross, 10,500 tons deadweight, 425 feet long by 57 feet beam, fitted with triple expansion engines with coal fired boilers and of typical American welded construction. In all 60 *Ocean* vessels were built for the British government in new yards which were specially laid out for their construction.

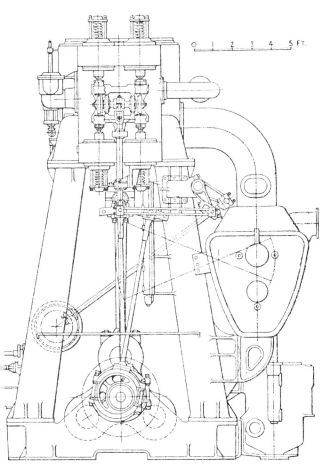

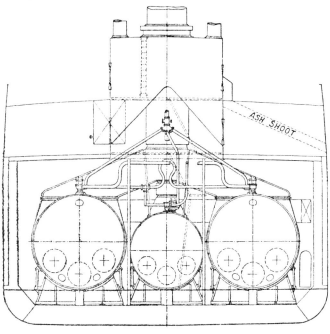

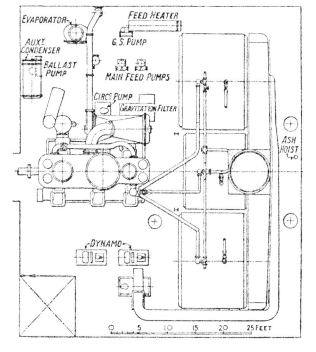

67. Machinery of the *Empire Liberty* showing (above) the triple expansion engine from the front end. Right top: The two main boilers and auxiliary boiler and below a plan of the engine room. The forced draught fan for the boilers is adjacent to the dynamos.

Shipbuilding & Shipping Record, 1942

In early 1942 the first of the Oceans arrived in the U.K. She was *Ocean Vanguard* 7174/41. The keel had been laid down on 14th April 1941, she was launched on 16th August and was delivered on 27th October. She arrived on this side with 8,000 tons of cargo including lead, canned foods, wood pulp, timber, wheat, borax, hides and aircraft. Shortly afterwards *Fort Ville Marie* arrived from Canada with wheat, apples and explosives. She had been laid down in May 1941, launched in October and delivered in time to sail before the St. Lawrence was closed to navigation by ice.

The U.S.A. had been planning to expand their shipbuilding production since before the war but when the time came to choose a prototype there was a divergence of opinion between those who favoured the adoption of an American design which would have had to be modified and an existing proven British design, the *Ocean* type. The decision was finally taken in favour of the *Ocean* design, although extensive revision was undertaken to suit American mass production methods utilising welding instead of riveting. Mass production then began on what came to be known as the Liberty ship. Called in the press 'ugly ducklings' and 'sea scows' they were built by the hundred and were credited with saving the Allied cause; in all 2,710 Liberty ships were launched. They were 441'6" overall by 57' beam with tonnages of 7,176 gross and 10,865 deadweight. The steam powered Liberty ships had 2,500 ihp. triple expansion engines fed by steam from oil fired water tube boilers built from standard designs. The all welded construction of the Liberty ships gave a lot of trouble due to cracking and a number were lost. It was said that one in thirty suffered major fractures, particularly in freezing conditions. Anxiety about the reports of structural cracking in the Liberty ships led to a study being carried out in 1945 when *Ocean Vulcan* 7174/42 (later *Cape Nelson* of the Lyle Shipping Co) was closely observed during a series of trans–Atlantic voyages over a period of eighteen months.

Rudder and propellor failures were common in all merchant ships at one time but in 1948 the frequency of failures in Liberty ships reached levels above the average and replacement of rudders with improved designs was undertaken. By this time, following modification to shafts, loss of propellors had become rare. Up to September 1949, 100 Liberty ships were reported as having shed their screws. Cracking around hatches was countered with reinforced corners, while cracking along the deckline was overcome by the fitting of riveted straps or angles. After these modifications reports of cracking dropped to one eighth of previous figures. However, as late as 1956, *Pelagia* broke in two in the open sea and *Seagate* broke her back after running aground, while in three months six ex–wartime standard vessels lost their screws, two Liberties, one Victory, one Park and one Fort. As designed the Liberty ships were 'stiff' in ballast trim, and when sailing in ballast it was usual to carry part of their ballast on the 'tween deck. At first no provision was made for shifting boards and several vessels were lost due to the ballast shifting in heavy seas. Even after shifting boards had been fitted *Leicester*, ex *Samesk* was almost lost. The welding at the base of the stanchions holding the shifting boards broke allowing the stanchions to swing and release the boards.

After the war the Liberty ships were sold in their hundreds to every maritime nation including well over 100 to British owners. Others found their way into this country's fleets by purchase from other nations.

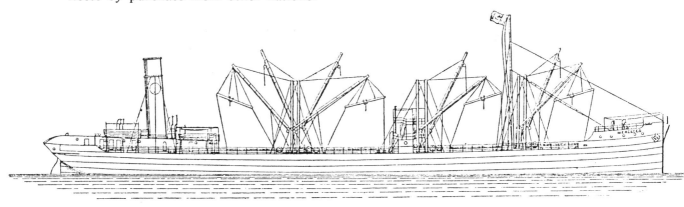

68. The coal steamer *Mercedes* 4482/01 of Christie & Co, Cardiff was built for the Australian coal trade to South America.   Engineering, 1901

3.

69.
Turret ready for launch-
ing at Doxford's yard.
Photo: The Engineer, 1892

Shipbuilders

The main builders of tramp steamers were concentrated in the Clyde area, south-east Scotland and north-east England. Although many tramps were owned in South Wales only one yard at Chepstow built tramps in the region for a short time. The same applied to Liverpool, though the main owners were involved in liner trading. Labour costs in the London area had driven out shipbuilding on the Thames by the time the main London tramp fleets were built up.

Ailsa Shipbuilding Co Ltd, Troon. The Ailsa yard opened in 1886 and was concerned mainly with passenger vessels, passenger/cargo ferries and tugs, but with slips up to 360 feet in length, a few tramps were produced for the intermediate trades such as *Maywood* 1188/01 for J.T. Duncan, Cardiff.

Ayrshire Dockyard Ltd, Irvine. The shipbuilding yards in Irvine were building only small craft until MacKie & Thomson took over in 1912. Under the name Ayrshire Dockyard Co Ltd 6 berths were laid down capable of holding hulls up to 450 feet. Among the tramp steamers built were *Baron Cochrane* 3385/27 (H. Hogarth); and *Blairmore* 4141/28 (George Nisbet). The post-war slump left the yard short of orders but it struggled on until 1934 when it was purchased by National Shipbuilders Security Ltd to be closed down and reduced to a ship repairing facility.

Ardrossan Dry Dock & Shipbulding Co Ltd, Ardrossan. In the 1870s the Ardrossan Shipbuilding Co was formed and expanded until there were 9 slips building tugs to cargo and passenger liners from 150 feet to 430 feet long. In 1894 the name was changed to Ardrossan Dry Dock & Shipbuilding Co Ltd, who built a new South Yard in 1916 (this was closed in 1931). In 1925 the company was taken over by Coast Lines Ltd and J.G. Kincaid and became Ardrossan Dockyard Ltd, which name it retained until closure in 1964. The yard launched mainly coasters and small tramps. Although Hogarth's tramps were registered in Ardrossan only one of their steamers was built in the yard, *Baron Elibank* 2579/19, but even this was purchased second hand and was launched as *Glassford.* Most of the cargo steamers were below 3,000 grt. and included *Hunstanworth* 2579/19, (R.S. Dalgliesh)

Campbeltown Shipbuilding Co Ltd, Campbeltown. This small coastal town on the Clyde is usually associated with fishing and holidays but in its day it had a busy shipyard. Opened in 1877 a number of quite large tramp steamers were built before closure in 1922, though its output was mainly for foreign owners. Two of the largest vessels built were *St. Quentin* 3528/14, (Geo. Bailey, Newport), built as *Lady Plymouth* and *Datchet* 3610/18, ex *Roquelle*, (E.H. Watts).

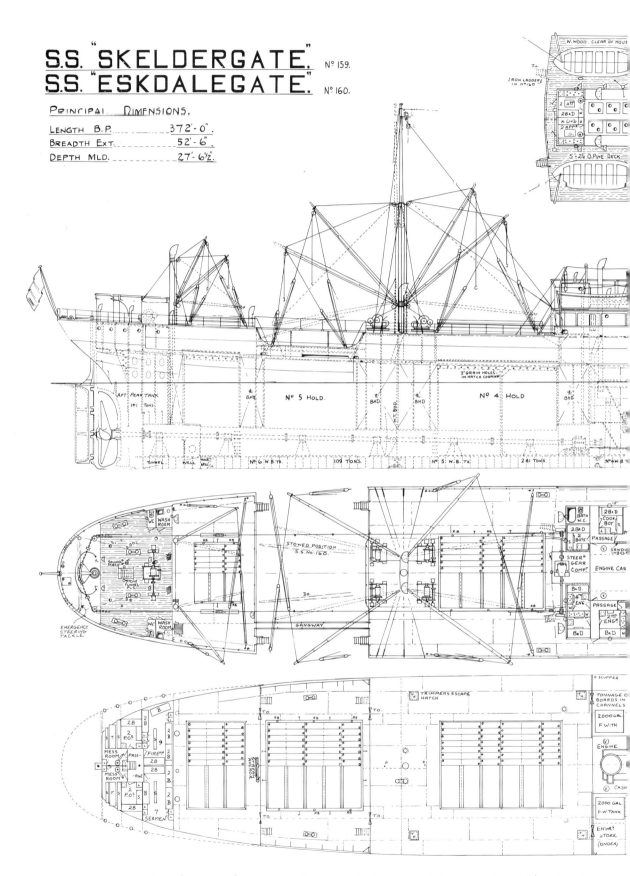

S.S. "SKELDERGATE." Nº 159.
S.S. "ESKDALEGATE." Nº 160.

PRINCIPAL DIMENSIONS.

LENGTH B.P.	372'-0".
BREADTH EXT.	52'-6".
DEPTH MLD.	27'-6½".

70. Burntisland 'Economy' steamers *Eskdalegate* 4250/30 (Turnbull, Scott Shipping Co Ltd) and *Skeldergate* 4251/30 (Redgate S.S. Co Ltd) were completed in 1930 and managed by Turnbull, Scott & Co, London. The triple expansion engines had cylinders

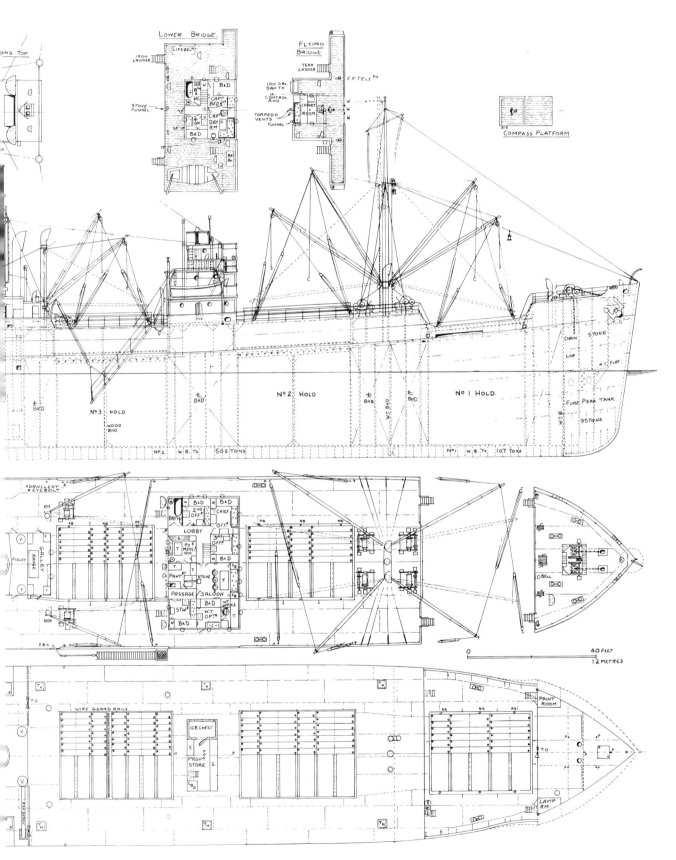

23", 39" and 65" in diameter with a stroke of 45" using steam at 200 lbs from 2 scotch boilers made by D. Rowan & Co, Glasgow. There was an auxiliary boiler to provide steam when in port. They carried 7,950 tons on a summer draught of 24'5".

Marine Consultants Ltd

Barclay, Curle & Co Ltd, Glasgow. John Barclay started shipbuilding in 1818 and was succeeded by his son Robert, who in 1845 took into partnership his yard manager Robert Curle, to form Robert Barclay & Curle. The name was changed in 1855 to Barclay, Curle & Co and in 1874 the company had to move their activities to Whiteinch. They built a variety of vessels, mainly passenger carrying, and ships for the liner trades such as *Bangalore* (8), with a few tramp steamers, *Lennox* 3677/95 for Warrack of Leith, *Onslow* 2722/98 for Harris & Dixon, London and others. After 1900 right up to 1950 the output of the yard was almost entirely destined for the liner traders though 7 standard Empire vessels were launched, 3 steam, 4 diesel. After 1950 a number of motor tramps were constructed such as *Trevalyor* 6501/59 for Hain S.S. Co. In 1965 shipbuilding ceased though the last ship credited to Barclay, Curle is dated 1967 in Lloyds Register of Shipping.

William Beardmore & Co Ltd, Dalmuir. The firm were steel steelmakers but in 1901 they took over the yard of Robert Napier & Sons in Govan, moving later to Dalmuir in 1905. The yard built warships, tankers, liners, even tugs, and from time to time a tramp steamer. The last two steamers to be launched were *Dalhanna* and *Daldorch* 5571/30 for J.M. Campbell & Son, Glasgow, steamers which attracted attention because of their advanced design. In 1931 the yard was closed by National Shipbuilders Security Ltd.

Blackwood & Gordon, Port Glasgow. This company moved from a small yard in Paisley in 1860 to give them the opportunity of building larger ships, as well as the tugs and coasters which were their bread and butter. In 1900 the title was changed to Clyde Shipbuilding & Engineering Co Ltd, and the slips were enlarged to take vessels up to 4,000 grt. Mostly they built small vessels for foreign owners but they did construct several medium sized tramps for British owners. *Fitzpatrick* 1168/69 for Burrell and *Hermia* 2050/03 for J. Neil, Glasgow. The company closed in 1900.

Charles Connell & Co Ltd, Scotstown. Charles Connell, formerly yard manager for Alex Stephen & Sons, started his own yard in 1861 and built a large number of high quality sailing ships. When the company began building steamers many famous liner companies came with orders, but Connell's were not noted as builders of tramps. However, during the first world war, 4 standard vessels were launched, and later they built *Ardangorm* 5200/30 (Clark & Service) and *Baron Kelvin* 3081/24 (Hogarth). Between 1931 and 1938 the yard lay idle. During world war two, 12 standard Empire steamers, such as *Empire Mordred* (98) were produced and afterwards their customers were mainly liner owners again though J. & J. Denholm went to Connell's for *Wellpark* 6722/46. In 1968 the yard became part of the Upper Clyde Shipbuilders Ltd.

Robert Duncan & Co Ltd, Port Glasgow. The Port Glasgow yard was established in 1862 on the ground previously occupied by John Wood. Close association with the big liner companies provided many orders for passenger vessels, but tramps were not neglected. Prior to 1900 most of the ships launched were sail, but after that date steam took over. Larrinaga & Co ordered *Domingo de Larrinaga* 4076/99 while W.S. Miller came here for their *Elsiston* 1619/04 and *Maplegrove* 3811/12 (12). The Duncan-built tramps were often large for the day; *Roseley* 4370/02, for W.R. Rea of Belfast. Their last order was for *Ardgorm* and *Ardgair* 5119/13 for Lang & Fulton. In 1914 the yard lay idle and in 1915 it was taken over by Russell & Co who were renamed Lithgows Ltd in 1918.

Harland & Wolff Ltd, Govan. In 1912 Harland & Wolff of Belfast took over the shipyard of the London & Glasgow Shipbuilding & Engineering Co Ltd and expanded further in 1916 when they bought over Caird & Co, Greenock, A. & J. Inglis of Pointhouse in 1919 and A. McMillan, Dumbarton in 1918. They built 6 dry cargo carriers to the standard War 'A' and 'B' designs including *War Jasmine* which became *Highmead* 5263/19 of Western Counties Shipping Co Ltd. Harland & Wolff were among the first builders to install diesel engines in tramps and A. Weir of Glasgow were one of their best customers with *Olivebank* 5154/26 and others. In world war two they built only 5 Empire's of the dry cargo type. Production ceased in 1962 and today a housing scheme occupies the site of the yard.

D. & W. Henderson & Co Ltd, Glasgow. The brothers David and William Henderson, marine engineers, purchased the yard of Tod & MacGregor in 1873 in partnership with the Anchor Line. The business was taken over in 1919 by Harland & Wolff and finally liquidated in 1935. In the early days they launched almost every kind of craft from ocean liners to river barges. Again a lot of their production went to Glasgow owners; Maclay & McIntyre took *Oceana* 4846/06. A.H. & E. Gunn of Cardiff ordered *Chalister* 5344/13.

73.
Gretavale, built 1928 by Lithgows Ltd for Andrew Crawford, Glasgow and mentioned below.

Photo: P.N.Thomas collection

During the war the yard built 10 standard vessels, and after the war 5 of them were bought by the Hain S.S. Co Ltd. Hogarth was a regular customer, one of many ships built for them was *Baron Napier* 3659/30.

Lithgows Ltd, Port Glasgow. William Lithgow was in the shipbuilding business as shipyard manager for Russell & Co, taking over the yard in 1891 but keeping the same name. His sons followed in his footsteps and finally renamed the company Lithgows Ltd in 1918. They concentrated on merchant ships and managed to keep busy even during the slump. They built for Clan Line, Hogarth and other well-known names and launched some of the first motor ships for the Lyle Shipping Co. Other tramp owners who ordered regularly from Lithgows were R. Fulton of Glasgow *(Bellailsa* 4553/24), Andrew Crawford *(Gretavale* 4586/28, (73)) and Pardoe-Thomas of Newport *(Knight Almoner* 4600/30 and 3 others). During the second world war the yard launched no less than 39 Empire type dry cargo vessels for the Ministry of War Transport, mostly the 7,000 grt. type. These found ready buyers after the war; *Empire Cyprus* 7200/45 became *North Britain* of Hugh Roberts of Newcastle. In 1968 the yard became part of the Scott-Lithgow group.

Lloyd Royal Belge (Great Britain) Ltd, Whiteinch, Glasgow. One of the shortest lived yards on the Clyde, this company occupied a site in Whiteinch from 1916 to 1921, building 25 vessels. The British Government provided the yard for the Belgians to build ships for their country while it was occupied by the Germans, and it was managed by the shipowners Brys & Gylsen Ltd. As might be expected it was called on to produce standard types of which 8 were built, including two which operated in the fleet of the Henley S.S. Co Ltd of London in the intermediate trades, *Acton Manor* 1480/19 and *Chiswick Manor* 1484/19. After the war the yard was sold to Barclay, Curle & Co Ltd.

A. McMillan & Sons Ltd, Dumbarton. Situated at Dumbarton, this yard was overshadowed by their better known neighbours, Denny, despite their not inconsiderable total of over 500 vessels launched. Well known as sailing ship builders they also put a useful number of tramps into service, mainly for overseas buyers. Vessels for British owners included *St. Kilda* 3518/99 for Rankin, Gilmour & Co of Liverpool and *Kelvingrove* 3092/99 for J. Black of Glasgow. The yard opened in 1834 and continued until 1930 when it was closed by the National Shipbuilders Security Ltd.

Murdoch & Murray Ltd, Port Glasgow. Formed in 1875, the company built ships for 37 years, apart from a spell in 1895 when the slump forced them to close temporarily. Mainly a small ship specialist, they did include in their production a number of intermediate traders such as *Ormesby Broad* 1277/01 for G.H. Elder of London and *Rosneath* 1779/90 for Gow, Harrison & Co, Glasgow. The yard had 5 berths with capacity for vessels up to 350 feet In 1912 the name was changed to Port Glasgow Shipbuilding Co Ltd, which survived until the slump which forced closure in 1927. Among the tramp steamers built in later years was *Windermere* 2815/21 belonging to Balls & Stansfield of Newcastle.

Napier & Miller Ltd, Glasgow. Originally known as Napier, Shanks & Bell, the yard was established in 1877 in Yoker by Robert Napier's grandson. With a change in management in 1898 the name was altered to Napier & Miller Ltd. When Rothesay Dock was constructed in 1906 the yard had to move to Old Kilpatrick, further down river. Napier & Miller built a large number of good-sized steamers including tramps for Glasgow owners who came back with repeat orders. Hugh Hogarth for his *Baron Murray* 3103/24, G. Nisbet & Co for *Blairatholl* 3319/25 and Raeburn & Verel for *British Monarch* 5661/23. Other owners also came: Reardon Smith for *Braddovey* 3359/27 and Watts, Watts of London for *Ascot* 4334/02 – she was still in their fleet in 1930, the year the yard was closed by National Shipbuilders Security Ltd.

Scott's Shipbuilding & Engineering Co Ltd, Greenock. Claimed to be the oldest working shipyard in the world (the first vessel was laid down in 1711) the company has traded under a variety of 'Scott' names, building nearly 900 vessels of all kinds, passenger liners, steam yachts, cargo carriers and warships. Although the yard was renowned for its passenger liners, quite a number of the humble tramps went down the slips of this famous yard. J. & J. Denholm took delivery of *Deerpark* 928/01 and at the other end of the scale *Eldonpark* 5184/28, while owners from other parts of the country came too; Mungo Campbell of Newcastle for his *Dalblair* 4608/26. In 1968 the company merged to form Scott-Lithgow Ltd.

Harland & Wolff, Belfast. G.W. Wolff was born in Hamburg but came to England to study. He went to Belfast to work in the shipyard of Hickson & Co and in 1885 the yard was taken over by the manager, E.J. Harland. In 1861 Wolff was taken into partnership and the famous name Harland & Wolff was born. The yard grew in size until by 1920 there were 15 slips and an engine works ready to build anything from a tug to a trans-Atlantic liner. They built mainly for the liner trade though several tramps were launched for local owners, *Lord Lansdowne* 2753/84 for T. Dixon & Sons, *Torr Head* 5911/94 for G. Heyn & Sons. During the first world war they built a large number of vessels for the government, both naval vessels and standard cargo carriers. There were 16 steamers of standard construction, 3 'A', 8 'B', 2 'D' and 3 'G' types. These vessels were disposed of to liner traders and foreign shipowners, but one of them became *Adderstone* 5255/20 owned by the White Shipping Co (R.I. James), Newcastle. She had originally been fitted with twin turbines but in 1934 these were replaced by a double compound engine with a White pass-out turbine, one of the approaches to the problem of improving fuel efficiency. They built, in addition, 15 of the 'N' type prefabricated ships which were taken up by the liner trade companies after the war. In the meantime the company had begun to expand, taking over three yards in Glasgow in 1912 and purchasing controlling interests in other firms on the Clyde, D. & W. Henderson, A. & J. Inglis, and A. McMillan. After the war some more tramp ships were built but these were mostly diesel powered.

Workman, Clark & Co, Belfast. In 1879 Frank Workman left Harland & Wolff and set up on his own by the River Lagan. He started off well with a number of orders from the City Line for the liner trades and then in 1883 the local Head Line ordered *Teelin Head* 1668/83 the first of many for that company. In the meantime, in 1880 he had taken into partnership George Clark, the company becoming Workman, Clark & Co Ltd. The new company also established ties with Corry's 'Star Line' (later part of the Commonwealth and Dominion Line). The yard was soon building for other passenger lines, and, although not noted for tramp steamers, tramps were not ignored. Clark & Service came here for their *Ardenearg* 3218/95. Indeed during the war a large number of standard dry cargo vessels were built by Workman, Clark, 7 'B' and 10 'G' types. Most of these went to liner trades but *War Peewit* 5179/19 went first to G. Heyn as *Ballygally Head* and then to the West Hartlepool Steam Navigation Co as *Kepwickhall.* During 1919 the Northumberland Shipping Co acquired a controlling interest in the yard but by 1923 the yard was in financial difficulties. It soldiered on, was reorganised in 1928, but in 1935 was forced to close through lack of orders.

The Caledon Shipbuilding & Engineering Co Ltd, Dundee. Over the years the company grew to occupy 10 building slips capable of launching vessels up to 700 feet and 20,000 grt. They built all types; passenger liners, liner traders, dry cargo carriers and coasters. Up until 1896 the yard had been under the management of W.B. Thompson & Co Ltd, who had built such ships as *Ailsa Craig* 3451/90 one of the Clyde Shipping Company's deep sea traders. As an illustration of the close ties which often existed between builders and owners, W.B. Thompson built 10 coastal liner traders for the Clyde Shipping Company while Caledon built 20, plus the two deep sea tramps *Ailsa Craig* and *Longships* 4461/93. As part of the war effort in 1918/19 Caledon built 5 tramps and 9 coasters. Between the wars more tramps were built including *Wanstead* 5486/28 for Watts, Watts & Co (2) and *Norman Monarch* 4718/27 for Raeburn & Verel.

Dundee Shipbuilding Co Ltd, Dundee. In 1894 the Dundee branch of Alexander Stephen, (the same family as the Glasgow yard) was bought over by the Dundee Shipbuilding Co, promoted by H.F. Craggs and C.H. Pile, both north east coast shipbuilders. The output of the yard was mainly trawlers, coasters and short sea traders such as *Ochilbrae* 1492/19 (D. Anderson of Glasgow).They built their last ship in 1922 and the plant was finally disposed of in 1927.

75.
Eskdalegate, built 1930 by the Burntisland Ship- building Co Ltd, Burnt- island. See below.

Photo: Alex Duncan

Gourlay Bros. & Co, Dundee. The Camperdown Yard, as it was known, laid down its first vessel in 1855. Many of their products were for local owners like *Emerald* 658/77 for P.M. Duncan & Son of the Dundee Gem Line. Most of the vessels launched were trawlers, coasters and liner traders but there were a few tramps among them. *Keats* 4336/05 of Glover Bros, London, originally *Den of Kelly* of C. Barrie of Dundee. From time to time a steamer was registered in the name of the builder. Such a one was *Grampian* 692/64 which the company built and ran for several years before being sold. In 1908 the company got into financial difficulties and was forced to go into liquidation.

Ramage & Ferguson Ltd, Leith. In 1878 this company was established in Leith and from their slips launched vessels up to 5,000 grt., tugs, steam yachts, coasters and liner traders for which they were well known and a few smaller tramps like *Dunmore Head* 1682/98 owned by Heyn of Belfast and *Inver* 1543/18 of the Shamrock Shipping Co, Larne. In 1935 the yard was acquired by Henry Robb Ltd.

Burntisland Shipbuilding Co Ltd, Burntisland. With the huge demand for building capacity in mind, a new shipyard with 4 berths was laid out early in 1918 to build 'C' type standard vessels. By September the 4 berths were occupied and the metal working shops had been arranged to provide some degree of prefabrication. The first vessel launched was too late for the war and was completed as *Sunbank* 3099/19 for Mitchell, Cotts' Sun Shipping Co of London. Most of the vessels from Burntisland were dry cargo carriers, liner traders and coasters. Many shipowners went back for repeat orders, *Pentreath* 2475/24 and others for Lambert, Barnett & Co, London, *Usk Valley* 2480/29 and others for R.W. Jones of Newport. Here were built two 'Arch' steamers, one for W.A. Souter; *Sheaf Brook* 2179/24 and *Eleveen* 1687/22 for W. Swanston of Newcastle. In an effort to beat the slump the company designed their 'economy steamer' in the 1930s and built *Eskdalegate* 4250/30 (70,75) and the shelter decker *Dan-y-Bryn* 5217/40 (137) for the Brynmore S.S. Co Ltd (Ambrose, Davies & Matthews Ltd, managers), Swansea. During the second world war 6 Empire ships were launched. The company ceased shipbuilding in 1968 and went into liquidation.

Blyth Shipbuilding & Dry Docks Co Ltd (later Cowpen Dry Docks & Shipbuilding Co Ltd), Blyth. Founded on the site of an existing shipyard in 1883 a continual stream of cargo vessels came from this builder, many owners coming back for repeat orders. Several of W.A. Souter's 'Arch' steamers were built here including *Sheaf Don* 2172/17 (46) and *Sheaf Crest* 2730/24. The Thompson Steam Shipping Co of London came here for their 'Rio' named vessels; *Rio Claro* 4086/22, Ropner for *Cragpool* 5127/28 and others. After the slump few tramps were built for the British flag and production finally ceased in 1966.

Armstrong, Whitworth & Co, (Shipbuilders) Ltd, Newcastle. Charles Mitchell set up in business as a shipbuilder in 1852 and constructed all manner of craft from paddle steamers to warships, with iron hulls, among them *Jesmond* 1435/78, Watts, Watts, London. In 1882 the company was acquired by W.G. Armstrong, builder of cranes, machinery and armaments, being renamed Sir W.G. Armstrong, Mitchell & Co, and featuring warships high on their list of products. Many tramp steamers were built for local owners, *Strathcona* 3942/04 for W. Petersen for one, and in later years *Kitty Taylor* 4640/29 for Lambert Bros of London. Another company which was taken over was the Tyne Iron Shipbuilding Co Ltd, founded in the late 1870s. One of their earliest tramps was *Beaconsfield* 1736/77 for G. Cleugh of North Shields. By 1920 the yard had 15 building slips in use able to build vessels up to 1,000 feet in length and the company was launching ocean liners, oil tankers, icebreakers and train ferries. Around 1927, shortly after *Kenton* 3930/27 was built for A. Stott of Newcastle, the yard was taken over by Armstrong, Whitworth & Co Ltd. This company in turn was acquired in 1927 by Vickers of Barrow and retitled Vickers, Armstrong, Ltd.

W. Dobson & Co, Newcastle. In the early 1880s W. Dobson's yard was opened and commenced building cargo vessels for well known tramp steamer owners like Nye, Clare & Co, London *(Rodney* 3472/01) and *Cairnglen* 1565/91 for Cairns, Young & Noble. Government contracts were placed in 1918 for 5 of the War standard vessels. One of the last ships to be launched from the yard before it was taken over in 1929 by Armstrong, Whitworth & Co Ltd was *White Crest* 4365/28 for Hall Bros of Newcastle.

R. & W. Hawthorn, Leslie & Co Ltd, Hebburn, Newcastle. This company was formed in 1886 when Andrew Leslie & Co, shipbuilders, amalgamated with R. & W. Hawthorn, engine builders since 1817. The Leslie yard had produced around 250 vessels, mainly built of iron, tramps such as *Howick* 1543/78 for H.E.P. Adamson of North Shields and *Thomas Melville* 1706/82 for J. Coull, also of North Shields. Under the Hawthorn, Leslie name more tramp steamers were built, of steel and of larger size, including *Birdoswald* 4013/92 of Lunn & Maccoy, Newcastle (built as *Tropea*) and *Llangollen* 5056/28 for E. Thomas Radcliffe. Despite their experience in the building of tramp steamers little use was made of it in either war as they built only 4 dry cargo vessels in all for government contract. By 1939 the yard had begun to build motor ships, and in 1968 merged to form Swan Hunter & Tyne Shipbuilders Ltd.

Northumberland Shipbuilding Co Ltd, Howden-on-Tyne. This shipyard was established in 1883 by H.S. Edwards, Sons & Craig, who were already in the ship repair business elsewhere on the Tyne. The company was named H.S. Edwards & Sons, later Edwards Shipbuilding Company. In 1898 the yard was sold to a newly formed company, the Northumberland Shipbuilding Company Ltd, controlled by Sir C. Furness. The Edwards yard had built some assorted tramps including *Harlyn* 1452/91 for the West Hartlepool S.N. Co. Under the new regime a decision was taken to specialise on a standard tramp steamer design of 7,300 dwt, 4,300 grt., 360 ft. b.p. The first one off the ways was *Rosalie* 4350/00 for John Cory & Sons, Cardiff. In the next 9 years 45 of the standard designs were built, though owners individual requirements were not ignored: Orders & Handford of Cardiff took delivery of *Ladykirk* 2300/04. With their experience in building standard ships the yard was an obvious choice for orders for War type ships and 16 were built in the yard. The design of the 'F1' type (58) was prepared by the managing director of the Northumberland yard and, although it differed from the Government standard, the Admiralty was so impressed that they gave the go-ahead for 13 to be built. *Saint Dunstan* 5662/19 (ex *War Keep*) of Rankin, Gilmour & Co, was one of the 'F1' group (77). In 1918 Furness, Withy & Co sold Northumberland to a combine associated with Sperling & Co. Overcapitalized, the combine soon found itself in difficulties and crashed in 1926. In 1927 a new company was formed, the Northumberland Shipbuilding Co (1927) Ltd, but this lasted only until 1931 when the yard was sold to National Shipbuilders Security Ltd. Their last steamer *Redsea* 5224/30 was built for Wm. Brown, Atkinson & Co of Hull. During the first world war the company created a record by handing over one of their ships 63 hours after it had been launched.

Palmer's Shipbuilding & Iron Co Ltd, Hebburn. Palmer's of Jarrow was founded in 1851 and during its life span of 83 years over 1,000 vessels of all types were launched from its slips. The pioneer collier *John Bowes* of 1852 was a product of the Palmer yard and indeed most of the early vessels were of the collier type (the company having been floated to build steam colliers). In later years many tramps entered the Tyne here, *Hazeldene* 2204/81 (ex *Bracadale*) owned by Isaac Crocker of Newcastle, and *Throstlegarth* 1566/95 built for R. & J.H. Rea of Liverpool. In 1911 the firm took over another yard at Hebburn to give more and larger building capacity. During world war one the efforts of the yard were directed towards naval vessels and only 6 standard types were built. One of them, *War Sparrow* 5169/18 became Andrew Weir's *Haleric.* By 1920 the yard had 12 building ways which had seen the launching of battleships, torpedo

77.
War Keep was completed
as the *Saint Dunstan*.

Photo: Alex Duncan

boats, cargo liners, coasters, steam yachts, oil tankers and even floating docks. The slump hit the yard in the late 1920s and the shipyard was sold off in 1933, to be closed by National Shipbuilders Security Ltd, though the ship repairing side survived under the name of Palmers, Hebburn Ltd.

John Readhead & Sons Ltd, South Shields. Originally founded in 1865 as J. Readhead & Softley, a firm which built tugs, coasters and similar small craft, the firm became John Readhead & Co in 1872, moving to a larger shipyard in 1880 and beginning to build larger ships. Around that time John Readhead met Edward Hain and a friendly association was formed between the two companies resulting in the construction by Readhead's of 87 tramps for the St. Ives company, vessels such as *Trelawny* 1658/88. Other owners ordered regularly: Runciman's Moor line ordered 30 ships before 1925 including *Pearlmoor* 4581/23: G.T. Readhead's *'cliffe'* steamers took *Headcliffe* 3654/15. The Readhead yard was not geared for warship work but in world war one they were only called on to build 6 standard vessels. It was a different story 30 years later when the Government ordered no less than 23 Empire type ships from the company of the dry cargo design. *Empire Scott* 6150/46 became *Walter Scott* of the Chine Shipping Co of London. The company built a several raised-quarterdeck engines-aft vessels such as *Rookwood* 6246/52 (53). In 1968 Readhead's became part of Swan Hunter & Tyne Shipbuilders Ltd.

Swan, Hunter & Wigham Richardson Ltd, Wallsend-on-Tyne. C.S. Swan took over an existing yard in 1872 and began building small coasters. He was drowned at sea in 1879 and in 1880 G.B. Hunter joined the firm which was renamed C.S. Swan & Hunter. By this time larger ships were being built for tramping service such as *Cilurnum* 2123/81 for Dunford & Elliott, Newcastle, and by 1900 still larger tramps were launched to meet the new demands for increased tonnage, for example Raeburn & Verel of Glasgow's *Osborne* 4296/98. They had also acquired a reputation for quality vessels of other types, ocean liners, cable ships, oil tankers, icebreakers, train ferries etc. In 1903 the company amalgamated with Wigham Richardson & Co Ltd of Walker. In 1913 the firm took over control of Barclay, Curle & Co in Glasgow. During world war one the yard was busy with the construction of naval vessels and were only instructed to build 11 of the standard dry cargo vessels and coasters. As happened with so many of these wartime ships they were too late to take part, like *War Warbler* 5293/19 which was completed as *Bretwalda* for Hall Bros of Newcastle. After the war they resumed production of their varied types including a number of tramps, among them *Gracefield* 4631/28 for E.J. Sutton of Newcastle, this vessel being somewhat unusual as it was equipped with an exhaust turbine driving a steam compressor, part of the drive for higher fuel efficiency. As with so many of the north-east coast yards customers kept coming back, among them Arthur Stott, & Co Ltd of Newcastle who managed a series of tramps, the first steam powered, *Hopestar* 5267/36, and another 7 of similar size, but diesel engined. These Hopemount ships with *Hope*...names were owned by Swan, Hunter & Wigham Richardson subsidiaries, managed by Stott. In world war two the yard was again busy on naval work and only 4 dry cargo standard vessels were built.

Tyne Iron Shipbuilding Co Ltd, Willington Quay. Shipbuilding started in this yard in 1876 and right from the start fair sized vessels were built, few being below 1,000 grt.

Yard No.3 was *Beaconsfield* 1736/77 for G. Cleugh of North Shields. Orders came from all over the country even as far away as Cornwall where E. Handcock of Falmouth had *Carn Brae* 1685/82 and *Carn Math* 1687/84 in their fleet. Many owners came back for repeat orders: Robinson's 'Stag' line, Stephens & Mawson and West Hartlepool Steam Navigation Co. Although not a large yard, (in 1920 there were only three slips in operation), they were called on to build 8 of the standard ships in world war one, the last being completed as late as 1921. *War Combe* 3090/18 became *Watsness* of the Reardon Smith fleet. In 1928 the company was taken over by Armstrong, Whitworth & Co Ltd and in 1935 the yard was dismantled by National Shipbuilders Security Ltd.

Wood, Skinner & Co Ltd, Bill Quay, Newcastle-on-Tyne. Established in 1883 the company launched its first vessel, a small coaster of 205 tons, in 1885, but it was not long before medium sized tramps were under construction. They built *Cairnmore* 1627/77 for the Cairns, Noble fleet. Eight standard ships were laid down during the war but not completed until after the Armistice - *War Down* 3099/18 went to the Graig Shipping Co as *Graig.* Although the yard had at one time 6 slipways only about 240 ships were built, the last being *Usworth* 1985/25 for R.S. Dalgliesh.

S.P. Austin & Son, Sunderland. This old established Sunderland yard was founded in 1826 and in 1846 moved to its present site just below the Wearmouth Bridge. By 1860 there were 58 yards building wooden ships in Sunderland and between 1871 and 1890 several of these were taken over by Austin's as each went out of business. At first the yard was not renowned for building large vessels, indeed it was 1902 before the 3,000 grt. mark was passed and E.W. Morgan of London took delivery of *Grangewood* 3422/02. During world war one they were called on to build the 'D' type standard vessels of 2,300 grt. to designs which they themselves were asked to produce (55). Even then they only built 4 out of the 27 ordered by the government to that design. Later they were asked to produce another design for the 'H' type vessel of 2,800 grt., but again they built only 2 out of the 31 completed in various shipyards. Of the 'D' type *War Drum* 2352/18 went tramping with the Meldrum & Swinson fleet as *Ashwin.* In 1920 the yard had only 3 slips limited to vessels up to 350 feet, and 3,600 grt., and was concentrating on colliers, dry cargo carriers, barges and small oil tankers. *Harraton* 2795/30 for the Tanfield S.S. Co Ltd of Newcastle was a typical Austin vessel. When business was bad they complained that orders for the colliers in which they specialised were 'poached' by other yards. A few standard coasters went down the ways between 1939 and 1945 and many coastal colliers. The yard amalgamated with Wm. Pickersgill & Sons Ltd in 1954 to form Austin & Pickersgill Ltd.

Wm. Pickersgill & Sons Ltd, Sunderland. The firm of William Pickersgill and Sons was founded in 1838 as builders of wooden sailing ships. They changed over to iron in 1880, and the same year saw the launching of their first iron hulled steamship, *Carmago.* A typical early product was *Gwalia* 1348/81 for E.C. Hurley of Cardiff, one of the well-decked steamers also favoured by the north-east coast owners. Their tramps were well respected and many famous owners came to buy, such as the Temple S.S. Co Ltd (Lambert Bros), of London for *Temple Mead* 4427/28, the Lancashire Shipping Co Ltd for *Corby Castle* 3607/98. Theirs was not a large yard having only 3 launching ways in 1920 but they could build up to 7500 grt. In 1954 amalgamation took place with S.P. Austin & Son, the combined name being Austin & Pickersgill Ltd. This company became well known for their modern standard motorships of the SD14 and B26 designs, the former a liberty ship replacement.

Bartram & Sons Ltd, Sunderland. The first vessel launched from this yard was the wooden sailing ship *Crown* built in 1838 which provided a profit to her builders, Lister & Bartram, of £71. The firm was restyled Bartram & Haswell & Co in 1871 and in 1872 they built their first iron hulled steamer, *Ardmore* 928/72 for J. Wood, Maryport. In 1890 the firm's name was again changed, this time to Bartram & Sons. Up to 1877 they made a name for themselves building fine sailing ships, a good name which continued after the change over to coasters, colliers and tramp steamers. They built for owners such as F.W. Ritson, (the 'Branch Line') with their *Hazel Branch* 2623/89, who came back many times with repeat orders. Even the canny Scots by-passed their Clyde builders when Hugh Hogarth came to the Wear for *Baron Eldon* 3705/99. The Cardiff firm of E. Thomas Radcliffe placed many orders after they took delivery of *Llanwern* 4966/28. Only a small yard with 2 slips, they nevertheless delivered 10 of the wartime standard vessels of the War type, including *War Collie* 5114/19 which became *Easterly* owned by Brown, Jenkinson & Co of London. The yard survived the slump and went on

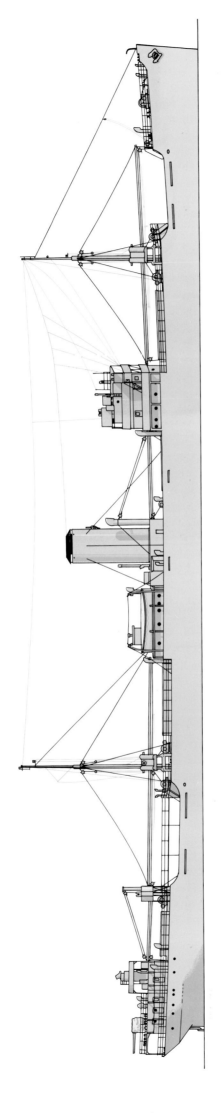

79. *Clearpool* 5404/35 was built by William Gray & Co Ltd, West Hartlepool for the Pool Shipping Co, managed by Sir R. Ropner & Co Ltd of West Hartlepool, but registered at Cardiff. Her registered dimensions were 427.5' x 55.2' x 27.2'. She had two steam turbines geared to a single shaft for a service speed of 11.5 knots well suited for charter to the liner trades. She is shown here in wartime grey as sailing in November 1942, equipped with various machine gun positions and a heavier calibre gun on the stern. Dazzle painting was not used as she would almost always be sailing in convoy.

to build standard ships in world war two to a design which they themselves had produced, among them *Empire Rock* 7064/43 which became *Admiral Codrington* of S.G. Embiricos, London. In 1968 the company was absorbed by Austin & Pickersgill Ltd.

John Blumer & Co Ltd, Sunderland. In 1859 John Blumer and others began building wooden sailing ships on the North Sands. In 1864 a move was made to the North Dock and a start was made on steamer building, concentrating on cargo vessels and colliers at first. Tramps came later though they were smallish like *Anerley* 1857/81 for Watts, Watts & Co. As the demand developed for bigger vessels so the company built larger; *Pennmanor* 3809/01 for Hill & Cassap, London. A number of tramp steamers were launched for the Runciman fleet, starting with *Arranmoor* 2452/97, a name to be repeated twice for the same owner. Eight 'C' type standard vessels were built for the war effort, one, *War Sun* 3050/19, passing to W.A. Souter and being renamed *Sheaf Spear.* The yard closed during the slump following the war, lay idle for four years and was re-opened in 1926. Only two more ships were built, *Usworth* 3535/26 for R.S. Dalgliesh and *Cydonia* 3517/27 for Robinson's 'Stag Line' before final closure.

John Crown & Sons Ltd, Sunderland. John Crown acquired his shipbuilding business at Monkwearmouth in 1847, known locally as the Strand Slipway Company for a while. Production consisted mainly of colliers and coasters with the occasional small tramp such as *Specialist* 2844/90 which was built for Pickering, Wallis & Co of London. The yard specialised in self-trimming colliers but their range did include sizes suitable for the intermediate trades, *Cedar Tree* 1557/28, Shamrock Shipping Company, Larne, and *Hillcroft* 2268/12 (ex *Sheba*), R. McNeil & Son, Cardiff. At the end of the second world war the yard was taken over by J.L. Thompson & Sons Ltd.

William Doxford & Sons Ltd, Sunderland. The Doxford family started shipbuilding in 1840 and moved to the Pallion site in 1857. Wooden ships at first, then in 1863 their first iron-hulled vessel went down the ways. By 1880 they had 5 slips in action for ships up to 4,500 grt., at that time quite a large vessel, though most of the ships which they were building were moderately sized, e.g. *Wexford* 2104/83 for W.J. Bassett, London. The company introduced their 'Turret' ship design in 1892 (33, 42, 69, 81), but as shipowners were very chary about buying one, Doxford's had to set up a special company, the Turret Steam Shipping Co Ltd, to buy and operate the first turret steamer, *Turret* 1970/92. Once proved, the design turned out to be very popular and the company built no less than 176; they had joint ventures or issued licences to Hawthorn, Leslie & Co Ltd, Swan & Hunter Ltd, Vickers Sons & Maxim Ltd and Fried Krupp AG, who built 7 turret steamers between them. The company kept up to date with developments in shipbuilding and turned out self-discharging colliers, vessels with side ballast tanks and steamers with geared turbine drives. In 1912 the first oil engine was built though it was 1921 before Doxford's installed their own design diesel engine, considerably altered from the prototype. The motorships were not an instant success and by 1931 only 55 diesel powered vessels had been built, only 13 of which were for tramp operators, including 6 for Walter Runciman, and so barely two per year had been sold. Between 1918 and 1920 no less than 19 standard vessels had been built to government order. They went on to survive the lean years of the '20s and '30s. Again in the next war they were called on to make great efforts and 26 of the Empire type dry cargo vessels were built of which 10 were lost by enemy action. The company became part of Doxford & Sunderland Ltd in 1966, Sunderland Shipbuilders (Court Line) Ltd in 1973, and in 1977 the yard became a member of British Shipbuilders Ltd.

Sir James Laing & Sons Ltd, Sunderland. Philip Laing, a shipowner, came to Sunderland in 1793 and set up as a shipbuilder at Monkwearmouth. Several moves were made before he settled at Deptford in 1818, and in 1832 James Laing took over the running of the yard. The first iron-hulled vessel from the yard was launched in 1853, but sailing ships were still launched alongside iron and steel steamers for many years to come. *Wychwood* 1216/79, an iron ship, beside *Edendale* 1109/79, a steel steamer for Dixon & Wilson, Sunderland. As the years passed Laing's built bigger and bigger ships; oil tankers and ocean liners, but always among them colliers and tramps, like *Langdale* 3930/03 and two others belonging to the Laing S.S. Co Ltd which was run by the Deptford Yard. Between the wars the company had a hard time like the other shipbuilders but among the vessels launched were *Saltwick* 3775/29 for Rowland & Marwood and *Aelbryn* 4980/38 for Ambrose, Davies & Matthews, Swansea. During the two wars the main call on the yard was for oil tankers and post war the vessels launched were motorships.

81. The 'Turret' steamer *Turret* framed up at Doxford' yard, see opposite.

Photo: The Engineer, 1092

Osbourne, Graham & Co Ltd, Hylton. The yard of Osbourne, Graham & Co was established at Hylton in 1871, building sailing vessels, steam coasters and colliers. The yard was the pioneer of the 'corrugated' hull which they built for the Ericsson Shipping Co, *Monitoria* 1904/09 and *Nervion* 1920/12 for owners in Norway. Their position on the river limited the size of vessel which they could launch but a number of usefully sized tramps were built; *Virent* 3771/02 (J.Westoll) and *Ericus* 2700/19 (Ohlson S.S. Co of Hull). Only 6 War standard vessels were produced in the Hylton yard. The depression of the 1920s forced the closure of the yard, their last vessel, *Copsewood* 969/25 being a collier for Joseph Constantine of Middlesbrough.

J. Priestman & Co, Southwick, Sunderland. After a period as a ship draughtsman and designer John Priestman set up in business in 1882 at Southwick, building *Isle of Cyprus* 1149/83 for Dixon, Robson & Co. The yard launched coasters, colliers and tramps at first, seldom above 2,000 grt., but in the late 1890s began tackling larger vessels such as *Roefield* 3089/96 for Woods, Tylor & Brown, London. In 1894 Priestman took out a patent for a self-trimming steamer with the sides sloping inboard from a low gunwale (see page 35). The idea did not catch on and only 3 vessels were built to the design, among them *Enfield* 2124/97, W. Ormston, Newcastle, (3). John Priestman himself owncd shares in a number of tramp shipping companies and had money invested in the collieries which provided the cargoes for the ships. He built steamers on speculation when orders were lacking. Tramps were the backbone of the yard, tramps such as *Maindy Court* 3792/17, Maindy Shipping Co, Cardiff, but during the first world war the Priestman yard had to put its own designs aside to build 6 'B' and 'C' standard vessels. The slump which followed the war hit the yard badly and only 14 more vessels were launched before the last ship left the slips in 1933. Among the last of the steamers to be built was *Knight of the Cross* 3857/29 and two others for the new fleet of Pardoe-Thomas of Newport. *Sandyford* 3207/04 belonging to Sandy Simpson of Newcastle became the Q5, the decoy ship which was credited with sinking two submarines in world war one. (The press gave the number as 17 or even 22). During world war two the yard was operated by Wm. Pickersgill & Sons Ltd.

Short Bros Ltd, Sunderland. This yard, which is reputed to have launched more ships for local owners than any other on the Wear, was opened in 1850. The company kept in the forefront of hull design and received awards at various exhibitions in 1877 and 1883. Good relations were established with many owners who kept coming back with orders, companies such as J. Westoll (e.g. *Lizzie Westoll* 2858/95) and Nitrate Producers' with their larger tramps like *Anglo-Saxon* 4263/02. In 1929, Lawther, Latta & Co were still placing orders with Short Bros, Sir John Latta having married into the Short family. Never a large yard there were only 4 building ways for ships up to 10,000 grt. During the two world wars the Short yard did its share with 8 standard War type ships in world war one and no less than 22 of the Empire dry cargo types in world war two, including *Hollybank* 7041/46 built as *Empire Southey* and sold to the Bank Line of Glasgow. The yard was not renowned for motor ships and by 1952 only 11 had been built. The business closed in 1964.

Sunderland Shipbuilding Company Ltd, Sunderland. The yard at South Dock was opened in 1866 by Iliffe, Mounsey & Co and they launched many excellent sailing ships and small steamers. In 1873 the name changed to J.W. Mounsey & Co, later to Mounsey & Foster, then to Robert Foster, until in 1880 the yard finally became The Sunderland Shipbuilding Co Ltd. Many of the vessels which had been launched had been of the popular well-decked type like *Ashbrooke* 1419/79 owned by the Gordon S.S. Co of London. As with many Sunderland yards, ships were built 'on spec' when times were bad and 1886 saw them with 3 such vessels on their hands, one of them for 3 years. Liner traders, colliers and tramps were the main product of this company; some liner owners each ordering a number of vessels over the years. During world war one they built only 6 standard ships of the 'B' type including *War Warbler* 5293/19 which was completed as *Bretwalda* for Hall Bros of Newcastle. They only constructed two naval vessels, the River Class gunboats *Mantis* and *Moth*. After the war some liner traders and tramps were built but in 1926, unable to survive the slump, and having been idle for over a year, the company went into liquidation. The last vessel to be launched was Yard No. 331, *Linaria* 3385/24 for Robinson's 'Stag Line'.

Joseph L. Thompson & Sons Ltd, Sunderland. The origins of shipbuilding in the Thompson family go back to 1819 when Robert Thompson and his sons began shipbuilding on the river, rather spasmodically at first, until in 1846 a site on the North Sands was occupied. In 1861 J.L. Thompson was left on his own to carry on the business. As so often happened with the Sunderland shipyards, owners kept coming back to the same yard for new vessels, and to Thompson's came Rowland & Marwood for their 'Cross' boats, e.g. *Blue Cross* 3028/92 and others, the Bolton Steam Shipping Co with their 'artists'; *Raphael* 1860/85. It was a busy yard and in 1907 launched 12 vessels totalling 48,218 grt. which stood as a record for over 30 years. They received orders for 8 standard steamers of the War type, mostly the 'F' design, which were too late for the war and went straight into civilian hands. The Byron S.S. Co Ltd of London had *Lord Guildford* 6635/20 in their fleet for some years. The company survived the slump and kept the tramps, oil tankers and refrigerated vessels going down the ways until the war when the orders for Empire vessels came in reaching a total of 27, 23 of them the 10,000 dwt. class designed by the company (page 61), 7 of which were lost by enemy action. Among those which survived the war was *Empire Tristan* 7167/42, which became J. & J. Denholm's *Hollypark* and later Andrew Crawford's *Gogovale.* In 1968 the company became part of the Sunderland Shipbuilders Ltd.

Robert Thompson & Sons Ltd, Sunderland. When Robert Thompson left the family firm of J.L. Thompson & Sons in 1854 he set up on his own in Southwick. He built a number of attractive sailing ships but it was not until 1870 that his first steamer was launched, an iron steamer of 768 tons for Culliford & Clark, Sunderland, the *Canadian.* In 1881 a second yard was purchased, Bridge Dockyard, from which hulls had to be launched broadside. All sizes of ships were built from steam trawlers upwards. The smallest was *Protector* 45/99 for fisheries protection work. The Thompson family held shares in the firm of V.T. Thompson for whom they built *Langham* 2748/92 and two others between 1892 and 1900. Among the 6 standard vessels built between 1918 and 1920 was the 'C' type *War Tempest* 3122/18 which traded with a minimum change of name as *Wye Tempest* in the fleet of T.G. Berg, the Wye Shipping Co of London. During the difficult days of the 1920s Thompson's managed to keep their building ways occupied but 1930 saw the last tramp steamers going down the slips, *Harmonic* 4558/30 and *Harmattan* 4588/30 for J. & C. Harrison. Two motor trawlers followed and when the new owners could not pay for them they lay two years before buyers could be found. This was too much for the Southwick Yard which was wound up in 1933 by the National Shipbuilders Security Ltd after 341 ships had been built. The repair yard remained open for another year before it also went into liquidation.

Craig, Taylor & Co Ltd, Stockton. Originally established at Thornaby in 1884 this yard turned out around 227 vessels of all types. At first they specialised in the usual coasters, colliers and tramps, well-deckers such as *Eleanor Mail* 1772/99 for Mail Bros, Newcastle, and *Sir Walter Raleigh* 1870/89, owned by Pearse & Haswell of Plymouth. During world war one a number of orders were held up so that priority could be given to the standard vessels which had been allocated by the Shipping Controller, among them *War Peacock* 5242/19 which sailed as *Portfield* of W.E. Hinde, Cardiff, one of the 8 'B' types which they built. As with so many other yards on the north-east coast the company did not weather the slump in shipbuilding and closed in 1930 after completion of *Portregis* 4409/30, another tramp for W.E. Hinde. In 1931 National Shipbuilders Security Ltd closed the yard.

Richardson, Duck & Co Ltd, Stockton. In 1854 Joseph Richardson and George Nixon Duck combined to found the shipyard at Stockton known as the South Stockton Iron Shipbuilding Company and launched the first iron ship on the Tees, *Advance*. They specialised at first in sailing ships and short sea traders (steamships), and as with other Tees-side shipbuilders they built 'on spec' from time to time, trading themselves until a buyer came forward. *Dione* 849/68 which was eventually sold to the Tyne-Tees Shipping Co, was put into the Baltic trade. *Burgos* 1773/84 for Briggs & Son, Hull was one of the first steamers to be fitted with a triple expansion engine, reducing coal consumption from 12/14 tons per day to 8.25 tons. As with other builders, satisfied owners returned with orders time and time again. In 1904, Farrar, Groves of London had in their fleet of 12 steamers 9 built by Richardson, Duck from *Start* 2419/89 to *Dungeness* 2750/04. During the war, in addition to a number of sloops and oil tankers, the company built 8 'A' and 'B' types which included *War Vulture* 5204/18 which traded after the war as *Bradavon* of the Leeds Shipping Company of Cardiff. The yard was improved in post war years but in 1921 the slump bit deep and in 1924 the last ship was launched, *Southborough* 4542/24 for the Hazelwood Shipping Company. The yard closed its gates in 1925 and the assets were finally sold off in 1929, the company being wound up in 1933.

Ropner Shipbuilding & Repairing Co (Stockton) Ltd. Robert Ropner was born in Germany and as a boy ran away from home and settled in West Hartlepool. He worked in the broking business, started a shipowning firm, got involved in the shipbuilding firm of Pearse & Lockwood and finally in 1888 set up in shipbuilding in his own right as Ropner & Son, building tramp steamers for rival shipowners as well as for the 'Ropner Navy'. Watts, Watts & Co of London had 22 Ropner-built tramp steamers in their fleet of 23 in 1904, of which 5 had been built on the well known 'trunk' principle which had been patented by Ropner (35) as an answer to the Doxford 'turret'. Among them were *Windsor* 4074/97 and *Chatham* 2074/98. During the war the yard launched 10 cargo steamers to Government account, 6 of the 'A/B' type and 4 of the smaller 'C' group. *War Scilla* 5276/19 which was completed as *Innerton* for R. Chapman of Newcastle was one of the old ships scuttled in 1944 as part of the Gooseberry breakwater at Arromanches (147). After the war the yard became Ropner Shipbuilding & Ship Repairing Co (Stockton) Ltd, but a few years later the slump forced the yard to close down. The last vessel was appropriately enough for their own fleet, *Willowpool* 4816/25. Smith's Dock took over the yard in 1930 but it was then acquired and dismantled by the National Shipbuilders Security Ltd. During its existence the Ropner yard built no less than 71 vessels for the parent fleet.

T. & W. Smith & Co, Stockton. H.S. Edwards & Sons, and Edwards Bros, joined forces in 1899 and created Smith's Dock Co Ltd. Originally their shipbuilding yard was on the Tyne, but in 1908 it was moved to Stockton-on-Tees where a large number of small vessels were built. They took over Ropner Shipbuilding & Repairing Co (Stockton) Ltd and carried on launching colliers, coasters, trawlers and whalers. They also built liner traders and from time to time a tramp steamer. Down their slips went *Alstruther* 3811/24 for F. Carrick & Co Ltd, Newcastle (see front endpaper), *Stonepool* 4803/28 for R. Ropner, and *Kyloe* 2820/30 for the Sharp S.S. Co Ltd, Newcastle. In 1966 the yard became part of the Swan Hunter Group.

R.Craggs & Sons Ltd, Middlesbrough. A smallish yard founded in the 1870s which built a few sailing ships before turning to steam. Most of their production of tramp steamers went to owners abroad.

Furness Shipbuilding Co Ltd, Middlesbrough. In 1918 Lord Furness established a shipyard at Haverton Hill-on-Tees to provide tonnage for the Furness Withy fleet, although a management buyout of Furness, Withy & Co Ltd in 1919 ended the association apart from newbuilding contracts. Within two years 12 slipways were in production and passenger cargo liners, oil tankers and tramps were being launched. In the years which followed Crosby & Sons of West Hartlepool ordered *Levenbridge* 4342/28 and *Ousebridge* 5601/29. By 1930, 190 ships had been launched. In world war two only 4 dry cargo Empire's were ordered, but 16 oil tankers were built. In 1951 the yard was acquired by Sears Holdings Ltd and later, in 1969, they were taken over by the Swan Hunter Group.

William Harkess & Son Ltd, Middlesbrough. In 1853 William Harkess, a shipbuilder, came from Sunderland to Middlesbrough. For the first 20 years the state of the river prevented him from building vessels larger than coasters, trawlers and the like, but as the river was deepened and widened intermediate tramps were introduced. O. & W. Williams of Cardiff came back again and again for vessels such as *Ordovician* 1112/00. Until the war the yard launched vessels up to a limit of 2,000 grt. During the war only 3 standard ships were built but the Admiralty ordered a number of minesweepers and patrol boats. The company was hit by the slump and launched their last vessel in 1922.

Sir Raylton Dixon & Co Ltd, Middlesbrough. Raylton Dixon quit his job as manager at the Richardson, Duck & Co yard to start up in business as Backhouse & Dixon. In 1873 the company became R. Dixon & Co, expanding to produce large numbers of small and medium sized vessels from trawlers to tramps, from *Cousins Arbib* 2163/82 for E. Arbib of London, to *Tuskar* 3043/92 for Farrar, Groves, also of London. The Dixon-Harroway ballast tanks (34) and cantilever construction featured on many of the vessels which were launched, like *Kwarra* 4426/10 which became *Charterhouse* of the Charter Shipping Co of Cardiff. Not a large yard, having only 4 berths, they produced 8 standard vessels to Government order. One of the 7 'C' type built, *War Ocean* 3067/19, was completed as *Castillian* for Westcott & Laurance of London. Shortly after the war, after launching its 629th vessel, the yard closed in 1923. The last vessels launched were big cantilever framed colliers for French interests.

Furnesss, Withy & Co Ltd, West Hartlepool. In 1869 Edward Withy and Edward Alexander commenced business as Withy, Alexander & Co in the yard vacated by Denton, Gray & Co. Alexander left in 1874 to join Capper, Alexander & Co, Cardiff, and in 1884 Withy emigrated to New Zealand, having sold the business (now E. Withy & Co) to Christopher Furness. Thereafter the yard was kept busy with a wide range of output, many being standard tramp types built 'on spec'. Although never implemented, the yard held the first 'turret' licence issued by Doxford. *Zanzibar* 2964/90 was typical of the standard approach, the first of 21 vessels produced as either well-deck or part awning deckers. Another group of 18 spar deckers was led by *Apollo* 3829/96. In 1908 Furness introduced his Co-Partnery Scheme, an innovative worker participation proposal which, after early promise, was killed off by union opposition in 1910. E. Withy & Co had amalgamated to form part of Furness, Withy & Co Ltd in 1891, and during 1909 rationalisation saw the shipyard transferred to the ownership and management of Irvine's Shipbuilding & Dry Docks Co Ltd.

William Gray & Co Ltd, West Hartlepool. In 1836 a J.P. Denton opened a shipyard in Hartlepool, and in 1862 took into partnership one William Gray, the firm then becoming Denton, Gray & Co. In 1869 the business was transferred to West Hartlepool and in 1872 became known as Wm. Gray & Co. In 1887 the yard was expanded from 3 to 5 building ways capable of accommodating vessels up to 500 feet in length. There were plenty of tramp steamers among the vessels launched, for scores of different owners. Moore, Innes & Co of London took *Vauxhall Bridge* 3391/01, J. Coverdale, a local owner, came to them for *Miles Coverdale* 2308/98, while *Waverley* 2292/01 was built for J. Morrison of Newcastle. By the end of 1919 the yard had expanded to 13 slipways on the banks of the Tees and 4 on the banks of the Wear, where a small shipyard had been opened in 1917 in co-operation with three shipowners, Sir J.R. Ellerman, Lord Inchcape and F.C. Strick, under the name of the Egis Shipyard Ltd. As might be expected from a company this size their war effort was tremendous and among the ships launched were 2 'A', 12 'B', 8 'C', 2 'D', 2 'E', and 5 'H' type standard ships. Among the owners who took delivery of these vessels after the war was Jas. Bell of Hull who added *War Currant* 2505/19 to the fleet under the name *Leicester*. Despite the ups and downs of the 1920s Gray's continued to build and launch vessels and in 1929 celebrated the launch of their 1,000th ship which had included no less than 25 for Ellerman Lines. Unfortunately the Wear yard had to be shut down in 1930. Once more during the second world war the Gray yard was called on to help replace shipping losses and from the yard came 29 of the 10,000 dwt. class of which 5 went into the Runciman fleet after the war, including *Empire Crest* 6715/41 which became *Clearpool*. Then there were 10 of the 4,300 dwt. Empire Malta type (60) with engines aft: *Empire Barbados* 3538/45 went to the fleet of Thomas Stone of Llanelli under the name *Berylstone*. Another group of standard ships built at Gray's was the 'Scandinavian type' a three-islander with masts at the ends of the wells (64), as in the Baltic traders, of which they built 24 including *Empire Lorenzo* 2865/42 which was bought by Hogarth's and renamed *Baron Elcho*. The business was wound up in 1962.

Irvine's Shipbuilding & Dry Docks Co Ltd, West Hartlepool. Captain Robert Irvine was marine superintendent for the West Hartlepool Steam Navigation Company until 1865 when he opened a shipyard in West Hartlepool. He found it difficult to make headway against the existing large shipbuilders and frequently built ships and managed them himself until he could find a buyer. One of these, *Colina* 1590/79 was not sold until 1900 when she was purchased by Abram & Addie of Glasgow. In 1897 the yard closed for renovation under the name of Robert Irvine & Co after launching *Jacob Bright* 2718/97 for J.G. Bright of Manchester, its 100th vessel. When reopened as Irvine's Shipbuilding & Dry Dock Co Ltd in 1897 Furness, Withy & Co Ltd had taken a controlling interest. Up until the war a considerable number of tramp steamers were built, tramps such as *Pengreep* 4806/14 for the Chellew Navigation Co. In 1909 the yard of Furness, Withy & Co Ltd was transferred to the ownership of Irvine's Shipbuilding & Dry Docks Co Ltd. Though not a very large yard they managed to build 14 standard ships during the first world war, one of which was *Emlynian* 5112/20, laid down as *War Unicorn,* which sailed under the colours of Emlyn Jones of Cardiff. Furness, Withy & Co sold Irvine's in 1917 but the difficult post-war period was to prove terminal. In 1924 *Heworth* 2855/24 was built for Burnett & Co of Newcastle. Two more vessels were launched and the shipbuilding side closed down in 1924. The repair yard remained open but went into liquidation in 1930. A new company was formed as Irvine's Shipbuilding & Dry Docks Co (1930) Ltd which struggled on until 1938 when National Shipbuilders Security Ltd dismantled the yards.

Earle's Shipbuilding & Engineering Co Ltd, Hull. C. & W. Earle set up in business in 1848 as engineers and in 1853 opened a shipyard at Victoria Dock. In 1863 a move was made to a new site on the banks of the Humber. They built under their original name until 1871 when the title was altered to Earle's Shipbuilding & Engineering Co Ltd. Their output was mainly tugs and trawlers with some naval vessels, but among the ships launched were some tramps from *Holderness* 1703/82 for Alexander & Arthurs of Glasgow to the larger *Apple Branch* 4452/20 for F. & W. Ritson, Sunderland. This was another yard which was killed off by the slump in shipbuilding and it was closed in 1932 when acquired by National Shipbuilders Security Ltd.

Thomas Turnbull & Son, Whitby. To most of us Whitby is a sleepy seaside holiday resort, but once it was the home and birthplace of enterprising shipowners. Here too was a shipyard which built tramp steamers; Thomas Turnbull, founded in the 1850s. The family also owned a tramp shipping fleet which early in the 1900s consisted of 13 vessels all built in the family yard from *Matthew Bedlington* 2141/82 to *Broomfield* 2386/02 which was the last vessel built.

Edward Finch & Co Ltd, Chepstow. On a site on the banks of the River Wye which had a tidal rise of as much as 48 ft. Edward Finch established a small shipyard in the late 1870s. At first the yard launched only small coasters, tugs and pleasure steamers, but from time to time something larger went down the ways, *Maroon* 1509/83 for Maclay & McIntyre, Glasgow and *Radyr* 1042/83 for J. Cory of Cardiff. In 1916 the site was taken over by the Standard Shipbuilding & Engineering Co Ltd, owned by a consortium of leading British shipowners for the purpose of building standard vessels for their account and the yard was expanded. In 1917 the yard was nationalised to build for Government account. The company was renamed Edward Finch & Co (1916) Ltd and carried on building on its own site while the extension was requisitioned but produced nothing by the end of the war. In the meantime the Finch yard had built 3 standard ships plus several coasters and barges to government order. In 1920 Finch's yard and the adjoining yard were taken over by the Monmouth Shipbuilding Company which constructed 3 of the 'H' type standard vessels and 5 of the 'N' type prefabricated ships. Among the 'H' type vessels was *Charterhague* 2568/20, E.L. Williams of Cardiff, which had been built as the *War Fig.* Shipbuilding ceased in 1925 and the company turned to the prefabrication of industrial steelwork.

T. Royden, Liverpool. In the mid-1810s Thomas Royden began business as a shipbuilder in partnership with James Ward, but in 1819 the firm of Thomas Royden was formed. Shortly afterwards a shipowning company was established, running between Liverpool and the River Plate. The yard made a name for itself with the sailing ships which they built but as steam pushed its way in, the company began to launch steamships, including tramps such as *St. Bernard* 2222/80 for G.B. Harland of West Hartlepool and *Westminster* 3859/90, Raeburn & Verel (built as *Indrapura*). In 1893 their last vessel, a four masted barque was built and the yard closed.

86. *Kurdistan* of Common Bros, loading coal at Leith, April 1933.

4. Cargoes

COAL

The most important export cargo carried by the steam tramp was coal. Large scale export of coal built up rapidly from the middle of the last century. Newcastle had exported coal to the continent for hundreds of years but the South Wales coal trade did not start in earnest until 1840 when the original dock in Cardiff shipped its first cargo of coal overseas. The inefficient engines of the early steamships consumed large quantities of coal and to enable them to cover long distances, coaling stations had to be established along the trade routes. The coaling stations were at first kept supplied by sailing ships until the development of the compound engine and later the triple expansion engine enabled the steam tramp to carry coal as a cargo on an economical basis. The expansion of the railway systems all round the world gave an additional impetus which increased the quantity of coal being consumed. 'Coal out, grain home' was the watchword of the tramp shipping business for close on 80 years. The graph (14) shows the rise and fall of the coal exports of this country and include associated fuels.

In the coal trade coal came in a huge variety of types, each with its own particular properties, each with its own name. There were 'steam coals' of which the Welsh variety were acknowledged as the best for steamships. These were called Smokeless Best, Smokeless Second Quality, Best Drys, Ordinary Drys, Steam Small (8 types), Washed Smalls, Best Washed Peas and Beans, and Unwashed Duffs. Then came 'Bituminous Coals', Household, Smalls, Gas Through. The 'Anthracites' covered Breaking Large, Red Vein Large, Machine Made Cobbles, Seconds and Thirds. Other forms of coal based fuels were taken as cargo, such as Patent Fuel and Coke, which came on the borderline between measurement and deadweight cargo, surprisingly enough being mainly measurement. The stowage rates were as follows:

Welsh coal	small	40–41 cu.ft./ton
	large	43–44
Scotch	small	43–45
	large	45–48
North Country	small	45–48
	large	47–50
American		42–46
Japanese		43–47
Lancashire		43–46
New South Wales (Australia)		44–48

Coal was a very dangerous cargo. Between 1875 and 1883, 57 vessels, both sail and steam were known to have been lost due to fires in coal cargoes, while a further 328 coal laden vessels were reported missing, many of which must have been lost due to fire. The fires were caused by spontaneous combustion, a generation of heat within the cargo which depended on a number of factors:

(1) Investigations into the weight of cargo carried showed that fire was more frequent in large cargoes:

Cargo below 500 tons	Casualty rate 0.25%
500 to 1,000 tons	1.0%
1,000 to 1,500 tons	3.5%
1,500 to 2,000 tons	4.5%
2,000 tons upward	9.0%

(2) The longer the cargo was in the hold the greater the danger: 26,631 short voyage cargoes suffered 10 casualties, 4,485 deep sea voyages produced 60 casualties. This increase was partially blamed on the higher temperatures encountered while passing through the tropics.

(3) The type of coal carried: Coal shipped from the Clyde, Virginia U.S.A., New South Wales and Calcutta were all particularly liable to spontaneous combustion. The latter was so notorious that in 1911 the following paragraph appeared in a shipping paper-"Three steamers were reported during the week with fires - *Blake* 3740/06 A.W. Pickard & Co. at Colombo, *Rokeby* 3788/99 G. Pyman & Co. and *Claveresk* 3829/07 B.J. Sutherland & Co. at Bombay. It will be remembered that this year the underwriters inserted a clause containing a warranty 'No Calcutta Coals', so that vessels in this trade have to pay an additional premium."

(4) Small coal was more liable to catch fire than large coal although less gas was given off.

(5) Temperature; a great number of fires occurred in bunker coal. In 1911 no less than 103 vessels were reported with fires in their bunker coal and 24 with the cargo on fire. In 1919/20, in a twelve month period, 204 steamers reported fires in either their bunkers or cargo. On 27th November 1929 *Euclid* 1911/4770 A.Woods, Liverpool, arrived at St. Vincent, Cape Verde Is. with the coal in the bunkers on fire and a fire in No.3 hold. An explosion occurred on 24th carrying away 'tween deck beams and hatches causing the 'tween decks cargo of bulk and bagged wheat to fall, cutting off the bunker coal supply, since when the vessel had been steaming on wheat.

(6) It was generally agreed that coal shipped wet was not more liable to spontaneous combustion than dry coal. The problem here was that if the coal dried out on the voyage the steamer off-loaded 3% less weight than she had shipped.

There was little that could be done to prevent spontaneous combustion but it was recommended that when the coal was being loaded suitable pockets be left so that thermometers could be inserted to check the temperatures within the coal at regular intervals during the voyage.

A second problem with coal was the formation of coal gas. When coal was loaded it was usually dropped by some means into the hold and would break up on impact exposing fresh surfaces from which the gases were released. Steamers were usually in a hurry and the holds would be closed as soon as loading was complete, with the result that the gases were trapped. In the days of the candle and paraffin lamp explosions were frequent as the gas seeped into areas other than the holds. In September 1895 *Westbury* 420/84 loaded coal in Burryport for Rouen. One hour after departing the mate and two men went into the hold to trim the coal to correct a slight list and almost at once there was an explosion which injured all three men. It was generally recommended that the hold should be kept ventilated to clear the gases as they formed and a good sized ventilator fore and aft on each hold was to be used. The flow of air was to be across the surface only; at one time there had been a school of thought that through venting would be a certain cure, but this did not last long. Four colliers were loaded at Newcastle all with the same type of coal. Three were bound for Aden and were through ventilated and these three were lost by fire during the voyage. The fourth, which was equipped for surface ventilation only, arrived safely at her destination, Bombay. From time to time new methods of loading were introduced with a view to reducing breakage during loading.

The main exporting ports in the United Kingdom were on the South Wales coast and the north-east coast, and to a lesser extent Glasgow and the Mersey. The ships spread out like a fan as they left these ports, as the fixture list for 15th June 1904 shows:-

Cardiff to:

Bordeaux	*Universal* 1274/78	Taylor & Sanderson, Sunderland
Alexandria	*Newcastle* 3403/99	J.J. and C.M. Forster, Newcastle
Naples	*Llanover* 3840/99	E. Thomas Radcliffe, & Co, Cardiff
Port Said	*T.R.Thompson* 3538/97	J. Westoll, Sunderland
Tenerife	*John H. Barry* 3083/99	C. Marwood, Whitby
Venice	*Begonia* 3653/99	J.Robinson & Sons, North Shields
Gibraltar	*Volunteer* 837/01	Fisher, Renwick & Co's, Manchester-London Steamers
Lisbon	*Calgarth* 1730/98	R.& J.H.Rea, Liverpool
Bermuda	*Miles Coverdale* 2308/98	J.Coverdale & Sons, Hartlepool
Malta	*Clara* 2431/98	Burdick & Cook, London

Tyne to:

Genoa	*Loch Lintrathen* 2789/99	A. Leitch, Dundee
Carthagena	*Grenada* 2158/96	G. Christall, Glasgow.
Lisbon	*James Westoll* 1990/84	J. Westoll, Sunderland
Barcelona	*Queen* 1785/82	Taylor & Sanderson, Sunderland
Rendesburg	*Ancient Briton* 1003/82	E.R. Newbigin, Newcastle
Carloforte	*Ardlethen* 1063/83	Adam S.S. Co, Aberdeen

Cardiff to:

Hong Kong	*Algoma* 2933/85	Eeles & Ruston, Cardiff
Santos	*Melbridge* 2868/91	J. Temperley & Co, London
Buenos Aires	*Llanthony Abbey* 2425/90	Pyman, Watson & Co, Newport
Constantinople	*Trevethoe* 2097/95	E. Hain & Son, St. Ives
Trincomalee	*Brighton* 3463/98	R. Chapman & Son, Newcastle
Diego Suarez	*Candleshoe* 3799/99	Bennetts & Co, Grimsby
Sierra Leone	*Cairngowan* 1181/83	Cairns, Noble & Co, Newcastle
Rio de Janeiro	*Glengoil* 2963/82	Lindsay, Gracie & Co, Leith
Aden	*Baron Innerdale* 3344/96	H. Hogarth & Sons, Glasgow

The British tramp steamers were also kept busy transporting coal between ports overseas. In fact these voyages accounted for 39% of the tonnage of coal carried in 1935 in vessels over 3,000 grt.

Route	No.of vessels over 3,000 grt.	Average tonnage carried	No. of vessels under 3,000 grt.	Average tonnage carried
Empire to Empire	386	7,607		
Empire to Foreign	18	7,331		
Empire to U.K.				
Foreign to Empire	18	3,098	28	1,543
Foreign to Foreign	279	6,542	161	3,607
Foreign to U.K.				
U.K. to Empire	282	6,565	31	3,171
U.K. to Foreign	890	6,505	4,079	1,788

The following are just a few of the voyages undertaken:

1938   Durban to Rangoon *Glendene* 4420/29, Dene Ship Management Co, Whitby
       Mariupol to St, Lawrence *Induna* 5086/25, MacLay & McIntyre, Glasgow.
       Calcutta to Tuticorin *Clumberhall* 5198/30, West Hartlepool S.N. Co.
       Port Redon to Montreal *Somersby* 5170/30, R. Ropner

1909   Calcutta to Singapore *Craighall* 4402/05, Biggart, Fullerton, Grier, Glasgow
       Taku to Hong Kong *Maori King* 3808/90, M.Ginsberg

1900   Calcutta to Pondicherry *Deepdale* 2598/80, A. Laing, Sunderland
             to Norfolk (Va.) *Gymeric* 4002/99, A. Weir, Glasgow
       Sydney to Colombo *Florence Pile* 3358/92, J. Weatherill, Dublin

The method of loading coal varied from port to port. On the north-east coast it was customary to load from 'staithes' where coal from the railway wagons was tipped into chutes which led directly into the ship's hold. In some areas the ground was high above water level, in others the ground was too low and the 'staithes' had to be built up of timber to the appropriate height. Elsewhere the coal was tipped direct from the wagon into the ship's hold, while in others the wagons were emptied on to a conveyor which then raised the coal high enough for it to be fed into the waiting ship.

Before world war one, coal was the most important cargo carried by the British tramp steamer. By 1935 the picture had changed considerably as during the war much of Britain's carrying trade had been lost. Figures obtained in 1935 showed that of the 39.53 million tons of coal, coke, etc. exported from Great Britain 7.64 million tons was carried in British ships of 3,000 grt. and over, while 7.39 million tons were carried in British ships of 3,000 grt. and less. The remaining 24.5 million tons were carried on foreign bottoms, i.e. British shipping carried only 38% of British coal. However in addition to the 15.03 million tons carried by British vessels, there was another 5.57 million tons of foreign coal which formed cargoes for British ships.

Figures produced in 1937 showed how unevenly divided was the proportion of coal cargo carried in British vessels in the intermediate trades:

Importing country	Percentage of coal cargo carried by British vessels	Percentage of timber return cargo carried by British vessels.
France	49.4	
Denmark	17.5	
Sweden	7.3	7.1
Germany	30.6	
Norway	6.7	7.4
Finland	7.8	
Holland	44.8	

Fire in coal continued to be a problem for the tramp steamer owner. During a three year period June 1925 to May 1928 272 ships reported 30 fires in coal cargoes and 280 fires in bunker coal. (Some vessels had fires on more than one voyage.) In 65% of the cases the blame was put on 'direct heating' where coal had been stored near boilers, funnel casings, steam pipes, etc. without proper insulation. In 11% of the fires new coal had been loaded into bunkers on top of old coal . Only in 14% of the outbreaks was spontaneous combustion blamed. In the remaining 10% of the fires faulty ventilation was the contributory factor. In the 1920s South Africa began to export coal but after a spate of fires marine insurance underwriters prohibited carriage of some types of South African coal. After world war two, coal from Danzig caused an epidemic of fires and the under-writers laid down restrictions on voyages which could be made with Danzig coal.

GRAIN

The commonest homeward cargo was, before world war one, grain. For the first half of the 19th century British agriculture was protected by the Corn Laws which made it too expensive to import corn. It was only after the repeal of the Corn Laws in 1846 that the grain trade was able to develop. From Russia came wheat, barley, oats, maize and rye from her ports on the White Sea and Baltic Sea. From the northern coast of Europe came wheat and some barley. Grain from the Mediterranean, from Canada and from U.S.A. trickled into the ports of the United Kingdom. A trickle at first but as the years passed the trickle became a flood. Although the amount from each area varied from year to year as harvests prospered or failed, the total quantity inexorably increased. Sweden dropped from the list in 1880. India and Australia began to ship grain in small quantities in 1870. Grain from South America was carried in 'parcels' by cargo liners but in 1893 the quantities available attracted the attention of tramp shippers and as the tramp steamers entered the lists the amounts shipped increased dramatically.

The sailing ship was used at first for the longer voyages, the steamer for the shorter distances but as the commercial efficiency of the steamer improved these took over. On long voyages the grain might overheat and be spoiled. Maize was the most likely to suffer from heating and was shipped as 'sailing grade' – a well dried grain not liable to suffer from heating, or 'steamer grade' – a softer type not safe for long passages. One of the longest voyages for grain ships was from the Pacific Coast of North America, a trade which remained in the hands of the sailing ship owners until the Panama Canal opened and cut out the long haul round Cape Horn.

Grain was a dangerous cargo. It was 'fluid' and when poured in a heap it had what was known as 'an angle of repose' of 23º to 26º depending on the type. That is, if a quantity was poured freely it would form a conical heap, the sides of which would vary from an angle of 23º to 26º to the horizontal. This was the equivalent of saying that if a cargo of grain was stowed and levelled off, the grain would begin to shift if the angle of heel of the vessel reached 23º. In practice the shifting would begin earlier as the heaving of the ship created dynamic forces which started the shifting at a smaller angle. Shipping losses ran at such a high level even after the enforcement of the regulations for which Samuel Plimsoll fought for so long, that public anxiety was aroused. In 1876 legislation compelled owners to place a loadline on their vessels, but left the determination of the freeboard to them. The effect on shipping losses was negligible, and it was not until 1890 that the Loadline Act came into force laying down strict rules for the fixing of a vessel's freeboard. In 1875 and 1876 the Merchant Shipping Acts decreed that "no cargo of which more than one third consisted of any kind of grain, corn, rice, paddy, pulse, seeds, nuts, or kernels should be carried on any British ship unless such grain cargo be contained in bags, sacks or barrels or secured from shifting by boards, bulkheads or otherwise."

Because of this continued loss further laws were passed in 1888 laying down the precautions to be taken when stowing grain,. These could be summarised as follows:
(1)   A bulkhead was to be built along the centreline of the hold, of timber at least 2" thick, close fitting to be graintight, supported by strong uprights. These were called shifting boards.
(2)   The maximum unsupported span between the uprights was determined by the plank thickness:

Thickness	Span
2"	8'
2½"	11'
3"	13'

(3)   Uprights supporting the shifting boards to be of wood not less that 10" x 2". Alternatively closely spaced steel hold pillars could be used.
(4)   Uprights to be stayed with 3" circumference steel wire rope.
(5)   Where hatchways were used as feeders to allow for the settling of grain they should not contain less than 2½% of the capacity of the hold. In fact grain can settle up to 6% in volume, equivalent to about one foot below the deck beams of a good sized steamer.
(6)   Where holds were partly filled with loose grain, the cargo had to have a 4 foot deep layer of bagged grain laid on its surface. Alternatively other bulk cargo in bale form such as cotton could be used, provided that suitable separation was arranged to ensure that contamination could not occur.
(7)   Where a bulkhead backed on to a heated space such as a boiler or engine room a further bulkhead had to be built leaving a 6" wide ventilated space.
(8)   Where a vessel had more than one deck, loose grain was not to be stowed on upper decks, only bagged grain.

These regulations were extended to cover foreign vessels bringing grain to British ports, but they were frequently ignored. The fines imposed when captains were prosecuted were small compared to the saving effected by improper stowage, and the additional profit from overloading.

The captain of a tramp steamer had to keep his eyes open for other problems which could arise when carrying a cargo of grain.
(1)   If the grain was shipped damp it could heat and deteriorate. This could also happen with water penetrating through cracks or holes in the deck.
(2)   The holds had to be thoroughly cleaned out before taking in a new cargo as grain left from previous voyages on stringers or in corners where frames and stringers met would rot and contaminate the new cargo.
(3)   Ample ventilation to cargo spaces was essential.
(4)   The captain or his mate had to keep an eye on the tallying, i.e. keeping a record of the quantity of grain being shipped. Preferably he was to sign the bills of lading as 'weight and quantity unknown, said to be .... tons.' or '.... bags said to be ....weight and quantity unknown.'

This last comment was important as grain was measurement cargo:-

Grain type	Cu.Ft./ton bagged	Cu.Ft./ton unbagged
Barley	60	54
Kernels	48	
Linseed	58	51
Maize	54	49
Oats	83	76
Rape Seed	60	
Rye	55	50
Wheat	52	47

These were average figures and changes in climatic conditions during growing and harvest could produce a lighter grain. The steamer was filled to capacity but the grain was weighed during unloading and the shipper was only too ready to prosecute should he find himself apparently short-shipped.

The task of the captain was made more difficult by the wide variety of local measurements which could be encountered:

South America	Arroba, which varied from 25.35 lb to 32.38 lb. according to the country.
Russia	Pood: equivalent to 36.113 lb. (100 poods = 1.6121 tons).
U.S.A.	Short ton = 2000 lb.

Grain could be shipped in tons or in bushels, where one bushel = 1.2837 cu.ft. which meant that a bushel varied in weight with the type of grain: oats 32 lb. to the bushel, barley 48 lb. to the bushel, maize 56 lb. to the bushel, wheat 60 lb. to the bushel.

Grain was a handy cargo for the tramp steamer owner as it gave him a round the year cargo as harvests occurred in different months according to the location. In January shipments from the River Plate began, and the tramp steamers converged on the Plate ports. The River Plate ports (92) were a bit of a problem for the shippers as some of them were many miles upriver from the mouth where a bar restricted the size of vessel which came to load wheat, maize and linseed. At the mouth was Buenos Aires which had a depth at the quay of 19' to 20', with extremes of 16' to 23'. Vessels wishing to load deeper had to take on their extra cargo at La Plata, 35 miles to the south. San Nicholas was 150 miles above Buenos Aires with a limit of 15' to 25' in the river, depending on the season, with 18' to 20' alongside the wharf. A further 50 miles upriver was Rosario where the depth alongside the quay in December to July was 19'. Fourteen miles further inland was San Lorenzo where the steamers were loaded by chutes from the top of the high river bank. The river could drop as low as 15' to 16' at this point. Finally, 310 miles above Buenos Aires was Colastine with a widely ranging bar depth of 12' to 24', though in the port itself the water was considerably deeper. Here cargoes had to be loaded manually. Opposite Buenos Aires, in Uruguay, was Monte Video with a depth of 17' to 18' in the harbour and 24' in the outer roads. No wharfage or cranage was available. Deep draughted steamers loading upriver took on part cargo and proceeded to the river mouth to complete their loading from lighters.

The Black Sea trade began in March although earlier shipments were sometimes possible. In the River Danube the main loading ports were originally Galatz and Ibrail, about 80 and 93 miles respectively from the river mouth, to be replaced in importance in later years by Sulina, at the river mouth (92). The river at Galatz was 16' to 24' deep and at Ibrail 18' to 22', and the Danube Commission insisted that steamers loading should only take on as much grain as would leave one foot clear below the hull. The additional grain to complete the loading was taken down river in lighters and put on board below Sulina beyond the bar which restricted draught to 24'. In the very early days the steamers towed their own lighters, but the Commission later insisted that their tugs be used for this work. The alternative was to load the steamers down to their marks, off-load into lighters when the bar was reached, and to reload the grain after the bar was crossed. With all this handling there was frequently trouble in establishing the actual quantity of grain shipped. Another problem with the Danube trade was the delay which was frequently encountered as the number of loading berths available was usually less than the number of steamers arriving for cargoes. On August 2nd 1910 there were 75 steamers in the Danube with 24 of them waiting their turn to load. The waiting was strictly controlled by gunboats and on one occasion, when a British captain tried to jump the queue his ship was fired on by the attendant gunboat, whereupon he took his place in the line of waiting steamers. British shipping formed only part of this armada of tramp steamers. In 1905, 949 steamers and 190 head of sail left Sulina, 792 having taken their full cargo at Galatz and Ibrail, the other 317 having partially or fully loaded at Sulina. British vessels formed 40% of this total, followed by Greece with 23%, Austria with 11% and the remainder Italy, Turkey, Holland, France, Roumania, Germany and Russia.

A number of ports in the Black Sea shipped grain from Russia, many with strange sounding names. Odessa had the best artificial harbour in the Black Sea with a depth of 30'. Theodosia was also well equipped with a depth alongside of 21' to 26'. Nicolaieff provided grain elevators to facilitate loading and could accommodate steamers up to 24' draught. Kertch was limited by the bar at Yenikale to vessels drawing less than 22' and shipment was by lighter. Taganrog had no anchorage and the grain had to be carried 25 miles to the anchorage where the steamers were waiting. Rostof near Taganrog suffered the same drawback. Novorossisk was another modern port with depths alongside of 24' to 26' and the visiting steamers were loaded by elevator. Other names which crop up are Kherson and Azov (92, 93).

American wheat was shipped from July onwards from the west coast ports, Gulfport, Galveston and Louisiana, and from the ports in the 'northern range': Boston, New York, Norfolk (Virginia), Philadelphia. In Canada, Quebec and Montreal were the grain shipping ports on the east coast, while more cereals came out through the west coast port of Vancouver. An alternative route which was developed was through Port Churchill on Hudson's Bay. In 1932 general cargoes were carried experimentally in to Port Churchill and grain cargoes were brought out. The first steamer was R.S. Dalgliesh's *Pennyworth* 5388/16 and because the magnetic compass was not reliable at those high latitudes she was specially fitted with a gyro compass. In the autumn of the same year the steamer *Bright Fan* struck an iceberg and sank on her homeward voyage. This made the insurance underwriters very wary, but despite this the voyages were repeated. In 1952 a Dalgliesh steamer was still making the round trip, among 21 vessels which lay alongside the modern facilities at Port Churchill. Their *Warkworth* 7133/43 managed two voyages in the short season between August and October. Another steamers was *Essex Trader* 6966/41 (Hugh Roberts & Son). From time to time there were casualties. In 1936 *Avon River* 3661/13 (Mark Whitwill & Son, Bristol) was lost and *Grelhead* 4274/15 (Derwen Shipping Co Ltd) suffered bow damage and lost two blades of her propeller when she made contact with ice.

Some statistics are available which show how the sources of the grain imported into the United Kingdom developed up until 1900. After this date the figures show only the

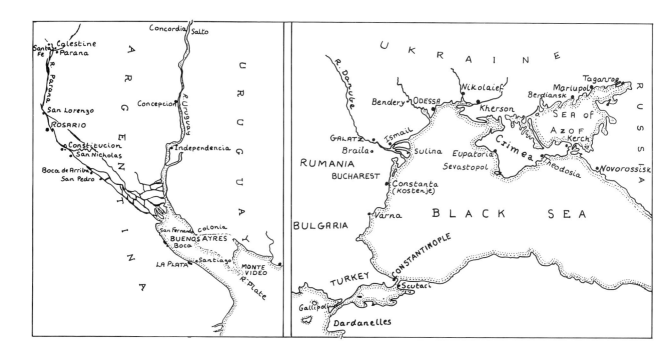

92. Grain ports of the River Plate (left) and the Black Sea (right).

93.
Hain's steamer *Trevanion* 2437/91, with a grain cargo from the Sea of Azof discharging in Weymouth, 1909.

Photo: I.W.Rook collection

total imports of wheat, barley, maize, oats, rye, meal, flour (millions of tons):

Source Year:	1860	1870	1880	1890	1900	1910	1930	1938	1950
Baltic	0.51	0.93	0.89	0.12	0.81				
Near Europe	0.77	0.40	0.35	0.18	0.25				
Black Sea	0.54	1.07	0.45	1.48	0.46				
Mediterranean	0.02	0.08	0.06	0.12	0.07				
North America	0.60	0.95	3.80	2.37	5.00				
Australia/India			0.39	0.61	0.20				
South America		0.03	0.08	0.15	0.94				
Pacific			0.35	0.60	0.53				
Totals	2.44	3.40	6.37	5.63	8.26				
TOTAL; all cereals	2.81	3.71	6.71	7.78	9.48	10.19	8.89	9.52	5.53

It is unfortunate that the method of presenting the figures of importation of grain was altered as the above does not show how the importance of the River Plate grain trade increased steadily. The falling total figures from 1920s onwards were the result of improving home production of cereals.

There are no early statistics to show how much of the world's grain was carried by British tramp steamers. It was not until 1937 that fully documented information was gathered and tabulated: The following figures relate to the year 1935.

Route	No. of vessels over 3,000 grt.	Average tonnage carried	No. of vessels under 3,000 grt.	Average tonnage carried
Empire to Empire	18	6,836		
Empire to Foreign	101	7,822		
Empire to U.K.	227	7,775		
Foreign to Empire	46	6,268		
Foreign to Foreign	416	7,552	12	2,060
Foreign to U.K.	392	7,322	404	684

The figures indicate that barely half of the sea-going tramp steamers were bringing grain to this country. The 1,200 ships carried a total of 8,977,951 tons of grain - 7,482 tons per vessel.

ORE

Another of the cargoes which featured high on the list was ore, which came in many varieties. These, with one exception, were definitely deadweight cargoes with very low storage factors (cubic feet per ton). Bauxite [aluminium] (40) cu.ft./ton, Stibnite [antimony] (20), Chrome (12-14), Cobalt (18-20), Copper (14-20), Galena [lead] (12-14), Hematite [iron] (12-17), Manganese (17-18), Wolfram [tungsten] (16-17), Zinc (18-24).

Although not in itself a dangerous cargo ores had to be treated with respect due to their great density. It is on record that a vessel 300' in length which took ore on board in one hold only, shortened by 11½" at her main deck due to the sagging caused by the concentrated load. It was advisable to load all holds evenly, moving the vessel back and forth below the tips. Finely crushed ores, when wet, could form a slurry with the vibration of the ship and in this condition could be highly dangerous with shifting causing a capsize. With two decked vessels it was usual to carry part of the ore cargo on the 'tween deck so as to ease the roll of the ship. However if care were not taken the 'tween deck could be overloaded and collapse could occur due to failure of the hold pillars. Sometimes ore was carried as part cargo on the bottom of the hold and overstowed with a lighter measurement cargo such as bagged grain, seeds, oil cake etc. It was important to ensure that good separation was provided, overlaying the ore with impermeable dunnage and matting as contact with damp ore could easily damage the dry cargo. To avoid making a vessel too stiff by putting all the ore flat in the hold, it was customary to form a wedge shaped mound along the centreline, although this could shift under violent pitching and rolling. It was better to bag the ore and then stack the bags in a wedge shape. Another solution was to build a strong wooden trough along the centre line to contain the ore and to raise its centre of gravity.

Towards the end of the 1870s home supplies of iron were running out and more had to be brought in from abroad. The graph (14) shows how the demand for imported iron ore rocketed to a peak in the 1900s, to fall away during the depression of the '20s and to shoot up again in the post-war boom of the 1940s, providing the impetus for the design of the specialised ore carrier.

The sources of ore in the earlier years of the century were within the range of the intermediate steamers. Lulea in Sweden, Narvik in Norway, Bona and Benisaf in Algeria, Almeria and Bilbao in Spain. The latter had a breakwater protecting the harbour and several British tramp steamers came to grief on this when entering or leaving in bad weather. Ore came also from Italy, Turkey, Morocco and Finland. As the various countries developed their own iron and steel industries there was less ore available for export and so the tramp steamers had to go further afield for their cargoes, to Rio de Janeiro, Goa, Malaya, Hainan, Peru and Brazil. Longer voyages meant more tonnage of ore on the move, but the trend towards specialised vessels meant that there was less for the ordinary tramp steamer. By 1959 it was estimated that only 0.4% of Britain's iron ore imports was carried by tramp shipping. This figure is a bit misleading as many tramps were in fact chartered to the specialist companies, but no figures are available of the numbers involved.

Specialised ore carriers were not a product of the post war period. The Swedes had in fact developed vessels specifically for the carriage of ore before world war one enabling them to push up their share of their trade to 53.1% while the British share dropped to a mere 1.1%. By comparison the Scandinavian countries carried 77% of the British coal which they imported in their own flag vessels.

As the 1935 statistics show almost half the ships employed in the iron ore trade were below 3,000 tons.

Route	No. of vessels over 3,000 grt.	Average tonnage carried	No. of vessels under 3,000 grt	Average onnage carried
Empire to Empire	5	8,170		
Empire to Foreign	67	7,778		
Empire to U.K.	14	8,074		
Foreign to Empire				
Foreign to Foreign	123	7,460	62	3,400
Foreign to U.K.	189	6,542	261	2,409

WOOD

One of the traditional cargoes, especially for the smaller tramp in the intermediate trades, was timber (95). Apart from one or two types of timber it was a measurement cargo (cubic feet per ton). Oak (36-45) cu.ft./ton, Pine (55-75), Teak (37-49), Fir (59-70), Ash (47), Cedar (48-75), Mahogany (42-64), Lime (64), Maple (53). At the extreme end of the scale came cork at 149 cu.ft./ton.

Timber was shipped in a variety of forms a few of which were:

Battens	Sawn timber between 6" and 7" wide and thicker than 4".
Boards	Sawn timber 2" and less in thickness.
Deals	Sawn timber 9" to 10" wide and thicker than 2".

95. Turret steamer *Turret Bay* with a timber cargo in the 1890s.

Staves   Timber already shaped for the manufacture of casks or case, shipped in bundles.

Sleepers   Railway sleepers, usually of Baltic Fir.

Logs   A heavy piece of timber either round, hewn or sawn.

Cargoes of timber were frequently made up of a mixture of several of the above, hence the abbreviation D.B.B. (deals, battens and boards).

Each country of origin had its own unit of measurement (standard), but the most common were:

'Standard':					
Petrograd	120 pieces	1½"x11"x12"	=1,980	Board Feet	=165cu.ft.
Christiania	120 pieces	1.25"x9"x11"	=1,237½	"	=103
London	120 pieces	3"x 9"x 12"	=3,240	"	=270
Quebec	100 pieces	2½"x11"x12"	=2,750	"	=292
Drontheim-sawn deals			=2,376	"	=198
	square timber		=2,160	"	=180
	round timber		=1,728	"	=144

The American 'mille' (1,000 sq.ft. of 1" timber) =1,000 " =38½

In addition a 'load' of unhewn timber (40 cu.ft.) A 'load' of hewn timber (50 cu.ft).

In order to estimate the carrying capacity of his vessel the shipowner was recommended to use the following formula:

$$\text{Capacity in Petrograd Standards} = \frac{\text{Bale capacity x 100}}{12 \times 1,980}$$

Because of its high stowage factor timber usually had to be carried with part of the cargo on the decks which were not generally designed to carry loads. Precautions had to be taken to support the decks using wedges between the beams and the cargo in the hold, and by spreading the loading by covering the decks with diagonal boards. Stanchions were fitted along the bulwarks extending 4' above the height of the deck cargo. These were stayed across with chains and turnbuckles and were provided with manropes to act as rails. All deck openings which were no longer accessible had to be sealed off but essential openings such as companionways had to be kept clear as had steering chains, lifeboats etc. Deck loads of timber were frequently excluded from insurance cover due to their vulnerability in bad weather (96). Ships intended for the trade had lugs fitted to the deck to take these wood stanchions which were part of the cargo. One such ship intended for the trade was *Pacific* 2816/23 completed by Murdoch & Murray Ltd, Port Glasgow, for Sir W.H. Cockerline of Hull (97). There was always a considerable timber trade to Hull and apart from the lugs on the deck the derricks were set high on the masts to be clear of a timber cargo (45). Typical of reports from timber carriers was: 20.10.1895 *Rotherfield* 2831/89, F. Woods, London. Pensacola to Greenock, cargo of timber and deals. Lost deck cargo in bad weather; 47°10'N, 42°158W. One man killed.

Although most tramp steamers carried timber cargo at some time or other, it was common practice that, when a vessel was to specialise in the timber trade she would be rigged with her masts at the extremities of the well decks to leave a long space between them clear of rigging and deck machinery. Holds were also made as long as practical clear of obstructions such as hold beams and stanchions. Such a vessel was *Brynymor*

96.
Alacrity of Witherington and Everett, Newcastle, with the remains of her timber cargo and main mast hanging over the side, September 1928.

launched in 1921 by the Dublin Dockyard Co Ltd for Letricheux & David of Swansea. (The Polecrest S. S. Co Ltd) 289.9' x 44.1' x 20.9', 2,600 grt. The hatches were large to facilitate the handling of long logs, but it was not possible to dispense with hold pillars because of the weight of the deck cargo (below). As the vessel was intended to trade extensively with Norway, attention was paid to the requirements of the Norwegian Board of Trade which called for two men only per cabin, separate mess rooms for seamen and firemen, bathrooms with hot running water and even a hospital, luxuries as far as British tramp steamers were concerned. *Brynymor* even carried wireless equipment. She was soon sold to E.T. Lindley of London who kept her for a short time before passing her on to Norwegian owners who renamed her *Braaland*.

Steamers began to carry timber from the Baltic in the mid-1870s only as an alternative to returning home in ballast after delivering a cargo of coal or coke, though there was a steady demand for pit props (100). Timber itself as a cargo did not make any profit, but covered the costs of the return voyage. In the early 1910s 7% of the

96. *Brynymor completed 1921 for the timber trade to South Wales.*

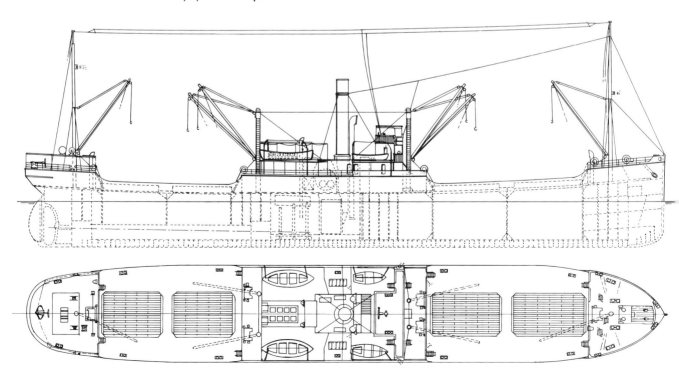

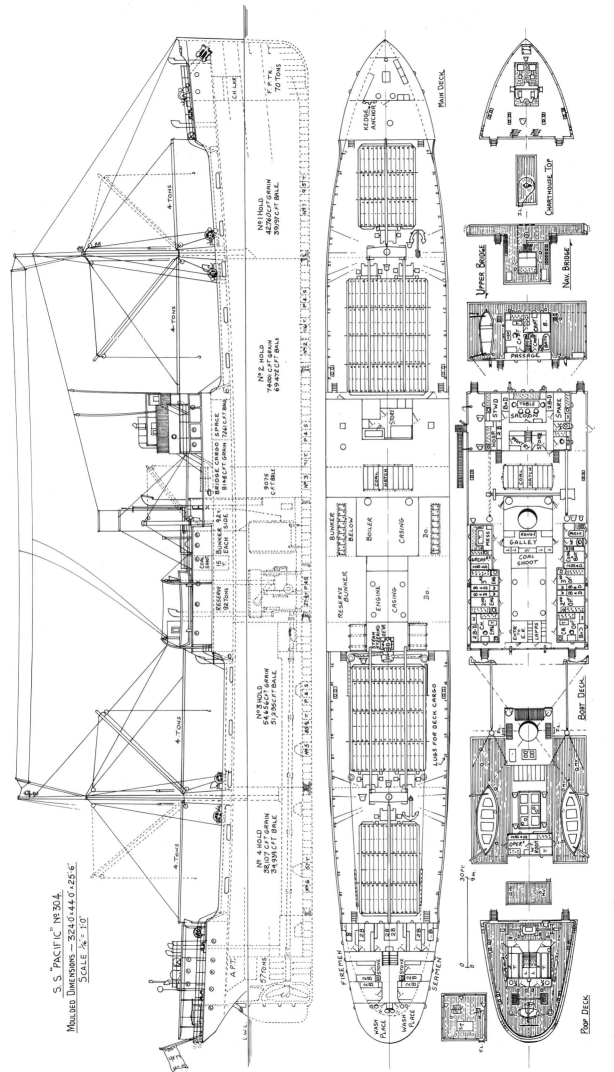

97. Single deck steamer *Pacific* 2816/23 was built by Murdoch & Murray Ltd, Port Glasgow for Sir W.H.Cockerline of Hull. Registered dimensions were 324.0 x 44.2' x 23.1'. Two scotch boilers supplied a triple expansion engine.

P.N.Thomas

GENERAL ARRANGEMENT
s.s. "EMPIRE MORDRED"

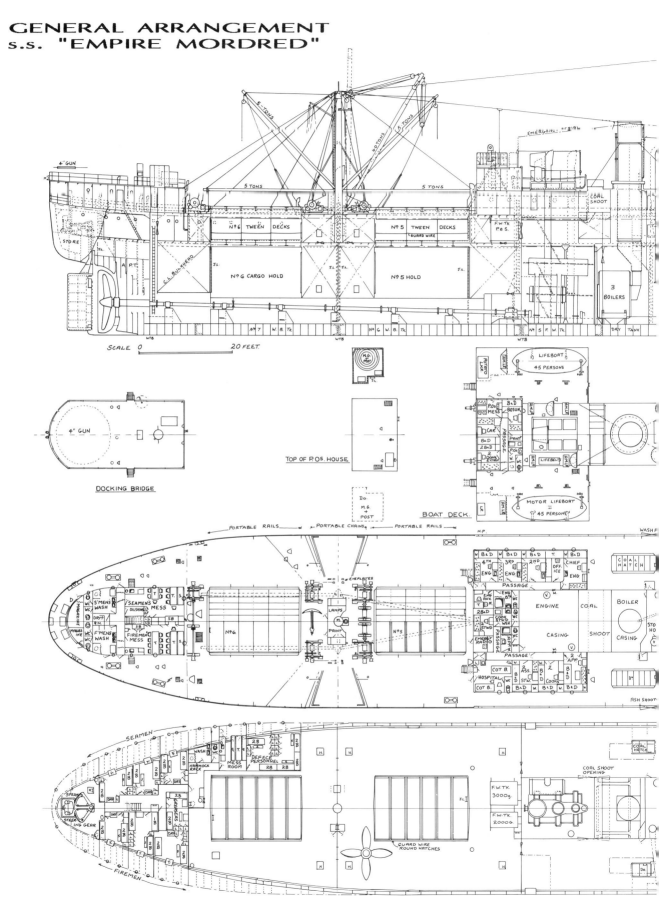

98. The two deck steamer *Empire Mordred* was a 'B' type standard ship completed in 1942 by Charles Connell & Co Ltd, Glasgow. Management was allocated by the Ministry of War Transport to G. Nisbet & Co Ltd, Glasgow. She had the dimensions

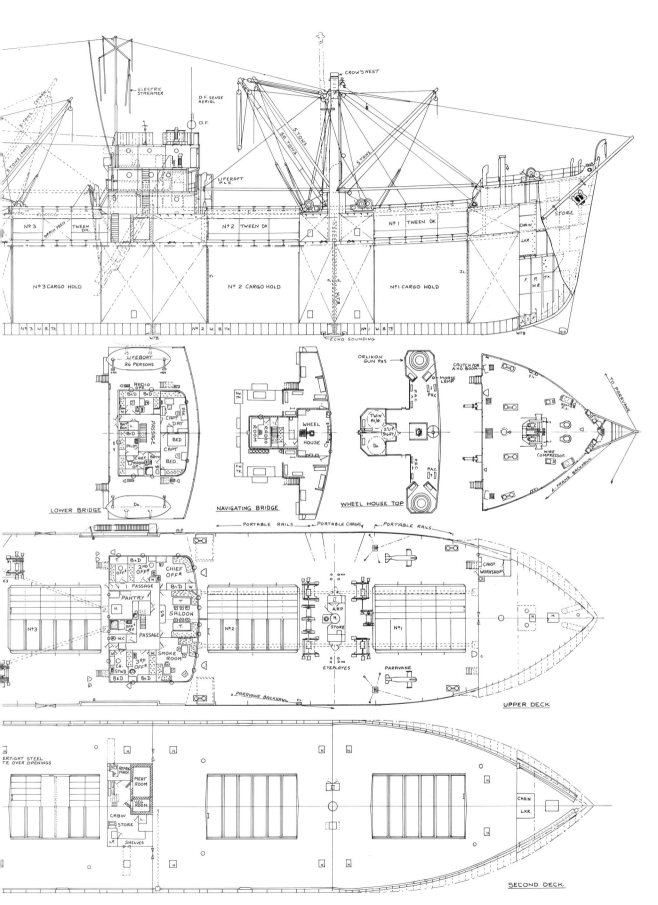

431.3' x 56.3' x 35.2' and was powered by a triple expansion engine with cylinders 24½", 39" and 70" diameter with a stroke of 48" supplied by Barclay, Curle & Co Ltd, Glasgow. Steam was supplied by 3 scotch boilers working at 220 lbs.

Scottish Record Office

100.
Isleworth 2648/89 of Watts, Watts & Co Ltd, London at Union Dock, West Hartlepool, unloading a cargo of timber.

Shipbuilding & Shipping Record

timber imported came from Canada, 21% from the U.S.A., and 35% from Russia. The small quantity from Canada was again the result of economics; the long distance involved compared to the short routes from the Baltic. After world war two Canadian timber became more popular as a cargo, partly due to its quality.

In 1935 most of the timber coming into Britain was from European sources. Where timber was carried by deep sea tramps most of it was intended for countries overseas.

Route	No.of vessels over 3,000 grt.	Average tonnage carried	No.of vessels under 3,000 grt.	Average tonnage carried
Empire to Empire	56	7,300		
Empire to Foreign	61	7,300		
Empire to U.K.	4	1,479		
Foreign to Empire	7	7,286		
Foreign to Foreign	38	6,500	24	3,500
Foreign to U.K.	34	5,715	349	2,952

Timber to the U.K. came from a whole variety of ports, both large and small:

1881 Cronstadt to London (Oats with deck cargo of lathwood) *Stanton* 800/70 R.T.Nicholson, Sunderland.

1881 Riga to Kings Lynn (Sleepers) *Glenavon* 2985/81, Elliott, Lowrey & Dunford, Newcastle.

1882 Simo, Russia to London (Deals) *Craiglands* 709 nrt/78, R. Hardy & Co, Hartlepool.

1883 New Brunswick to Liverpool (Phosphorous and deals), *Palmerin* 1150/75, A.J.Kay, Durham.

1883 Wyborg to Brest (Deals) *Dissington* 628/80, G. Humble, Newcastle.

1883 Uleaborg to London (Deals) *Medusa* 1413/62, J. Laing, Sunderland.

1884 Danzig to Tunis (Sleepers) *Annan* 1025/72, J.D. Turner, West Hartlepool.

1884 Sandvik to London (Deals) *Hamsteels* 1679/78, Pyman, Bell & Co, Newcastle.

1884 Iggesund to Hull (Iron ore and deals) *Hesperus* 878/71, F. Good, Hull.

1890 Narva, Finland to London (Deals, boards, battens) *Troutbeck* 817/82 G. Renwick, Newcastle.

1904 Grelfort to Bordeaux (Pine not hewn) *Aureola* 2346/93, J.F. Wilson & Co, West Hartlepool.

1904 New Orleans to Bordeaux (Oak staves) *Sir Walter Raleigh* 1870/89, Pearse & Haswell, Plymouth.

1904 Celestine to U.K. (Quebracho wood) *Zoe* 2255/89, Turner, Brightman, & Co, London.

1904 Oporto to Cardiff (Pitwood) *Cornelia* 903/72, W.Monroe, West Hartlepool.

1909 Arachon to Barry (Pitwood) *Melrose Abbey* 1211/77, F.Jones & Co, Cardiff.

1925 Gulf to Buenos Aires (1,375 stds.) *Kildale* 3877/24, Rowland & Marwood's S.S. Co, Whitby.

1929   North Pacific to East coast U.S.A. (4,500 mille) *Illingworth* 6067/21,
        R.S .Dalgliesh Ltd, Newcastle.
1930   Bay of Fundy to U.K. (900 stds.) *Saima* 2177/24, Chr. Salvesen & Co, Leith.

Archangel was also on the list of timber ports but the expense involved left little room for profit and it was not a popular trade with British shippers. After world war two it became more attractive economically and British tramps were time chartered to carry pit props to the U.K. In 1954, 5 steamers were taken:

Angusbrae 2905/43   Dundee, Perth & London Shipping Co, Dundee.
Burnhope 2915/43   Burnett Steamship Co, Newcastle.
Moto 2932/42   Pelton Steamship Co, Newcastle.
Sea Fisher 2997/40   Jas. Fisher & Sons, Barrow.
Tintern Abbey 2471/39 F. Jones & Co, Cardiff.

It is interesting to note that *Angusbrae* and *Sea Fisher* belonged to companies usually associated with the coasting trade. The first three steamers on the list were of the 'Scandinavian Type' of Empire vessel specially designed for working North Russian ports (see *Angusburn,* ex *Empire Bard,* 64).

Vessels engaged primarily in the timber trade were allocated additional freeboard marks on a different basis trom the ordinary cargo steamer, for use when carrying timber. The ordinary marks were: Tropical Fresh (TF), Fresh (F), Tropical (T), Summer (S), Winter (W) and Winter North Atlantic (WNA). The prefix 'L' indicates the marks used when carrying timber:

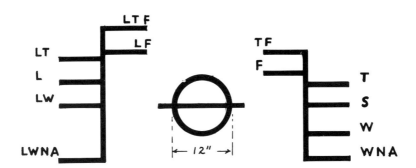

COTTON

Cotton was a raw material which was brought into this country in large quantities. Most of the countries of origin were served by the big liner traders and quite a lot of cotton was imported as part cargoes. In 1905 for instance only six cargoes of more than 10,000 bales were landed at Manchester, the remainder being shipped in parcels. One of the problems was that cotton was sold to brokers in relatively small quantities and unless loaded and unloaded methodically, taking care to separate the different markings, no end of trouble could arise with merchants claiming short shipment or wrong delivery.

The Southern States of the U.S.A. were the biggest exporters (102), while other sources were Egypt, India and Peru. Cotton was a measurement cargo, packed in large bales pressed to obtain maximum density, covered with coarse cloth and bound with steel bands or rope. Typical stowage factors were: U.S.A. [the standard bale weighed 500 lb.]. High density (85 to 88 cu.ft./ton), Hand stowed (130 to 135), Turkish (110 to 130), Indian High density (55 to 60), Egyptian [the standard bale weighed 750 lb.], (68 to 72 cu.ft./ton)

Cotton baled clean and dry would not come to any harm. Wet, it would heat and deteriorate but there was no danger of fire. However, cotton was frequently dirty with oil or grease and in this case spontaneous combustion was highly likely to occur. In 1906 a commission sent out to Savannah by the Lancashire spinners reported that: "American bales are dirty, damaged, disreputable, water soaked, wasteful, slovenly, clumsy, and highly inflammable" (at this point they seem to have run out of adjectives!) Worse still the stevedores in the cotton ports were careless in their smoking habits and it was generally felt that fires in cotton cargoes were the result of discarded cigarette ends and burning matches. Sparks from wood–burning locomotives were also blamed and arson was not ruled out as a cause. This last belief was strengthened when, in 1894, fires

102. The steamer *Ormiston* 4843/07 loading U.S. cotton at Harbour, Gulfport.

occurred simultaneously on 9 steamers loading at Savannah:

Castlegarth	2615/92	G.E. Macarthy, Newcastle.
Skidby	3703/92	R. Ropner & Co, West Hartlepool.
Baltimore	2334/88	Furness, Withy & Co, West Hartlepool.
Armenia	2330/90	W. Gray & Co, West Hartlepool.
Petunia	1691/89	J. Lilley & Co, West Hartlepool.
County Down	2210/90	W.J. Woodside, Belfast.
Whitfield	2422/91	McLean, Doughty & Co, West Hartlepool.
Dalegarth	2265/89	G.E. Macarthy, Newcastle.
Stag	2052/84	J. Robinson & Sons, N.Shields.

It is interesting to note the small size of the steamers and that those marked * were of the well–deck type, a design more associated with coastal and intermediate trades. Every week during the cotton season fires were reported in the casualty columns of the shipping press, despite all the precautions that the shipper and the shipmaster might take. When the fire was discovered the usual procedure was to close all apertures leading to the hold and to introduce steam to 'suffocate' the fire.

Imports of cotton into the U.K. rose from 620,000 tons in 1860 to about 800,000 tons by 1900 and held a fairly steady level until the first world war after which the intake fell off, falling to 542,000 by 1930. Many nations abroad which had been major customers had begun to manufacture their own cotton goods and imports were down to 364,000 tons by 1940 rising to 452,000 tons in 1950.

ESPARTO

After delivering an outward cargo of coal at a Mediterranean port a common homeward cargo was Esparto Grass, used in the manufacture of paper and cordage. The usual ports from which Esparto was exported were Nemours, Oran, Susa, Bona and Aguilhas. Esparto was made up into bales of about 360 to 370 lb., with a stowage factor ranging from 135 to 155 cu.ft./ton. Being a measurement cargo, it was carried as deck cargo, sometimes as part of a full cargo of the material, sometimes with a cargo of ore in the hold. Esparto was highly inflammable and there was a constant risk that sparks from the funnel or from the galley chimney might ignite the bales. When a fire did occur the damage was serious (103). Loading was often pushed near to the limit of stability with the cargo stacked high on the decks, problems then arose in the Bay of Biscay when the weather side became wet and heavy, causing the ship to start listing. Most of the Esparto Grass coming into the U.K. was carried by the smaller type of intermediate trader. In 1935, seven vessels of more than 3,000 grt. brought in 2,365 tons each, while

87 steamers of less than 3,000 grt. carried 1,704 tons each into British ports. The trade continued post-war (105).

SUGAR

Sugar was shipped into this country in large quantities reaching a peak of 2.4 million tons in 1895 and again in 1938. Much was carried as parcels by the liner traders but there was always enough left to provide full cargoes for the tramp steamers. Some companies such as J. & J. Denholm of Glasgow traded steadily in the sugar business. Cane sugar came from the West Indies, India, Malaysia, Philippines and Mauritius and was shipped 'green', i.e. raw, or 'dry', i.e. with the natural syrup drained out. The sugar was packed in bags, hogsheads, or baskets. Dry sugar could be carried in bulk and had an angle of repose of 40º, which meant that there was little danger of cargo shifting. The stowage factor for sugar was: Hogshead (barrel) 52 to 56 cu.ft./ton, Bagged 40 to 48, Bulk 40 to 45.

Sugar was not an easy cargo. Dry sugar by itself gave no trouble but good separation was required where it was a part cargo, and the sugar had to be kept from contact with steelwork. Green sugar drained off a kind of syrup which could damage a cargo stowed beneath it. It also gave off fumes which could taint edible goods. In 1924 ten men were gassed in a ship's hold, overcome by the fumes from fermenting sugar. Holds intended for sugar in bulk had to be rigorously cleaned and dried to remove dirt, oil and acid. After the early 1950s specialised bulk sugar carriers (53) were introduced which took much of the trade from the ordinary tramp steamer.

In 1935 barely half the tramp steamers which carried sugar were bringing it to the U.K.:

	No. of vessels over 3,000 grt.	Average tonnage carried	No. of vessels under 3,000 grt.	Average tonnage carried
Empire to Empire	15	7,364		
Empire to Foreign	2	5,010		
Empire to U.K.	45	8,025		
Foreign to Empire	18	7,400		
Foreign to Foreign	48	6,057	5	511
Foreign to U.K.	76	6,831	3	511
U.K. to Foreign			10	511

From the West Indies rum was often carried in barrels as a part cargo stowed on top of the sugar. There was a lot of trouble with leakage which damaged the sugar and ship-owners associations discouraged the practice.

103. the 4,000 ton deadweight steamer *Colemere* under repair in December 1915 following a fire in the cargo of esparto grass. Note the deck beams, buckled in the heat yet to be replaced. *Colemere* was managed by Herbert Watson of Manchester.

SCRAP METAL

Scrap metal began to appear on the list of imports in the mid-1890s, 11,000 tons per annum at first, hardly enough to make four decent cargoes, building up as time went on through 113,000 tons in 1915, 600,000 tons in 1938, to 2,000,000 tons in 1940. In 1935 the figures showed that only a small proportion of metal scrap carried by the tramp steamer was bound for the U.K. ports and that the deep sea vessels involved were of a good size:

Route	No.of vessels over 3,000 grt.	Average tonnnage carried	No.of vessels under 3,000 grt.	Average tonnnage carried
Empire to Empire	4	7,872		
Empire to Foreign	5	9,446		
Empire to U.K.	5	8,206		
Foreign to Foreign	73	7,627	7	782
Foreign to U.K.	12	5,978	199	600
U.K. to Empire	–	–	–	–
U.K. to Foreign			56	857

Due to the nature of scrap metal it was not possible to give a normal stowage factor and so it was the practice to accept a figure of 50 cu.ft./ton when arranging a charter. As scrap was just dumped into the hold a lot of internal damage was liable to occur unless the ceiling was covered with old boards to absorb the shock. It was also recommended that the cargo be trimmed to avoid a build up of weight below the hatchway as small dense items found their way to the bottom of the heap and light bulky material slid down the slope into the bilges. This possibility of a concentration of load was particularly a problem with two decked steamers.

FERTILIZERS

As agriculture in the world expanded the demand for fertilizers increased. In the days of sail most of the fertilizer was guano (dried bird droppings) shipped from the west coast of South America round Cape Horn to the U.K. and the Continent. Through time the list of fertilizers grew to include basic slag (a by-product of the steel industry), bone meal, chalk, gypsum, phosphate and limestone, together with purely man-made materials such as superphosphates and nitrogenous fertilizers.

Basic slag at 30 to 32 cu.ft./ton was packed in bags and, although dusty, was fairly harmless. Bone meal, bagged at 44 to 46 cu.ft./ton was a more difficult cargo, being smelly and having a tendency to rot the bags in which it was packed. Chalk was shipped in barrels at 42 to 45 cu.ft./ton or in bulk at 36 to 40 cu.ft./ton and gave problems due to the dust associated with it. Gypsum was another dusty cargo stowing at 43 to 46 cu.ft./ton in bags. Phosphate rock was carried in bulk at 33 to 35 cu.ft./ton and was a very dirty cargo. It was essential to prevent moisture from reaching this material. It was customary to ship bales of cotton on the top of phosphate from the Southern States of the U.S.A. and as long as good separation was provided there was no trouble. Superphosphates were bagged at 38 to 40 cu.ft./ton and during the voyage gave off gases which attacked cloth, foodstuffs, iron and of course the bags in which it was packed. This gave rise to arguments when the cargo was unloaded over the difference between the number of bags loaded and the number unloaded.

The nitrates were a particularly dangerous cargo. Not inasmuch as they would cause fire, but, should fire occur for any reason, the nitrates would speed up the conflagration and in a confined space cause an explosion. In 1910 a new Ropner built trunk steamer belonging to Swedish owners, *Bismark* 4938/10, blew up at Iquique in Chile five hours after a fire had been reported on board. In April 1947 at Texas City, a French ship *Grandchamp* 7176/42 and an American ship *High Flyer* 7174/44 caught fire. Both were being loaded with ammonium nitrate fertilizers and in this disaster 500 people were killed and 3000 injured. Three months later, at Brest, *Ocean Liberty* 7174/42, managed by Mitchell Cotts & Co on behalf of the Ministry of War Transport blew up after catching fire with a similar cargo on board, killing 25 and injuring 100 people.

In the Pacific phosphates were discovered in 1902 on the Nauru and Ocean islands. The transport of these was dealt with by the Pacific Phosphates Company who chartered tramp tonnage as required. This company was replaced by the British Phosphate Commission which again chartered tramp steamers until its own fleet of specially

105. *Brettenham* heads up the English Channel with a cargo of esparto grass. She was built as the 'Scandinavian' type *Empire Bard* in 1942 and became the *Angusburn* in 1946 (see 45 and 64). In 1954 she was sold to the Brebner Shipping Co Ltd (British Empire Steel Products Co Ltd, managers), London to become the *Brettenham*. The following year she passed to Rederi A/B Hildegaard (F. Lundquist), Mariehamn, the owners when this photo was taken. She was broken up in 1971.   Skyphotos

designed ships were built, the names of Andrew Weir & Co and Houlder Brothers appearing frequently on the charters.

The carriage of fertilizers gave employment to a great number of British tramp steamers. The figures for 1935 were:

Route	No. of vessels over 3000 grt.	Average tonnage carried	No. of vessels under 3000 grt.	Average tonnage carried
Empire to Empire	68	8,250		
Empirc Foreign	5	5,123		
Empire to U.K.	–	–		
Foreign to U.K.	20	7,761		
Foreign to Foreign	92	7,369	40	2,000
Foreign to U.K.	–	–	146	1,074
U.K. to Empire	6	5,063	–	–
U.K. to Foreign	–	–	41	1,230

SALT

Salt is a very common, but very important household commodity and although used by the individual in small quantities, the total on the move in the world at any one time is enough to provide cargoes for a substantial number of tramp steamers. In 1935, 86 cargoes were carried totalling 695,740 tons. Average tonnage per cargo was between 7,000 and 8,100 tons. Most voyages were Empire to Empire or Foreign to Foreign with only 4 Foreign to Empire.

Packed in bags the stowage factor was 38 to 40 cu.ft./ton, in barrels 50 to 52 cu.ft./ton. Large quantities were carried in bulk at 36 to 38 cu.ft./ton with the salt kept from contact with the ship's steelwork by mats or burlap. There was some loss of weight due to evaporation, the moisture produced being liable to harm dry goods stowed nearby. Conversely, salt can absorb moisture which meant that it had to be kept away from wet or moist goods.

GENERAL & MIXED CARGOES

As has been mentioned before, the tramp steamer was frequently chartered by a liner trade company to substitute for one of their own vessels and in such circumstances would find itself carrying a general cargo. A general cargo was a combination of a number of completely different commodities, each with its own storage requirements. 'Keep dry', 'keep cool', 'do not stow below other goods', 'keep away from goods which smell'....and so on. This is where the shipmaster needed to keep his stowage manuals handy! Some goods were quite valuable and had to be kept in a locked compartment. Articles carried in one general cargo were itemised as follows: 350 tons of wheat, 1,950 bags of flour, 432 bales of wool, 950 cases of canned beef, 500 boxes of butter, 170 bales of hemp, 54 casks of skins, 260 sacks of peas and 6,155 pieces of timber, and all had to be tallied into the hold and counted out at the destination. Sometimes explosives and acids were carried. Often hazardous cargoes were carried on deck where they could do least damage should anything untoward occur. One vessel was lost in the Bay of Biscay in 1912 when her deck cargo of drums of oil and tallow broke adrift in a violent storm. The oil and grease got into the pumps and blocked them, while the spillage on the decks made it impossible to stand. In 1935 the pattern of voyages with general and mixed cargoes was:

Route	No. of vessels above 3,000 grt.	Average tonnage carried	No. of vessels below 3,000 grt.	Average tonnage carried
Empire to Empire	21	5,650		
Empire to Foreign	19	6,500		
Empire to U.K.	25	6,300		
Foreign to Empire	45	6,150		
Foreign to Foreign	100	5,430	22	744
Foreign to U.K.	59	5,250	294	980
U.K. to Empire	34	4,820		
U.K. to Foreign	11	6,016	52	500

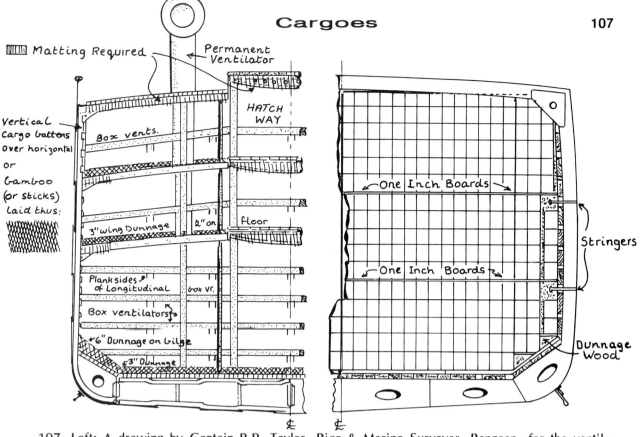

107. Left: A drawing by Captain R.P. Taylor, Rice & Marine Surveyor, Rangoon, for the ventilation of rice in a three deck steamer. Right: The stowage of case oil in a single deck steamer.

RICE

Rice was a household commodity which was moved around the world in large
quantities. Originating in the East Indies, it was eventually grown in all parts of Asia,
Africa and even the United States. Rice was generally shipped in gunny bags with a
stowage factor of 50 to 75 cu.ft./ton depending on the country of origin and whether or
not it had been cleaned. It was not an easy cargo. It was susceptible to damage by the
smell of other goods, and rice itself, if stowed damp, generated heat and emitted a foul
smell which affected other cargo. Rice bran, one of the many forms in which rice was
shipped, was liable to infestation by insects which moved to other vegetable cargo if
stowed nearby. Careful dunnaging was required and a complicated system of ventilation
was called for, comprising vertical channels and horizontal channels running both fore
and aft and athwartships, through the stacked bags of rice (107). This through
ventilation was most important at the beginning of the season; as the season progressed
the rice was usually drier. Late in the season it was shipped unventilated.

CASE OIL

A cargo which was frequently carried by the tramp steamers was 'case oil'. This was a
general term which covered kerosene, paraffin, petrol, turpentine, lubricating oils etc. It
was a cargo which was classified by the shippers as 'dangerous' or hazardous goods.
Generally it was contained in sealed five gallon cases (tin boxes), packed in twos in
wooden crates. The greatest problem with cases in the hold was at the sides where the
cases might be subject to uneven pressures. Here they had to be supported by dunnage
to keep them level and to keep them from being crushed against stringers. Periodically
between the layers, boards were laid to distribute the weight of the higher tiers (107).
The usual ports from which case oil was exported were Batoum and Poti in the Black
Sea and from ports on the western seaboard of the United States. There were instances
where the cases were stacked against the bulkhead which divided the hold and the
bunkers; a fire in the bunker could have had a disastrous result.
    The carriage of case oil continued for some time after the true oil tanker was
introduced, delivering cargoes of oil to ports which lacked bulk unloading facilities. It
was rather surprising to find some of the Empire standard world war two vessels being
designed for carrying case oil but in view of the very mobile nature of that war it was a
wise move. Among the shipowners who took on the carriage of case oil in considerable
quantity were Hogarth, the King Line, Hugh Roberts and Idwal Williams.

JUDGE & SON,

96 & 98, Leadenhall St.,

LONDON, E.C.

Telegrams—"LOGOGRAM."

Watkins, Scott's (1896 Edition) A 1, and Hinrich's Codes.

500/5/1909.

JAMES D. DUNN & CO.
SHIPBROKERS
GLASGOW

SCOTCH—PLATE.

STEAM.

WILSON, SONS & CO., Ltd.,

HEAD OFFICE—

Salisbury House,

LONDON, E.C.

ALSO AT

CARDIFF & BARRY.

CHARTERERS

AND

Coal Depot Proprietors.

MADEIRA,
LAS PALMAS,
ST. VINCENT, C.V.,
PERNAMBUCO,
BAHIA,
RIO DE JANEIRO,
SANTOS,
SAO PAULO.

CHARTER-PARTY.

(SALT—EAST).

Code Reference—"SALINASIA."

London, 24th Inch. 19 0

It is this day mutually agreed between — The Vale Steamship Co. Ltd (Andrew Crawford Barr & Co. managers)

OWNERS of the good Steamer *Galavale (Durret)*

of 2441/3830 net/gross tons register, classed *British Corporation*, and carrying about 6000 tons CARGO, now on passage to Antwerp, sailed Port Said 20th Inch. with liberty to drydock/load from UK or Continent to Mediterranean Adriatic or Islands and Messrs Salinera Española, Palma de Mallorca CHARTERERS.

1. That the said ship being tight, staunch and strong, and in every way fitted and suitable for the voyage shall, after discharge of cargoes as above, sail and proceed to TORREVIEJA, or so near thereto as she may safely get, and there load from the Charterers or their Agents in the customary manner where and as ordered by them, and which the said Charterers bind themselves to ship, a cargo of SALT in bulk and/or in bags not less than 1500 TONS but not exceeding 1200 TONS, and being so loaded shall forthwith proceed to *Calcutta* alongside any wharf, or vessel, or craft, or warehouse as ordered, or so near thereto as she may safely get and there deliver the same as customary, where and as directed by the Consignees, being paid FREIGHT at and after the rate of *Seven* shillings sterling per ton of 2,240 lbs. delivered. Winchmen, Dues, Duties, and ordinary

W. A. YOUNG & Co.
SHIPBROKERS
LIMIT ST. SQ., LONDON, E.C.

CHARTER-PARTY.

London, March 22nd 19 11. 190

It is this day mutually agreed between Ashmead S S Coy Limited (Messrs Hope Sloan Man)

Owner S of the good Screw-Steamer called the *Ashmead*

of 2249 Tons net register, 4900 tons deadweight, exclusive of bunkers, or thereabouts, Master, now in Antwerp, and expected ready to load about 5/10th April

and Messrs Nilson, Sons Coy Ltd Charterers.

1. That the said Steamer, being tight, staunch, and strong, and every way fitted for the Voyage, shall, after discharging inward cargo, if any, with all possible despatch, sail and proceed to Burntisland and there load in the customary manner, from the Charterers, in such Dock, or usual crane-loading Berth, as may be ordered by them on or before readiness, a full and complete cargo of Cowdenbeath

Coal not exceeding 5000 tons, nor less than 4500 tons, and not exceeding what she can reasonably stow and carry, over and above her Tackle, Apparel, Provisions and Furniture; and being so loaded, shall therewith proceed with all possible despatch to Monte Video for orders as to Port of Discharge (same to be given within 24 hours of arrival, or lay days to count), to discharge there or at LA PLATA, or BUENOS AYRES (in the Docks DARSENA, BOCA, BARRACAS or RIACHUELO)

or Vessel, and/or Craft, as ordered, or so near thereunto as she can red to shift, the expense of so doing to be paid by Consignees, rate of Eighteen Shillings nine pence intaken quantity less two per cent.

Strathclyde Regional Archives

5. Shipbrokers

In the Royal Navy it used to be said that there were about ten men ashore supporting each man who was serving at sea and so with the tramp shipping industry there was a huge organisation ashore arranging cargoes and finding ships to carry them. Chief among them were the shipbrokers. Most owners were also shipbrokers and often maintained offices in other ports apart from their home port, elsewhere they appointed local brokers to act on their behalf. The owners' brokers were employed to find cargoes or a charter for the shipowner. They were expected to obtain the most favourable freight rates for their principle and to ensure that the terms of the charter agreement were reasonable. On the other side of the fence were the chartering agents who were looking for suitable steamers to carry a given cargo, at the lowest freight rate and the most favourable charter conditions. There were other brokers who were more concerned with liquid fuel cargoes and with the liner trades. The sale and purchase brokers were, as their name implies, concerned with the buying and selling of ships on behalf of clients, keeping in their files details of hundreds of vessels, ready to open negotiations when an enquiry was received. They would also act as agents for the building of a new steamer, making out specifications, obtaining quotations from a number of shipyards and even recommending which quotation should be accepted.

At the other end of the chain were the agents, firms appointed by the shipowner in ports abroad to look after all the interests of their ships as they arrived with cargo. The agent had to be fully conversant with local laws and customs, especially with the correct procedures and with the paperwork. He had to be familiar with all the facilities available in his port area so that the most appropriate berth would be allocated. He had to be in a position to get the best out of the local stevedores so that loading or unloading would be carried out without unnecessary delay. It was an onerous appointment.

In simple terms the following is what was involved in the preparation of a charter. A merchant with a cargo to move approached a chartering agent with details of the cargo and the volume or tonnage in question, where it was and to where it was to be shipped, sometimes with a choice of destinations. The chartering agent made it known to the shipowners' agents that he had a cargo to offer and kept trying until he found one with a suitable vessel available. He had to determine where the vessel was located, when it would be available and what freight rate was acceptable. The cargo agent reported back to his client and after some bartering a charter party agreement would be drawn up and signed by both sides. It was seldom as simple as that as these agreements had to take into account all manner of eventualities. From time to time the North of England Protecting and Indemnity Association (of shipowners) published a book called "Suggestions to Captains" which gives an impression of a veritable legal jungle where it is only too easy for things to go wrong and for one of the parties in the agreement to suffer financial loss. The charter parties were drawn up in great detail and woebetide the captain or owner who strayed from the narrow path defined in the document. Some of the pitfalls are described elsewhere in the text.

When a steamer was proposed for a charter, the brokers would have a glance at Lloyd's Register to check if she was suitable for their client's purpose. Take for example the entry for *Garscube*. Built 1906, net tonnage 2,240, gross tonnage 3,568. The ratio gross:net=1.6, the accepted average which would mean that her deadweight was probably 2,240 x 2.4 = 5,400 tons. She was a single–decker, built on the deep frame principle making stowing of bales a bit awkward, or the cleaning of the stringers for a grain cargo meant extra work. The hull was classed '100 A.1.', and her machinery was certified by Lloyd's engineering surveyors. In other words she was a sound vessel. In later years the register contained details of cubic capacities, deadweight and bunkers to enable a more accurate assessment to be made. So these figures for *Arncliff* in 1922 were 6,200 deadweight including bunkers, permanent bunkers 14,940 cubic feet (about 340 tons), grain capacity 329,000 cubic feet, bale capacity 304,000 cu.ft. Knowing the bunkers allowed a guess to be made as to the vessel's range without refuelling abroad, an expensive business. Taking a 9 knot steamer burning 20 tons of coal per day would give 11 miles per ton burned. Considering a few typical routes it is possible to see what bunkers would have to be carried to complete a round voyage.

Route	Miles between ports	Bunkers for round trip + 10% contingencies & fuel used in port
Hull to Stockholm	888	177
Cardiff to Barcelona	1,652	330
Cardiff to Genoa	1,988	397
Glasgow to Montreal	2,693	539
Cardiff to Alexandria	2,924	585
Cardiff to Odessa	3,284	657
Liverpool to Savannah	3,618	724
Cardiff to River Plate	5,029	1,005
Dundee to Bombay	6,560	1,312
Cardiff to Valparaiso	7,142 (via Panama Canal)	1,429
	8,618 (via Cape Horn)	1,724
Cardiff to Sydney	11,365	2,273

Two points then had to be considered:
1. When the bunkers had been deducted from the deadweight, would the vessel carry the required weight of cargo?
2. If the bunkers had to be reduced to meet the cargo requirement, where would be the best place to coal and what would the extra cost be?

This is a typical shipping transaction with three parties involved. Grant & Graham, merchants, Aberdeen; Taysen and Townsend, brokers, London; Roth, agents for Bennett & Co, shipowners, Grimsby, owners of the steamer *Haverstoe* 2105/87, (1333 nrt.).

23.5.1895. Taysen's manager called on Mr. Roth looking for a cargo of maize for June/July shipment on behalf of Grant & Graham of Aberdeen. Mr. Roth offered *Haverstoe* which was booked for a charter (cancelling 15th August) to go to Buenos Aires and load maize. Taysen wired Grant & Graham: "Offer you *Haverstoe* 2,800 tons max. yellow Plate maize, load 15th July, cancel 15th August, a freight rate of 21/10½ per ton." Grant & Graham wired back: "Agree but try to get 1½d. reduction." Taysen wired Roth: "Accept *Haverstoe*." and wired Grant and Graham: "Booked *Haverstoe* 21/10½d, impossible to get her for less."

24.5.1895. Taysen issued contracts to Roth and Grant and Graham containing phrase "bills of lading to be dated 15th July." This was rejected by Bennetts and new contracts were issued stating: "loading 15th July, cancelling 15th August." Grant and Graham wrote Taysen and as a result 2,800 tons of maize were purchased, but included the clause: "shipment expected 15th July." Taysen sent Grant and Graham the contract, they wired back: "Shipment up to 15th August or buyers have the option of cancelling. Bennetts refused to make this alteration which gave the buyers the option of cancelling if *Haverstoe* was not loaded by 15th August.

29.5.1895 Grant and Graham wired: "Having failed to tender as per contract the purchase is off." (The maize was shipped in the *Haverstoe* and sold on the 5th September at a loss of £3,807).

24.7.1895   Bennetts issued a writ to recover damages for breach of contract. As might be expected there was a court case to recover the loss from Grant and Graham for breach of contract. The judgement was that a contract had been made and had been broken, but, that, any time after 24th July when legal proceedings were instituted, the grain could have been sold and a higher price obtained. Taking the grain price as at 24th July the loss was only £1,557 and this was what had to be paid.

Charter parties became so complex that it was found advisable, to protect signatories, to draw up standard charter party agreements for various cargoes and for various routes, each one being given a code name to be used in correspondence. The following are some examples of these standard forms:

Coal: East Coast Coal Charter Party 1922. Coal from the East coast between the Humber and Berwick to the Danube or River Plate. Code name MEDCON.

Wood: Pitch Pine Charter 1906. Timber from the Gulf of Mexico and Central America to the United Kingdom, the Continent and the Mediterranean. Code name PIXIPINUS.

Grain: River Plate Charter Party 1914. Homewards. Code name CENTROON.

Ore: Mediterranean Ore Charter 1921. Code name MEDITORE.

General: Baltic and White Sea Conference Uniform General Charter. Code name GENCON.

Time: Time Charter. Code name TRANSITIME.

The forms usually opened with the preamble: "It is this day mutually agreed between Messrs. X...... owners of the good steamship called the Y....... classed A1, of "a" tons nett register and "b" tons deadweight and Messrs. Z....... as agents for the charterers." The phrase 'good steamship' may seem antiquated but it simply meant that the vessel was guaranteed seaworthy in all respects.

UNSEAWORTHINESS: It is usual to think of unseaworthiness as relating to the hull of the steamer or to faulty loading of cargo, but this term was often applied for very different reasons. In 1897 E.P. Babtie of Glasgow signed a charter party to load their steamer *Vortigern* 3026/92 at Manila with a full cargo of Phillipine produce to be delivered at Liverpool – "Dangers of navigation or machinery, negligence, default or error of judgement of the owners, pilot, master or crew excepted." *Vortigern* left Manila on the 14th October 1897 with 155 tons of coal in her bunkers. She called at Cebu to take on a further 20 tons. On 27th October she arrived at Labuan with only 3 tons left and took on 470 tons of local coal. On 12th November she arrived at Colombo with 138 tons of Labuan coal left, having burned 25 tons per day instead of 18 tons per day for Welsh steam coal. 300 tons of Indian coal were shipped. On 29th November the master found that only 40 tons of coal was left in the bunkers and he authorised the mixing of 50 tons of copra from the cargo with the coal to be burned as fuel. The cargo owners naturally sued for recovery of £610, the value of the copra which had been burned, while the shipowner invoked the 'error of judgement' clause. However, the court held that the steamer had been 'unseaworthy' because she had not sufficient fuel in her bunkers to complete her voyage.

In another case a steamer was deemed 'unseaworthy' after seawater had caused damage to a sugar cargo, having leaked into the hold through a broken scupper pipe.

One of the strangest cases was that of *Trieste* 1512/83, Stott, Baker & Co, Liverpool. She arrived in Manchester with a cargo of linseed and oats from Riga and the dockers found a corpse in the hold. The sanitary authorities ordered part of the grain to be destroyed and the shipowner had to pay compensation as the court held that the ship had been 'unseaworthy'.

To return to the charter party, there then followed numerous paragraphs, each giving information or laying down a condition, among them the following:

(1)   The loaded draught had to be stated to ensure that the steamer would be able to enter the port of loading and to stay afloat at all states of the tide.

(2)   Where the ship was at the time of the contract being signed and when she was to be expected at the loading port. One owner entered into a contract and stated that his vessel was "in Finland bound for London". However he found time for her to perform another voyage in the interim and although his ship was available at the time stated he had to pay out compensation to the charterer who had incurred extra expense, because his vessel had not proceeded from Finland to London as stated in the charter party.

(3)   A description of the cargo and the weight or volume to be shipped laying down the maximum and minimum quantities acceptable to both parties.

(4)   A statement on how the cargo was to be carried, e.g. whether in bulk, in bags, in barrels etc.

(5)   The port of loading and the port of unloading.

(6)   If lighterage was involved, whether special conditions applied. At some ports a bar prevented steamers from loading fully alongside the wharf and loading had to be completed from lighters once the steamer was over the bar.

(7)   A statement laying down how the freight money was to be paid and whether or not any advance was to be expected.

(8)   Cancellation and lay days. The cancellation date was the last date on which the charterers were obliged to accept the vessel for loading. The lay days were the number of days allowed for loading or unloading. Sometimes the quantity of cargo to be handled each day was specified as the method of cargo handling at different ports varied. Sometimes the port provided cranage while at another the vessel had to use her own derricks.

(9)   A demurrage clause. Demurrage was paid to a shipowner to compensate him for delays in port due to causes outside his control .

One of the most extreme cases of demurrage was that of *City of Newcastle* 1973/82, R. Bell, Newcastle. On 11th February 1889 she arrived at Poti to take on a cargo of ore, but was not permitted to enter the port. On 4th March she was struck by another steamer and had to go to Constantinople for repairs. On 19th April she returned to Poti to load but due to overcrowding in the harbour she was unable to enter until 2nd June, completing her loading on 9th June. Her owners claimed, and won demurrage for 54 days, 18 hrs., 30 min. and received £994.17.6d.

(10)   A statement of the fee to be paid to the broker either as a lump sum or a percentage.

(11)   A deviation clause. The charter agreement frequently laid down the route to be followed by the ship; any departure from this was called 'deviation'. Whether or not deviation was permitted was stated in this clause. If the vessel had to coal during her voyage this had to be specified, otherwise, should the charterer suffer any financial loss due to 'deviation', the shipowner would face a law suit. Sometimes the deviation clause specifically refused to allow the chartered vessel to assist or salvage vessels in distress.

(12)   The general average clause. From early times it had been the custom of the sea traders that, if a part of the cargo had to be jettisoned to save the vessel, then the value of that lost cargo should be covered by the owners of the other cargoes in the vessel.

The above were the more important clauses in the charter party but there were many more to be found in the small print of the standard forms.

As a guide to all concerned the maritime press printed regular lists of 'fixtures' which indicated what goods were moved, between what ports, the quantity of goods and the freight rate being paid. In order to pack as much information as possible into a small paragraph the brokers adopted a system involving many abbreviations: A typical entry in the maritime press would read as follows: "San Lorenzo to UK/Cont. 6,700t., 10% 26/- heavy grain. Option two ports N.Spain 1/3 ton extra, Portugal one port 2/- extra, 2 ports 3/-, Med. one port 2/6 extra, 2 ports 3/6, same country, 3/9 different countries. 6d. less if Antwerp/Rotterdam.10–28 Jan.1929."

Translated into plain English this meant that the steamer had been chartered to load a cargo of heavy grain from San Lorenzo, 6,700 tons allowing 10% more or less at the owner's option. The vessel was to be discharged at a named port in the United Kingdom or the Near Continent for which the owner would receive 26/- per ton shipped. If the charterers wished they could order the steamer to two ports in northern Spain in which case the rate would be 1/3 more per ton, alternatively the steamer could be directed to Portugal receiving 2/- per ton extra, if unloaded at one port, 3/- if unloading was carried out in two ports. A further alternative was a destination in the Mediterranean at a rate of 2/6 extra for a call at one port, 3/6 if two ports, but should these be in different countries the rate would be 3/9 per ton extra. There was a further option of unloading at Antwerp or Rotterdam when 6d. less would be paid. The steamer had to be ready to load between 10th and 28th January 1929, both dates inclusive.

They also used abbreviations in the charter parties since little space was left to add comments or to make alterations.

a.a. – Always afloat. At all times during loading and unloading the vessel must not be allowed to touch bottom. A/H – Destined for any port between Antwerp and Hamburg. B.C. – Bristol Channel. B.D. – Bar draught. The minimum depth of water over the bar at ebb tide. B.L. – Bill of lading. b.t. – Berth terms. C.F.O. – Calling for orders. The tramp steamer had to put into a port such as Queenstown or Falmouth to ascertain to which port her cargo was to be taken. Many charter parties gave a vague destination such as "East Coast United Kingdom". D.B.B. – Deals, boards and battens. (United Kingdom). E.C.U.K. – East Coast United Kingdom. E.C.S.A. – East Coast South America. f.o.w.– First open water. Where ports were icebound throughout the winter this phrase was used to indicate when ships might be expected to enter the port.

n.a.a. – not always afloat. Indicating that the vessel might have to touch bottom during loading or unloading in a port where deep water was not available alongside the berth. n/n – not north of .... A charter party might include a phrase such as E.C.U.S.A., n/n Cape Hatteras, i.e. any port on the east coast of the U.S.A. but not one north of Cape Hatteras. p.o.c. – Port of call. p.o.r. – Port of refuge. Many ports were recognised as safe anchorage in time of storms and ships might run for such a port under stress of bad weather. s.b.s. – Surveyed before shipment. Where a difficult or delicate cargo was to be shipped a master was advised to have a survey carried out and to obtain a sworn statement from an expert that he had properly prepared his vessel to receive that cargo in order to eliminate possibility of damage. Such a certification might save considerable cost should a law suit be brought in the event of the cargo being spoiled. W.C.E. – West coast of England. Y.A.R. – York-Antwerp Rules. As early as 1877 the shipping fraternity, realising the differences between the way the nations applied the rules of General Average, formulated an internationally acceptable code which has been revised from time to time since that date.

The paperwork involved in administering a tramp steamer was considerable. The ship's papers which had to be produced on the request of port officials, customs officers and others included the following:

(a)   Bill of Lading. This was a form of receipt for the goods which were on board the steamer signed on behalf of the shipowner.

(b)   Bill of Health. A certificate confirming that there was no one on board with a contagious disease.

(c)   Certificate of Registry. A document issued at the port of registry giving full details of the vessel.

(d)   Ship's Articles. Listing every member of the crew giving details of his status, length of voyage, scale of provisions.

(e)   Manifest. A full list of all cargoes aboard with case contents, shippers names, and case marks.

(f)   A copy of the charter party.

(g)   Official log. A diary of every happening aboard the ship, including courses and speeds. It was no use, at the end of the voyage, in complaining that some untoward event had caused delay on the voyage or damage to the cargo unless it had been entered in the ship's log.

(h)   A list of dutiable stores.

(i)   A loadline certificate stating the statutary freeboard for the fully laden vessel.

When a vessel arrived at her unloading port the Master would expect the agent to meet him and to go with him to the Customs House to report his arrival and to produce the appropriate documents from the above list as required by local laws. If any damage had been received during the voyage to ship or cargo, the Master would go to a Notary Public and make a 'Protest' This procedure was very old established and allowed the Captain to put on record details of the bad weather or untoward events which had caused the loss or damage. The 'Protest' was very necessary as, at the time, the full extent of the loss or damage would not be known. Should a court case ensue, the absence of Noting Protest could result in the shipowner losing his case.

NOTING PROTEST: Sometimes a protest was just a statement about bad weather which had been encountered, made to cover the possibility of damage being discovered during unloading: "At Glasgow, the fourteenth day of September Eighteen Hundred and ninety-six, between the hours of ten and eleven o'clock forenoon. Compeared (appeared) William Pugh, master of the S.S. *Saint Jerome* of Liverpool registered tonnage 1845 who represented that he sailed from Norfolk, Virginia on twentysixth August last bound for Glasgow with general cargo, that he experienced heavy weather wind and seas in the Atlantic Ocean and arrived at Glasgow at two o'clock afternoon on the eleventh September current. Protests in common against wind and weather with power to extend."

As it happened, the captain of this steamer was back sooner than he thought to lodge another protest: "At Glasgow, the eighteenth day of September, Eighteen Hundred and ninetysix between the hours of four and five o'clock afternoon. Compeared (appeared) William Pugh, master of the S.S. *Saint Jerome* of Liverpool, registered tonnage 1845 presently lying in Queen's Dock Glasgow who represented that in the forenoon of the present day as the S.S. *Auretta* of Glasgow was being warped into her berth immediately ahead of the *Saint Jerome*, she collided with the *Saint Jerome*, striking her on the port bow and stoving in onc platc. Protcsts in common form against thc aforcsaid accidcnt with power to extend."
(The *Saint Jerome* 2864/94 was owned by Rankin, Gilmour & Co of Liverpool.)

Other noting protests were more specific and related to damage suffered by the cargo during the voyage: "At Glasgow, the first day of September in the year Eighteen hundred and ninetysix between the hours of three and four o'clock afternoon. Compeared (appeared) William McKintosh, master of the S.S. *Torgorm* of Glasgow, registered tonnage 1065 who represented that he sailed from Glasgow on the twentythird May Eighteen hundred and ninetysix bound for Barbados, Trinidad and Demerara with general cargo, including fortyone cases Galvanised Iron marked: I.T.& S.

V

Trinidad

that the said fortyone cases were properly stowed in the after part of Hatch number Two along with iron pipes, oil and bottled beer in casks, on top of coal in bulk, there being no sulphate of ammonia or any other chemical stowed in that part of the vessel, to the best of his knowledge and belief that the said fortyone cases were discharged at Port of Spain Trinidad in fair and good order with the exception of three of the said cases which were stained with oil which had leaked from the cask stowed in the same hatchway as above stated. Protests in common form with power to extend."
(The *Torgorm* 1676/89 was a small well deck steamer owned by Caw, Prentice & Clapperton & Co, Glasgow.)

The agent would arrange for the discharging of the cargo to start and as it was unloaded it had to be tallied, i.e. a record kept of each parcel of goods and the appropriate marks, as it left the steamer. With coal or grain in bulk the tallying would be done by weight. With bales, which were usually destined for a number of different purchasers, it was vital to tally the number of bales against each identifying mark. It was essential that one of the ship's officers should check on the tally regularly, as the shipowner was responsible for any shortage. In many foreign ports it was customary to try and cheat during the unloading. Similarly cargoes had to be tallied as they were taken aboard and where possible it was preferable to tally on an 'over the rail' basis, i.e. what was actually brought on board and not to accept a statement of what was on the quayside or in the lighter alongside for loading. Before departure the Master had once again to call at the Customs House with the necessary documentation to obtain permission to leave port.

CARGO SHORTAGE: There were frequent controversies about the quantity of cargo shipped. In 1912 *Auldmuir* 2747/03, Glen & Co, Glasgow, was chartered to load 68,645 bags of maize at Rosario, said to weigh 19,900 quarters. (4,266 tons). On arrival at Bristol the bags were broken open in the hold and the grain 'bulked' for discharge by elevator. The grain was not weighed but the bags were counted and found to be short by 409. The steamer owner demanded the full freight while the shipper withheld £125.10.8, being the value of 409 bags of maize. Evidence was called which showed that:
1.   It was common practice to put nails in the loading chutes so that the bags tore and provided loose grain which made it easier to stow cargo. The torn bags usually disappeared.

2.   Even had the grain been weighed out of the steamer there would in any case have been a shortage due to natural drying out of the grain ranging from 0.46 to 2.24%. The judgement was that the shipowner had agreed to deliver 68,645 bags and was therefore liable for the cost of 409 bags = £3.8.2, but nowhere in the Bills of Lading had he committed himself to deliver a stated weight of grain.

Other causes of shortage were:

1.   On one steamer the mate was tallying slings of four bags on board and marking "1" for each sling. For a short time he handed over the tallying to another person without explanation, and this individual marked '1' for each sack. Thus when the tally reached the mate's total of sling loads the loading was stopped, leaving a shortage.

2.   Officers sometimes accepted 'boat notes' when goods were trans-shipped from lighters without tallying the goods over the rail.

3.   'Sworn meters' used for checking cargo discharged in foreign ports were sometimes tampered with.

4.   In 1895 *Emir* 4090/89, W. & R. Thomson, Liverpool showed a shortage of 12 bales of jute, each weighing 400 lbs. It was stated in court that it was possible for a local tally clerk to allow a bale to be left in the sling after being checked in the tally, to go back over the side and to be swung in again to be checked in a second time.

5.   Corruption on the part of local officials, stevedores and others in foreign ports.

6.   Errors in calculation when each of the parties concerned were using a different basis of measurement, e.g. pounds, quarters, hundredweight, tons, bushels for grain.

7.   Confusion between marks on 'parcel' cargoes. Cotton cargoes were frequently marked for different consignees at the port of unloading and care had to be taken to tally out the bales against the correct marks and to store them in the quayside warehouses under the same marks. Marks were not always checked when the bales were removed from the warehouses and any consignee receiving too many bales would not make a fuss.

Although the maritime press gave the freight rates daily it was up to the individual shipowner to satisfy himself what rate he could accept for any given cargo and voyage and still make a profit by preparing a balance of income and expenditure. On the debit side was the cost of running the vessel plus 'disbursements'.

DISBURSEMENTS: This was the term used to cover the various expenditures incurred when a steamer arrived or departed from a port. Firstly there were the direct costs associated with the port itself; pilotage, harbour dues, towage, foy boats (boats whose crew handled the mooring lines from ship to shore.), light dues, etc. Secondly the costs relating to the cargo; import duty, stevedoring, cranage, tallying, the cost of dunnage, weighing, trimming, etc. Whether or not the shipowner was responsible for these depended on the terms of the charter party. Thirdly, there were the general expenses such as taxis, postage, cables or telephone charges and payments to agents.

On her tenth voyage from Wellington, New Zealand, to London early in 1898 Thomas Dunlop's *Queen Louise* 3385/93 ran up a bill of £229.5.0. for disbursements:

Wharfage	£37. 1. 9	Cleaning hold	£18.10. 9	Scaling furnaces	£10. 4. 0
Towage	21. 0. 2	Carting dirt	2. 6	Hauling ashes	2.10. 5
Running lines	1. 4. 8	Washing hold	18. 1. 7	Telephones	1.15. 0
Watchmen	13.15. 6	Wood for dunnage,	43.18.11	Cables	5. 3. 0
	73. 2.11	Winch driver	32. 9. 3	Consul	3. 4. 2
		Labour	6. 3. 7	Medicines	1. 0. 7
			£119. 6. 7	Laundry	1. 3. 7
				Optician	2. 1. 2
				Water	7.13. 3
				Charter expenses	2. 1. 2
					£36.16. 4

To assist shipowners in their estimate of total cost of a charter in order to fix a rate for the freightage, the nautical press published from time to time typical disbursements for a variety of ports and cargoes. Around 1913 The Shipowners Register of Port Charges was published detailing disbursement charges for hundreds of ports with various cargoes and various sizes of steamer and sailing ship. A typical entry was that for a 2,400 nrt. steamer arriving at Buenos Aires from Cardiff with a cargo of 4,897 tons of coal:

Pilotage	Boat attendance	Stevedore	Despatch money
Harbour dues	Customs	Winchmen	Charter commission
Light dues	Night watchman	Tallymen	Water
Health dues	Doctor	Cooperage	Cash to Captain
Anchorage	Car hire	Extra labour	
Wharfage	Telegrams		
Entrance dues	Postage		
Packet privilege	Sundries		
	Towage		
Totals for above	£318. 9. 4.	£239.19. 8.	£295.13.10

Overall Total – £854. 2.10

The turnround costs to load grain for Belfast cost, under the above headings were as follows £214. 0. 7., £191.12. 7., £991. 9. 7., a total of £1,397. 2. 9.

No comparable figures are available for the post world war two period, but in 1949 a cargo of grain from Montreal in a 2,673 nrt. steamer cost £2,002.14.06. for disbursements, not all that much higher considering that 36 years had passed, but in this case the grain had been loaded by elevator.

The careful shipowner kept notes of all titbits of information which came his way relating to shipping costs, as an old office notebook from P. McCallum & Co shows:
Barry: 1904. *Riverdale* (4206/00 J. Little, Glasgow) £304.
Baltimore: 3,512 grt. 5,400 dwt. Oats. £398.
Brisbane to Bombay: *Vermont* (4271/00 Gow, Harrison & Co, Glasgow) 7,000 dwt. Brisbane £306.11.0. Bombay £105.12.8., loading 5,000t. of manganese ore.
Calcutta: 7,000 dwt. £300 in. £200 out.
Janeta (3302/94, Maclay & McIntyre, Glasgow) 1900: New York to Algoa Bay, oats.
Hamburg: 2,779 grt. 4,400 dwt., discharging grain from River Plate, £210.
    4,053 grt. 5,200 dwt. Wheat £342.
Hull: 3,302 grt. 6,150 dwt. Discharging oats and maize £328.
New York: 4,307 grt. 7,080 dwt. Loading grain £587.
     2,576 grt. 4,500 dwt.   £251
     3,512 grt. 5,400 dwt. oats £255
Port Arthur: *Riversdale* 6,800 dwt. £334.
Rotterdam: 3,825 grt. 6,150 dwt. Discharging oats and maize. £294.
     3,302 grt. 5,200 dwt.   wheat £206.
Brisbane: Turret steamer *Elaine* (Weddel, Turner & Co, London) 3,687 grt. Aug.1904.
     Loading sleepers. £476.
Abram, Addie & Cousins say that the *Ardgowan* (4271/06 Lang & Fulton, Greenock) should take 3,900 loads=6,240 tons, hardwood sleepers + 800 tons bunkers.

FREIGHT RATES: Knowing the dead weight cargo capacity of his steamer and using the prevailing freight rate the shipowner could satisfy himself as to whether or not a venture would show a profit. As indicated in the following chapter, freight rates were never steady but fluctuated with market 'forces' – too much grain, too many ships, product price. The following is a summary of rates per ton for various commodities at five year intervals over various routes. These figures were published in all the shipping magazines as a guide to the prospective shipper.

Year	Coal Wales to Port Said		Coal Wales to Genoa		Coal Wales to River Plate	
	Min.	Max.	Min.	Max.	Min.	Max.
1900	10/–	14/3	8/–	12/3	9/3	25/–
1905	4/8	8/1	5/–	8/–	6/3	12/–
1910	4/9	8/3	5/1	8/3	11/–	18/–
1915	20/6	70/–	22/6	66/–	17/6	41/3
1920	15/–	80/–	17/6	72/6	22/6	58/9
1925	7/9	12/–	6/9	10/7½	10/8	20/–
1930	6/3	8/6	5/4	8/–	9/6	15/–
1935	6/5	10/–	6/3	10/6	8/6	9/9
1940	23/6	35/–	23/–	26/–	27/6	38/–
1945	44/–	90/–			40/8	57/–
1950	25/–	36/3			28/9	57/6

Where there are blanks in the above table no record of freights for that particular route were quoted for that year.

Year	Grain Australia to U.K.		Grain U.S.A. to U.K.		Grain Azov to U.K		Grain R.Plate to U.K		Grain Chile to U.K	
	Min.	Max.	Min.	Max.	Min.	Max	Min.	Max.	Min.	Max.
1900	32/6	37/6	15/6	24/-	10/9	21/-	17/-	29/6	30/-	35/-
1905	22/6	26/3	8/6	12/-	8/9	14/-	11/-	20/-	18/9	24/-
1910	20/6	27/-	7/9	13/6	7/6	14/6	6/9	14/9	14/-	20/-
1915	85/-	110/-	45/-	130/-			42/6	125/-	30/-	120/-
1920	100/-	150/-	29/-	60/-			40/-	200/-	59/-	130/-
1925	27/6	55/-	26/9	40/-	15/-	20/-	10/9	25/6	22/-	30/-
1930	20/-	37/6	6/5	10/6	9/9	13/9	9/6	20/-	16/-	30/-
1935	18/6	28/-	14/-	23/-	13/9	17/6	11/6	17/-	16/6	23/-
1940	55/-	150/-	57/3	130/-			42/6	155/-		
1945	95/-	120/-	108/6	110/6			82/6	86/6		
1950	52/6	87/6	56/-	90/-			40/-	67/6	57/6	60/-

Year	Rice Burma to U.K.		Ore Vizapatam to U.S.A.		Ore Huelva to U.S.A.		Jute Calcutta to U.K	
	Min.	Max.	Min.	Max.	Min.	Max.	Min.	Max.
1900	23/9	33/9					21/3	31/3
1905	16/3	25/-	18/3	20/6	9/-	11/6	16/3	25/-
1910	18/9	24/6	18/-	21/3	8/9	13/6	13/6	24/-
1915	30/-	127/6			10/6	17/-	34/3	150/-
1920	75/-	140/-			14/-	15/-	96/-	109/6
1925	20/-	36/-			9/9	11/6		
1930	16/9	20/-	9/9	12/6	4/6	5/11		
1935	18/-	27/-	13/-	22/6	10/5	12/3		
1940	55/-	110/-	75/-	90/-	16/-	21/-		
1945					(32/-	45/6 to the U.K.)		
1950	32/-	55/-			(18/6	43/6 to the U.K.)		

Voyage estimates did not always show a profit, as this one, done in 1931, shows. In this case the owner would have to decide whether to accept the loss or lay his ship up. His 6,750 dwt. steamer, steaming at 9 kts. burned 23 tons coal per day (2½ tons per day in port).

Voyage: Cardiff – Oran   coal
Oran – San Lorenzo   ballast
San Lorenzo – Las Palmas (for orders)   grain
Las Palmas – Hamburg (assumed)   grain
Hamburg – Tyne   ballast

Coal	*Miles*	*Days*	
		Port	Sea
Cardiff	– – –	7	–
Oran	1,383	2½	6½
San Lorenzo	5,786	10	27
Las Palmas	4,835	1	22½
Hamburg	2,018	5½	9
Tyne	430	–	2
		26	67

Bunkers – Cardiff to San Lorenzo
19½ days in port @ 2½ t.p.d.	48.75
33½ days at sea @ 23 t.p.d.	770.50
tons	819.25

Bunkers – San Lorenzo to Tyne
6½ days in port @ 2½ t.p.d.	16.25
33½ days at sea @ 23 t.p.d.	770.50
tons	786.75

Coal required	819.25	
	786.25	
in reserve	94.50	(4 days)
	1,700.00	tons

Cargo. Deadweight 6,750 tons
Stores	50			
	6,700		6,700	
Coal	1,700	from Cardiff	880	from San Lorenzo
	5,000	tons	5,820	tons

Balance	Income £.	Outlay	£.
Cargo to Oran		Disbursements-cargo	118
5,000 tons @ 6/6	1,625	– ditto –	354
Cargo to Hamburg		Port costs: Cardiff	410
5,820 tons @ 18/6	5,833	Oran	820
	£7,008	San Lorenzo	1,070
		Las Palmas	28
		Hamburg	635
	Wages.93 days @ £29.10.0		2,743
	Coal 1,606 tons @ 16/6		1,325
Loss on voyage £7,503–£7,008=£495			£7,503

An alternative would appear to be to carry only enough bunkers for the first leg and to coal overseas, but with bunker coal abroad at about 30/- per ton instead of 16/6, while the freight rate on the coal cargo was only 6/6 made this idea uneconomical.

Another employment for the tramp steamer was the 'Time Charter', where the hire of the vessel was on a time basis, not on the basis of carrying a given cargo between given ports (108). A Time Charter might occur when a liner company short of a vessel for a period of time would charter a tramp steamer to fill the gap. The ship owner might be paid in a lump sum or a sum per deadweight ton per month. In return the hirer was entitled to carry any cargo between any ports unless the charter party specifically excluded any particularly dirty cargo or any particular port or area. The ship owner appointed and paid the crew, fed them, paid insurance and maintenance. The charterer paid the running costs.

An extension of the Time Charter was the 'Demise Charter' under which the charterer became, for all intents and purposes the owner of the vessel with the master and crew coming under his authority. The only right of the registered owner was to receive the charter fee and to take over the vessel on the expiry of the charter.

PORTS OF CALL: As you read through the voyages of some of the tramp steamers you will come across many unfamiliar names, some of which do not even appear in the Lloyd's Atlas. The following list locates these less well known ports.

Port/Location	Main export
Akyab, Burma	rice, cotton
Aguilas, Spain (nr.Caragena)	ore. esparto
Bahia Blanca, Argentina	grain
Bjornborg, Finland	timber
Bussorah (Basrah), Turkey	dates, cotton, grain
Carloforte, Island off Sardinia	ore
Cette, Southern France	fertilizer
Cheribon, Java	hardwoods
Christmas Island, Pacific	fertilizer
Cienfuegos, Cuba	sugar, tobacco
Coosaw, U.S.A. (nr. Charleston)	cotton, timber
Ergasteria, Greece (nr. Athens)	
Eupatoria, Crimea	grain
Gefle, Sweden	timber
Girgenti, Sicily	sulphur
Horli, South Russia	grain
Hornillo Bay, Spain (nr. Cartagena)	ore
Huelva, Spain (north of Cadiz)	sulphur, ore
Imbetibe, nr. Rio de Janeiro	
Kilindini, nr. Zanzibar	
Kotka, Gulf of Finland	timber
Kustendje (Constanza), Roumania	grain
Licata, Sicily	sulphur

Port/Location	Main Export
Limone, Costa Rica	
Lulea, Sweden	ore, timber, phosphates
Martin River,Canada (Gaspe Peninsular)	
Massawa, Abyssinia	ore
Mazzaron, Spain (nr. Cartagena)	ore
Mezen, Russia (Baltic)	timber
Miramichi, New Brunswick	timber
Negapatam, India (south of Madras)	
Ocean Island, Pacific	fertilizer
Palembang,Sumatra	
Pascagoula, Gulf of Mexico	
Patras, Southern Greece	
Perim, Gulf of Aden	
Pernambuco, Brazil	cotton, hides
Porman, Spain (S. of Cartagena)	ore
Pozzuoli, Italy (Nr Naples)	
Poti, Black Sea	grain
Rio Mariana, Elba	ore
Rivadesella, (near Marseilles)	
Sagua la Grande, Cuba	sugar
Salaverry, North Chile	
San Domingo, Dominican Republic	sugar
Santa Fe, River Plate	grain
Sestri Levante, near Genoa	
Thermia, Island off Greece	
Villaricos, Spain (nr. Cartegena)	ore

6.
Diary

118. *St. Abbs* outward bound in later years with topmasts and bowsprit reduced, when owned by Robertson, McKie, Glasgow. She was built in 1879 by J. Laing, Sunderland.

STEAM TRAMPS IN WORLD EVENTS

After the disruption of the Crimean War in the latter part of the 1850s orders for steam vessels increased and in the 1860s they began to trade more widely. The shipping papers reported regularly on the trade and shipping situation and their comments have been summarised in the form of a 'Diary':-

1866. The story of this year was one which was to be repeated at regular intervals for a hundred years. "1866 has been marked by a more than ordinary depression in shipping notably in steam. Markets have been affected by the war between the Prussians, Italians and Austrians, a cattle plague, cholera and financial panic, all of which served to check trade. Shipbuilding has been adversely affected, at the beginning of the year there was an abundance of orders for new steamers but financial losses soon forced intending owners to cancel contracts. The only area where there was a bright spot was the Baltic where poor harvests gave the steamers profitable cargoes, taking in grain." This year the European Commision took over control of the navigation of the Danube under an act published last year.

1867. A slight improvement in trade. South America was beginning to attract attention and a new line of steamers was established. Export of coal was expanding rapidly, 9.74 million tons against 7.86 million tons in 1861. Nominally Spain and South American republics were at war but there was no actual fighting to interrupt trade.

1869: SUEZ CANAL. It is sometimes claimed that the opening of the Suez Canal in 1869 was the event which was responsible for the rapid expansion of the tramp industry. Be that as it may, there is no doubt that the new canal opened up the Far East to the steamer which now did not have to carry coal for the journey round the Cape of Good Hope. The Suez Canal was 6 years in the planning and 10 in the building. From 150 feet wide by 20 to 26 feet deep at the outset, the canal was widened and deepened to 240 feet by 34 feet, while in 1885 electric light was installed. Typical of the savings which could be made on voyages to the Orient were:

	Via Cape of Good Hope	*Via Suez Canal*	*Days saved by 10kt. steamers*
London to Freemantle	10,900 miles	9,340 miles	6½
London to Calutta	11,730	7,900	16
London to Shanghai	13,790	10,441	14

Despite the saving in distance and days, the charter party sometimes stated that the voyage had to be carried out "via the Cape".

From the outset the number of steamers using the canal increased rapidly:

1870	486 steamers	905 nrt. average
1900	3,441 (2,510 British)	2,820 nrt.
1932	8,682	2,304 nrt.
1939	5,277	

So the 1870s and early 1880s was a period of rapid expansion for the tramp shipping fleets. Design progressed from basically steam powered sailing ships to the well-deck and three island design which were to be the basic designs for the next 50 years.

1882. A fair year for shipping. Britain now possessed 71% of the carrying capacity of the world. 30,870,000 tons of exports were carried by British steamers. Steamers had moved into the Black Sea, Baltic and West Indian trades leaving the sailing ships to carry coarse produce such as wood, asphalt and phosphate. Shipbuilders were kept quite busy, prices were up 15% on 1880 and delivery was 10 to 16 months. America's protectionist policy made her a very poor customer.

1883. Looking back over the last 17 years there had been a vast improvement in the steamer. In 1866 a 700 dwt. steamer cost £14,000 and consumed 41 tons of coal per day. Today a 3,000 dwt. steamer cost £28,000 and had a consumption of 21 tons of coal per day. Steam tonnage using South Wales ports was on the increase:

1880	3,153 steamers	1,928,091 tons
1883	3,541 steamers	2,287,216 tons

Exports of iron and steel to America were dropping steadily but home demand was rising and the ore trade with Spain was expanding. Shipowners were complaining but profits of 10-30% were being made. The bar at Bilbao had been deepened and larger steamers were lifting cargoes. Few steamers below 1,500 nrt. were being built, most were between 2,100 and 3,100 nrt. The grain trade with the U.S.A. was being taken over by the steamer:

	Sail	*Steam*
1880	60,000,000	10,000,000 bushels
1883	19,000,000	53,000,000 bushels

The South Wales ports now owned 200 foreign going steamers, mostly between 400 and 900 nrt.

1884. Another shipping depression and shipowners were considering a proposal to lay up a quarter of their steam tonnage in an effort to push up freights, a move to come into force on 20th May. At Sunderland the import of timber was reaching quite high proportions with two thirds of the vessels arriving with timber being steamers. The shipbuilding 'boom' of 1883 had created a surplus of tonnage which reacted on freights which dropped. Shipowners were hoping that Britain would open new military operations in Egypt as a lot of tonnage would be chartered.

1885. WAR IN THE SUDAN. In 1885 Great Britain mounted a campaign in the Sudan against the Mahdi whose army had taken Khartoum and killed General Gordon. To carry the troops and cavalry together with their stores, and to provide support for the army after it had landed, the Government chartered a fleet of 27 vessels including a number normally engaged in tramping.

Loch Ard	1304/83	Dundee Loch Line (A. Leitch), Dundee.
Oceano	1004/71	Tatham & Co, London.
Nyanza	1870/67	Mercantile Steamship Co, Liverpool.
Zurich	1395/83	Turner, Brightman & Co, London.
Camel	293/83	J.E. Scott, Newport. (Watercarrier).
Edinburgh	2330/85	Adamson & Ronaldson, London. (Condensing ship).
Stroma	958/83	Napier Shipping Co, Glasgow.
Amethyst	533/83	Wm. Robertson, Glasgow. (Fitted with refrigerating machinery: to carry 300 cattle carcases.)

During the year the shipping trade was depressed and the Admiralty was paying only 17/6 per gross ton per month against the rate of 28/- per gross ton per month which had prevailed in 1882 when they had previously had cause to charter merchant ships. Over the next decade fleets expanded more slowly though some owners did well.

1898. A good year for the tramp trade. Wars and rumours of wars led to stockpiling of grain and shipments from the U.S.A. were particularly heavy. The needs of the Spanish-American war eased and a brisk export from the U.S.A. developed resulting in the chartering of tramp steamers for trading to the Cape of Good Hope, Australia and the East. Large stocks of railway material were shipped from the U.K. to the Russian Far Eastern ports.

BOER WAR: 1899 - 1902. When war was declared in South Africa in 1899 the Government chartered a large number of vessels to carry troops and supplies out to Cape Town. By February 1900 over 120 passenger liners and 70 dry cargo vessels had been chartered. Of the latter about 30 were from liner trade and 40 from tramp companies. Ropner's *Maltby* 2834/89 carried coal from Newcastle to the Cape. J.A. Black's *Kelvindale* 3092/99 was chartered to carry horses from London at £23 per head, while other steamers brought horses from Melbourne. Taylor & Sanderson's *John*

Sanderson 3274/89 was nearly lost in June 1900 when her cargo of hay caught fire as she lay in Algoa Bay and 3,000 bales had to be jettisoned to save her. A form of transport much used during the Boer War was the mule and *Knight Templar* 4188/89 of Greenshields Cowie & Co, Liverpool, carried a cargo of these animals from New Orleans to Cape Town at £17 per head.

Among the tramp steamers chartered were:

Eversley	2866/96	H. Scholfield & Son, Newcastle.
Mab	2833/91	Pyman, Bell & Co, Newcastle.
Trevanion	2437/91	E. Hain & Sons, St. Ives.
Meath	2295/79	R.M. Hudson, Sunderland.
White Jacket	2237/89	George Hallett, Cardiff (121).
Penarth	3035/96	Morel Ltd, Cardiff.
Graphic	2490/95	W.H. Cockerline & Co, Hull.
Gloxinia	2450/97	J. Robinson & Sons, North Shields.

With the sudden influx of shipping some vessels were anchored off Cape Town for several weeks before they could be discharged.

1899. An anxious year for tramp steamer owners with expenses increased all round. Coal went up to 25/- per ton against the 13/- which they had paid in 1898. When shipping was chartered for the war in South Africa it was anticipated that there would be a shortage and that freights would rise. Unfortunately there was a general slump in trade and freights remained fairly static. There was a demand for coal in South Africa and the early boats got good rates. The American government chartered a number of tramps to carry stores to the Far East. The Argentine harvest was heavy and gave employment to a large number of steamers at good rates. The Black Sea crops failed and many tramps sent there for grain had to turn back for ore cargoes from the Mediterranean.

1900. A fairly satisfactory year though coal prices remained high keeping bunkering costs up, making long voyages expensive. A large number of tramps were taken up on time charter by the British government for South Africa and China (the Boxer Rising), while the American government was still taking tonnage for the Philippines, some for two to three years. In some markets this resulted in a shortage of tonnage which pushed rates up. American coal was by now cheaper than British coal and many steamers sailed with low stocks aboard and bunkered in the States, many taking on a cargo of U.S. coal which was selling better than the British.

In September a cyclone struck Galveston while a number of steamers were in port loading, among them the tramps: *Kendal Castle* 2885/96, J. Chambers & Co, Liverpool (Barry to Galveston, ballast); *Norna* 2242/90, Herskind & Co, West Hartlepool (Barbados to Galveston, ballast); *Red Cross* 2877/90 (121), Rowland & Marwood, Whitby (Rio de Janeiro to Galveston); *Roma* 2721/89, Rowland & Marwood, Whitby (Boston to Galveston, wheat); *Taunton* 3973/98, Young, Ehlers, London (Rio de Janeiro to Galveston); *Whitehall* 2776/92 (121), T. Turnbull & Son, Whitby (Galveston to U.K., cotton).

1901. The freights this year were abnormally low. The shipping which had been released from government charter had flooded the market. Cargoes from the U.S.A. were difficult as many liner traders were taking on cargoes which had previously been handled by the tramp steamers. Shipbuilding was at a low ebb and there were few ships on the stocks.

1902. A monotonous year with low freights all round and tramps were being run at a loss. Good crops in the Black Sea area drew large numbers of steamers, leading to congestion and long delays. There was a steady demand for ore from the Mediterranean but again too many vessels offering kept the rates down. Coal was being exported from the U.S. again but the liner traders were poaching in the trade, this also applied to the export of grain from America.

On the 8th of May the volcano Mount Pelee, near the port of St. Pierre in the island of Martinique blew up destroying the town and killing about 30,000 people. There were a number of British ships in the harbour and 3 of these were total losses, a cable ship *Grappler* and two Canadian vessels, the barque *L.W. Norton* and the steamer *Roraima.* Only one tramp steamer was present at the time, *Roddam* 2378/87 belonging to W. Young of London. She was unloading general cargo at the time and her crew of 23, together with 21 shore workers were on board. Of these 10 of the crew and 15 of the shore hands lost their lives.

1903. Whereas Samuel Plimsoll had campaigned for control over the loading of ships,

121.

The *White Jacket* was
one of the vessels chart—
ered by the Government
to carry supplies to South
Africa for the Boer War.
She belonged to the
White Jacket S.S. Co Ltd
managed by George
Hallett, Cardiff. *White
Jacket* had the dimensions
290.0' x 38.6' x 19.7',
2,237 grt.

Red Cross, 2877/90, a
survivor of the Galveston
cyclone of 1900, was
built by J.L.Thompson &
Sons, Sunderland for the
Rowland & Marwood
S.S. Co Ltd of Whitby.
She was later sold to
W.S.Miller of Glasgow
and renamed *Luciston.*
Dimensions were 316.0'
x 40.6' x 20.8'.

Also caught in the
Galveston cyclone was
Whitehall 2776/92. She
was managed by T.
Turnbull & Son of
Whitby. She survived the
cyclone and is seen here
approaching the locks at
Bristol.

Photos: I.W.Rooke collection.

a new situation arose in 1903 when the collision between the steamer *Darleydale* 3095/99, Lucas & Co, Bristol and a barque drew attention to the underloading of vessels. A committee was formed to look into the question of fixing a light load line. Other cases came to light where the insufficient ballasting of steamers had led to their being difficult to manoeuvre, thereby causing an accident. These included *Buckingham* 2879/91, Raeburn & Verel, Glasgow, *Ashmore* 2519/98, Adam S.S. Co, Aberdeen, *Kildonan* 2118/98, John Cory & Sons, Cardiff.

A drop in freight rates to the South American ports forced the owners of some large tramps to send them to the Black Sea, which in turn led to an excess of tonnage there which brought down the rates in that area. It was a bad year for the insurance market with 67 British steamers reported as casualties. The total losses were 6 foundered, 40 stranded, 11 collisions, 6 fires, 4 missing.

1904. Another year of low freights reflected in the prices being asked for new construction. Steamers which cost £8 per dwt. ton in 1900 could be bought from the builders for only £5:5:0 per dwt. ton. The war between Japan and Russia was affecting shipping. The Japanese bought 60 old vessels from Britain while the Russians were buying from Germany. The Russians were stocking up with coal for their Baltic fleet for what was to be its destruction at the Battle of Tsushima. Shipments were arranged by the Hamburg America Line who chartered 60 or more colliers, mainly British and German. Unrest in Russia had affected grain production and little was on offer for shipment. British owners were sending their steamers in ballast from the Mediterranean to Bombay and Karachi to take advantage of the good rates being offered for the carriage of rice. Gulfport at the mouth of the Mississippi was re-opened for the export of timber after it had been reconstructed and expanded.

WEEK by WEEK DIARY for 1904. Just as the conditions in the freight market varied from year to year so they varied from week to week. Owners frequently had to gamble on what their vessels might find when they arrived at their loading port. 1904 has been taken as an example and the weekly variations shown:

13.1.04. Owners prefer to keep steamers laid up rather than to charter at a dead loss.
20.1.04. Very few charters from Mediterranean ports, rates barely maintained. Steady rates for the East but very few cargoes.
27.1.04. Rice ports show better demand, rates fractionally up.
3.2.04. Black Sea. the large amount of tonnage offering is depressing the rates. Few fixtures for Mediterranean; charterers are holding off on a falling market.
10.2.04 Port Arthur requirements brisk. (Russo-Japanese war imminent), good rates. Admiralty have chartered a fair amount of tonnage to Bermuda. Black Sea surplus of tonnage still having effect on rates. Mediterranean – fair number of charters from ore ports but too many vessels available. River Plate trade de-demoralised by labour and political trouble.
17.2.04 Black Sea rates improving with owners holding out.
24.2.04 East: Rates steady, enquiries numerous.
2.3.04 Good week for coal exports. Position favourable to owners. Black Sea: Owners still holding out for better rates. Americas: Charterers still holding out for better terms.
9.3.04 Rates have fallen as has the price of grain. Strike at the River Plate has paralysed that business. East: good demand for handy boats.
23.3.04 Less cargo and more boats has resulted in fall in rates. East: Rates for rice cargoes show a rising tendency.
30.3.04 Glut of tonnage in all trades; outlook gloomy.
6.4.04 Homeward market from Mediterranean very slack.
13.4.04 Cargoes from Black Sea few and far between. Americas: very little doing except timber from North America.
20.4.04 Every trade at its lowest, great glut of tonnage forbids hope for the future.
27.4.04 Black Sea rates never worse due to glut of tonnage. River Plate has picked up.
4.5.04 North America: demand almost nil.
11.5.04 Outward: owners reluctant to lose money by chartering. East: lower rates accepted as so many vessels want return cargo. Trade quite demoralised.
19.5.04 Black Sea: after many vessels had been ordered home in ballast, rates steadied.

25.5.04 Market miserably dull.

1.6.04 Mediterranean: Ore charterers are demanding lower rates, shipowners reluctant to give unremunerative quotations.

8.6.04 Black Sea: fair amount of tonnage fixed; rates improving. Americas: few cargoes except case oil.

15.6.04 Few fixtures, rates weak. Some timber from North America. East: Good rates but few fixtures.

6.7.04 Market poor, few fixtures, rates nominal.

13.7.04 Feeling that Black Sea freights will improve with new grain crop. Poor crop reports from rest of world, improving prospects for River Plate freights.

27.7.04 Americas: fair demand for vessels, quotations steady.

17.8.04 Americas: cotton and general cargo doing better with firm rates.

24.8.04 Coal freights depressed. India and rice ports improving in homeward trade. Odessa has enormous amount of idle tonnage. Americas: crops are likely to be small so liner trade capacity should suffice.

7.9.04 Heavy export of coal from N.E. coast ports to Mediterranean but rates only average. Java sugar crop mainly booked. Rice from Bassein and Rangoon has improved; possibility of vessels going out via the Cape of Good Hope in ballast for it. Danube trade nil due to Roumanian prohibition.

14.9.04 Demand in River Plate good but rates steady due to abundance of tonnage. A lot of coal from Cardiff to Mediterranean. Shipment of steam coal to Russia continues but German vessels are carrying the bulk of it. Improvement in the Black Sea owing to better arrival of grain at Odessa. Most of the tonnage which has been encumbering the port is now worked off. Mediterranean; currant crops poor. Less demand for tonnage this year.

21.9.04 As predicted boats going out in ballast for rice. Owners in all trades are holding out and there is no disposition to make concessions. Although freights generally are poor for coal, very heavy tonnages are being shipped, undoubtedly for Russian account for Cape Verde, Canaries, Madeira and the Far East, also to the Baltic. Our own Admiralty has taken up at least 8 steamers for the Far East. Owners in coal out, freight back are breaking even. (In respect of higher rates it is noticeable that small, handy vessels fully maintain their advantage, as working more saleable cargoes, though the difference is not always enough to discount the relatively higher running expenses.)

28.9.04 Freights from the Black Sea will drop with the rush of boats in ballast ever ready to snap up cargoes, including ships free from the surplus lying at Marseilles.

5.10.04 Northern Baltic ports will close soon and rates will improve for Southern Baltic ports.

12.10.04 Last week saw an improvement in coastal coal rates for the humble ordinary cargo boat, enough to cover increased winter risks. Ore freights are now forming an important part of the market, 75,000 tons shipped from Lulea to Holland, 36,000 tons from Pomaron to Leith.

19.10.04 Freight markets are good with a scarcity of ready vessels. A feature calling for notice is the increased use of steamers in the nitrate trade, one of the last strongholds of sail. On the Tyne 3 or 4 large steamers are loading coal out to W.C.S.A. (West coast of South America) for nitrate cargoes back.

2.11.04 A fillip was given to outward freights by the extensive taking up of tonnage for the Admiralty, together with the continued demand for the Baltic Fleet. The Sea of Azov is again overcrowded.

9.11.04 The spurt in coal freights has suddenly ended. The Baltic season has ended releasing a large number of handy sized steamers which would normally turn to the Mediterranean, Black Sea or Continent. Many boats are laid up, especially in the North-East ports. Shipments of coal from Blyth have increased enormously but two thirds is carried on foreign bottoms while some 30 British vessels are lying idle in the Tyne. Coal for the blast furnaces at Bilbao is being carried almost entirely by Spanish vessels. The last homeward timber charters from the Baltic have been carried at enhanced rates.

16.11.04 A poor grain crop in Russia has discouraged forward chartering. A good deal of timber tonnage has been chartered from America.

23.11.04 With the Baltic and St. Lawrence about to close homeward freights are low.

The Admiralty continues to take up tonnage for coal to Gibraltar and Malta. The new season's rice charters have been fixed for Burma.

30.11.04 The Tyne nitrate round seems to be increasingly in favour with Valparaiso-Pisagua range. There is a demand for coal for Japan.

7.12.04 The market is oversupplied with seeking tonnage and rates are maintained with difficulty. With labour disputes on the railways at the River Plate forward chartering has been checked. Charterers are seeking large boats for coal for the Far East and Japan.

14.12.04 Several boats have been chartered for cotton from New Orleans to Europe and 60,000 qtrs. of grain from New York for Dec to Jan shipment. U.S. Navy has asked for quotes with no intention of using other than U.S. vessels. (Comparative quotes 7–7.5 for American ships, 4.23–6 for British ships.) Black Sea again has too many boats for available cargo.

21.12.04 With poor Black Sea freights at least one company regularly working the Black Sea has laid up its boats. There is little business partly due to a bad grain harvest, partly due to the Russian coal duties, and no coal is going to Russian Black Sea ports. (The Russians are attempting to promote their coal.)

RUSSO–JAPANESE WAR 1904-1905. When Russia and Japan declared war on the 8th February 1904 the British shipowners carried on business as usual and it is doubtful if, at first, they thought that they were blockade running when they carried goods to ports in Japan or to ports on Russia's Far East seaboard. However, each of the combatants regarded material bound for their opponents' ports as being subject to the rules of contraband of war. Basically this gave warring nations the right to seize supplies destined for the enemy even though they be carried by a neutral vessel. This meant that in time of war neutral vessels could be stopped on the high seas by a foreign warship for the examination of her papers and cargo to determine if they were bound for a hostile port and might be of use in furthering the war effort of that nation. If this was found to be the case the cargo could be seized as 'contraband'.

Many British tramp steamers were already at sea when the war broke out and without wireless they were not aware that they were in any danger. Within weeks *Frankby* 4182/04 (Macvicar, Marshall & Co, Liverpool) and *Ettrickdale* 3775/94 (R. Mackill & Co, Glasgow), both carrying coal were seized by the Russians, but they were subsequently released as they had sailed before the 28th February, the date on which the Russians declared that they intended to treat coal and other stated goods as contraband. Russia's failure to pay compensation for such seizures was probably a factor when W.R. Rea declared bankruptcy in 1908 (losses of £12,190 on *Allanton* and £4,200 on *Lethington*). Many British captains, not willing to risk capture, discharged their cargoes in Chinese ports. One of the first steamers to be stopped was *Allanton* 4253/01, W.R. Rea, Belfast, which was seized by a Russian armed merchant cruiser and taken to Vladivostok, where her cargo was condemned by the Prize Court. The steamer *St. Kilda* was less lucky: *St. Kilda* 3512/99, Rankin, Gilmour & Co, Liverpool. Voyage Hong Kong to Kobe and Yokohama. Cargo; cotton, rice, jute and general. Captured and sunk by *Dneiper* off Hong Kong 5.6.1905. Hull valued £30,000. Cargo valued £11,000 (part only).

The justification for the sinking of *St. Kilda* lay in a clause in the Russian 'rules' which permitted the captain of a warship to sink the blockade runner if it was not possible to take her to port for internment. Since the Russian warships were operating far from their base this clause was readily invoked.

Needless to relate British shipowners were indignant at being subjected to search and regarded the sinkings as quite unjustified. They demanded protection by the Royal Navy but the Government of the day talked a lot and did nothing. At the end of August the Russian armed merchant cruisers *Don* and *Ural* were waiting between Sagres in Spain and Gibraltar where they stopped a number of steamers which were in fact carrying coal to Italy, while the *Petersburg* and *Smolensk* were reported in the Red Sea. To avoid them many owners rerouted their vessels round the Cape of Good Hope. However in September the *Petersburg* and *Smolensk* vanished and there were reports that they had headed for the Cape Verde Islands, Cape Town or Madagascar. To add to the confusion the armed merchant cruisers *Korea* and *Kitai* were also reported to be at sea on blockade duty. The Japanese cruisers were not so active though *Crusader* 4210/01 (C.Smales & Son, Whitby) was stopped and taken to Hakodate despite the fact that her destination was Shanghai and not a Russian port.

Cheltenham 3741/01 (Galbraith, Pembroke & Co, London) made several successful runs to Japan with railway iron, contraband in the Russian book, but she ran out of luck when she was captured by the *Gromoboi*. 'Mines' were placed aboard her by the prize crew in case the Japanese attempted to free her. She was taken to Vladivostok and the ship and cargo were confiscated. Her crew was repatriated via the Trans-Siberian railway, a trip which took an uncomfortable 21 days, and by boat from St. Petersburg to the U.K. The members of the crew claimed, and received, £10 damages each; danger money, because they had not been warned of the risks that the vessel was running.

All the time that the Russians were stopping and searching British ships, they were chartering British ships to carry coal on Russian account to selected ports. During September 1904 thirty steamers left Cardiff alone carrying coal to Kronstadt, Libau, St. Vincent, Las Palmas, Madeira, Canaries, Manila, Colombo, Shanghai and Hong Kong, about half the vessels being British. They also purchased 7 steamers with the intention of running the Japanese blockade of Port Arthur, but soon lost them by capture. The significance of the Russian coal charters was all too soon made apparent when the Dogger Bank Incident took place. In September 1904 the Russian Baltic Fleet sailed for the Far East to break the Japanese blockade of Port Arthur and on the Dogger Bank, opened fire on and damaged several British trawlers. It was night time and the Russian lookouts, nerves on edge, claimed that they mistook them for Japanese torpedo boats. An international incident was narrowly avoided and the Russian government paid £65,000 in compensation. The Russian fleet finally reached the Far East in May 1905 and on the 26th was destroyed by a better trained Japanese force at the Battle of Tsushima.

In all the Russians seized 10 steamers, 6 of them British, of which they sank 5, while the Japanese seized 33 vessels of which 19 sailed under the British flag. Among the British vessels involved were:

Lincluden 2746/96, Sivewright, Bacon & Co, Manchester. Captured by Japanese. Original voyage was Nicolaieff to Vladivostok but because of war risks had been cancelled at Woosung on payment of 65%. Cargo had been insured from Woosung to Japan for £18,000. Later released. Reported 7.6.1905.

Oldhamia 3639/04, Sivewright, Bacon & Co, Manchester. Captured by Russians, prize crew put aboard south of Hong Kong. Voyage New York to Hong Kong. 165,000 cases of oil. Property of Standard Oil Company. Hull valued £34,000. Reported 7.6.1905. Later reported run ashore Urup Island and set on fire by Russians, 26.7.1905.

Cilurnum 2097/81, Dunford & Elliott, Newcastle. Under charter to Mitsui Bussan Co. Captured by *Rion* ex *Smolensk*, Russian cruiser. Voyage Shanghai to Kobe. Part cargo beans, cotton and antimony thrown overboard. Vessel later released. Reported 14.6.1905.

Oakley 3798/01, W.R. Rea, Belfast. Captured by Japanese and sent to Sasebo. Voyage Bristol Channel to Vladivostok with coal. Hull valued £40,000, cargo £20,000.

In the middle of the Russo-Japanese conflict, for some strange reason the British armed forces carried out a training exercise. A fleet of transports sailed from Southampton to invade the Essex coast, escorted by a force of cruisers. The troopships engaged were "usually employed in the cattle trade and consequently easily adapted as Army transports". 'Tween decks were used for emigrants, cattle or troops.

1905. The trouble in Russia and the lack of homeward cargo forced up the outward rates for coal to the Mediterranean as shipowners would not carry coal otherwise, with the prospect of a ballast voyage home. Britain and Cuba concluded a commercial treaty safeguarding trade between the two countries, a move which the Americans did not like. Britain was carrying 40% of the sugar exported from Cuba. There were several tramp steamer losses which shook the insurance market: *Aboukir* 3317/96, Glen & Co, Glasgow. (£134.000); *Dumbarton* 3495/03, McLean & Rodger, Glasgow. (£120,000); *Drumcruil* 3788/00, J. Chadwick, Liverpool. (£100,000); and a number of vessels carrying timber from the Gulf in the winter months were lost. These included: *Nutfield* 2566/91, Woods, Tylor & Brown, *Freshfield* 2730/92, J. Brown & Son, Liverpool, *Mars* 3856/92, Venus Steam Shipping Co, Newcastle. This led to a review of regulations regarding deck cargoes of timber.

Burrell & Son, who had sold their fleet five years previously, having judged that the price of ships would not go any lower, ordered 12 new steamers. Others followed suit and during the year the price of a 6,150 dwt. steamer rose from £33,000 to £41,000. However there was not enough profitable business to sustain the building boom and many owners had to dispose of their contracts at a loss.

1906. Another bad year for shipping with tramps coming home in ballast from the Mediterranean rather than accept low rates from the Black Sea. The River Plate trade was disappointing as was the ore and timber business from the Baltic. Ships were being laid up and there were few orders for new vessels.

The Admiralty, desirous of testing out plans to institute convoys in case of war with Germany, invited shipowners to take part in forthcoming naval manoeuvres. It was suggested that only 2 to 3 days delay would result from participation but shipowners were not very enthusiastic. Some small but important details had escaped the Admiralty's attention. Delays cost money in running costs, missing a cancelling date cost money and could lose a cargo. The proposals limited the operation to the area between England and Gibraltar. Liners and vessels carrying perishable goods would not be asked to take part. The convoys would be made up of groups of 12 vessels as they arrived at Falmouth or Milford Haven. Steamers would be considered 'sunk' if an enemy warship came within three miles and fired three shots. Compensation was promised at a figure between £40 and £60 with 2d. per 12 hours per ton for further delay. No mention was made of indemnity for loss of charter.

It seems strange that having considered the question of sailing merchant ships in convoy, in times of peace, that the Admiralty should delay, in the face of massive shipping losses, until 1917 before they instituted convoys in times of war.

1907. The year started with freight rates higher than normal and ended with rates as bad as they could be, except for the homeward freights from the River Plate. Tramp steamers suffered excessive delays in port both at home and abroad. One cause was that the coaling facilities in U.K. ports had not kept pace with the growth in the size of tramp steamers which slowed down loading. There were few coal charters for the Far East and in this area also the liner traders were taking homeward cargo away from the tramp.

1908. The liner traders started undercutting the tramp steamers in the grain trade from India and the Pacific coast of North America. A typhoon at Hong Kong caused a great number of casualties, among them *Powhatan* 2386/86 (Watts, Watts & Co, London), which was sunk and *Bara* 3761/05 (Japp, Kirby), *Carnley* 4644/03 (Harris & Dixon Ltd, London) and *Pocahontas* 2675/89 (Watts, Watts & Co, London), which were damaged in collision with other vessels.

1909. Despite improvements in homeward rates throughout the year, (grain from Odessa to U.K. from 6/- up to 8/3, ore from Bilbao to Middlesbrough from 3/6 up to 4/6), the year was generally a poor one for owners and builders. The year opened with 245 vessels laid up, 90 in the Tyne, and half the building berths were empty, new steamers could be had for £4:16:3 per dwt. ton. More tramp steamers than usual had been sold to the breakers, some younger than was normal. New cargoes had been introduced for tramp steamers, soya bean from Vladivostok, (400,000 tons were shipped), and also maize from East Africa.

1910. Another bad year of low freights, laid up shipping and many seamen out of work. Strikes in the coal mines also affected shipping, although about 500,000 tons were imported from Germany. A poor harvest in Argentina completed the gloomy picture.

1911. Despite shipyard lockouts and a coal strike this was a 'golden year' for the shipowner. The freight for coal from Cardiff to Lisbon rose from 5/8 to 8/3, grain from the River Plate to the U.K. from 15/3 to 18/-. The war between Italy and Turkey produced a heavy demand for coal to Italian ports. Drought in Germany brought internal traffic to a halt and coal was shipped to Stettin and Hamburg. The European sugar beet harvest failed and there was a big demand for tonnage to carry sugar from Java. There was such a demand for tramp steamers that owners brought them home in ballast rather than hang around awaiting cargo in the River Plate. The liner trade was short of tonnage and there was an extraordinary amount of time chartering of tramps. By the end of the year there were no ships laid up and there were so many orders for new tonnage that prices were up to £6:4:0 per deadweight ton and with long delivery delays.

1912: BALKAN WAR. In 1912 trouble flared up in the Balkans when Serbia, Bulgaria and Greece combined to fight Turkey. Turkey closed the Dardenelles and by May at least 210 vessels were held up in the Black Sea, while another 118 lay at Tenedos waiting to pass into the Black Sea. British shipowners were of course badly affected as the Black Sea was one of the mainstays of their coal and grain trade. It was estimated that at least half of the ships involved were British. One owner was not affected, Walter Runciman; by a stroke of luck not one of the Moor Line ships was engaged in the Black Sea trade at that time. After about 20 days the Straits were reopened and the loss to British shipping was put at about £101,025. Italian torpedo boats carried out an attack in the Dardanelles but fortunately no British ships were damaged and Turkey did not close the waterway. Instead she laid mines which restricted the width of the navigable channel. Needless to say all this warlike activity made shippers shy about fixing charters for the Middle East and they turned their attentions to less troubled areas.

The Balkan War became 'physical' when *Clumberhall* 3599/99 (West Hartlepool S.N. Co) was seized by the Italian cruiser *Piemonte* in May 1912. She was proceeding in ballast from Liverpool to Bombay when a serious leakage developed in one of her boilers, and she put into Hodeidah Roads to affect repairs. The Italians took her to Massowah and released her after 9 days. The owners lost the Bombay charter worth about £5,000, but the Italians refused to give compensation. The West Hartlepool S.N. Co appealed to the government but they were unable to get any satisfaction. There was more trouble when a Canadian and a French steamer were sunk by floating mines in the Gulf of Smyrna, but as the mines had been laid in Turkey's own territorial waters little could be done.

It was a year of boom in the tramp trades despite a bad start with a coal strike which paralysed the coal export trade for a while, and a dock strike in London. During the strike the coal carriers bunkered on the Continent and went in ballast to the Mediterranean to pick up their homeward cargo or to Nova Scotia or Virginia for coal for the River Plate. South Africa received coal from Australia. The Turks cleared a passage through their minefields and there was a rush of steamers to Danube and Black Sea ports. With too many ships offering, the rates dropped but later as the congestion cleared rates went up to good levels.

Second hand steamers sold this year at high prices. Owners who had bought in the periods of slump now sold at a good profit:
Wentworth 4656/92, R.S.Dalgliesh,Newcastle. Bought 1909 £12,000 Sold 1912 £24,000
Sylvia 2035/04, W.T. Mitchell,Glasgow.   Bought 1909 £16,750 Sold 1912 £23,000

1913. A fairly steady year with rates lower than 1912 and dropping towards the end. A poor crop in the Argentine left a shortage of maize from the River Plate. The harvest in the Black Sea area was hit by rain. In both areas a surplus of tonnage pushed freights down. Not only that but India's harvest did not come up to expectations either. With the trouble in the Balkans owners preferred to avoid problems and sent their boats out East through the Suez Canal only to find too many ships chasing too little cargo with the resultant drop in freight for those who did fix a cargo. Russia had mobilised troops because of the Balkan crisis, withdrawing labour from her coal mines. To meet shortages she imported coal from Britain. This gave many tramp steamers their outward cargo but flooded the Baltic market producing low freight for homeward cargo.

In 1913 there was a great deal of activity in the chartering of tramp tonnage, one of the liner traders was Clan Line Ltd who took three local tramps for their Far Eastern trades; they were all two decked steamers best suited to the trade. *Ormidale* 3560/93 R. & C. Allan, Glasgow, for Cape Town and other South African ports. *Earl of Elgin* 4448/09 Marshall & W.L. Dobbie, Glasgow, for Colombo, Madras and Calcutta. *Lancefield* 5761/13 John Black & Co, Glasgow, also for Colombo, Madras and Calcutta.

1914. The year opened with a depressed shipping industry. The harvest in the Argentine was again bad and many ships had to be laid up due to shortage of traditional homeward cargo. As the Baltic, St. Lawrence and the Danube opened and drew tonnage from the pool of shipping, there was some improvement in freights. Shipping strikes in Italy and Spain brought their tramp activities to a halt and British owners were quick to fill the gap. Trade from the Gulf was affected by trouble in Mexico. Russia put an embargo on the export of grain, the Admiralty prohibited the export of high quality steam coal in order to build up stocks for the possibility of war. Germany stopped importing ore via Rotterdam and Antwerp. These moves increased the number of tramps looking for cargo and many sailed in ballast for North America which had enjoyed a bumper harvest, flooding the market and forcing down freights. At home a strike of engineers and fitters held up dozens of tramps under repair which might otherwise have been in German ports when hostilities commenced. After the outbreak of war Italy demanded coal and grain in quantities that the tramp owners found hard to meet, and this, combined with a renewed U.K. demand for imports, took rates to high levels.

WORLD WAR ONE. In the middle of 1914 freights were dropping, there were too many ships seeking cargoes, and there was a shortage of ready cash to pay freights. The shippers held on to the cargoes so the ships lay idle. A paralysis was creeping over the shipping industry.

On August 4th war was declared by Britain and within days reports began to come in that German raiders were at work in the South Atlantic and Indian Ocean sinking British cargo vessels. The underwriters refused to insure and the charter market went dead. At the same time almost all of the North European ports were closed to British shipping which for over 50 years had visited them; St. Petersburg, Gothenburg, Copenhagen, Danzig, Hamburg, Emden, Antwerp, all ports which had received large quantities of imports. Turkey's entry into the war in November closed off further ports for the British tramp steamer, ports in the Danube and Sea of Azov. The queue of idle ships grew.

By the end of 1914 it had become obvious that the war was going to go on for a long time, that a large amount of arms and ammunition and raw materials would be needed and that ships would be needed to carry them. Not only that, but more ships would be required, as the East European sources of goods were not now available and longer voyages were necessary to bring back the cargoes. For example, before the war importing grain into Norway took 250,000 tons of shipping, in wartime 750,000 tons were needed to transport the same quantity. Now that there was a shortage of ships freight rates soared. Cotton from Savannah went up in leaps and bounds: July 1914 (25c. per 100 lb.), November 1914 (50c./100 lbs.), January 1915 ($1/100 lbs.), January 1916 ($3/100 lbs.), December 1916 ($5/100 lbs.). Other amazing prices were paid for freight: June 1917: Coffee from Rio de Janeiro to Marseilles 400/- per ton, June 1917: Coal from U.S.A. to Argentine 125/- per ton, October 1917: Rice from Burma to Cette (France) 600/- per ton, January 1918: Syrup in barrels from U.S.A. to London 35/- per 100 lbs.

Time charter rates also increased: 1914; 2/6 per ton per month, 1917; 47/6 per ton per month. The price of ships rose as well though not as dramatically. For example, a 2,250 grt. shelter deck steamer: 1910 (£17,500), 1912 (£22,500), May 1914 (£21,500), November 1914 (£23,500) January 1915 (£32,000)

Several factors gave rise to the shortage of shipping:
1. Vessels were being lost to U-boats and surface raiders.
2. There was an increase of the total tonnage of cargo being shifted.
3. The longer voyages meant more ships at sea at any one time.
4. Shipbuilders were concentrating on building warships.
5. Not only were voyages longer but detours to avoid enemy attack were adding to the length of the voyages.
6. There was congestion in the ports.
7. Control of shipping was in the hands of 'amateurs' in government departments.

Congestion in ports was widespread; on 28th May, 28 steamers were at anchor off Marseilles waiting entry to the port. In April 1915 over 70 vessels were anchored in the Mersey waiting for berths in the docks at Liverpool. In January 1916 at Genoa, 40 vessels loaded with grain and coal were anchored in the outer harbour. On the 25th February 1916 the Thames was so crowded that it was taking 2 weeks to unload. (Part of the problem was that conscription had reduced the size of the dock labour force.)

In Norway it was soon evident that British dry cargo vessels would be diverted to home needs and that they would have to build up their own cargo fleet. They approached British shipbuilders but they were busy with warships. The Norwegians then went to the U.S.A. and placed orders for steamers many of which were eventually sold to Britain at greatly enhanced prices. All over the world shipbuilding nations stepped up production but even in 1918 world output had not reached the level of the losses incurred during the three years of war.

On 7th August 1914 the government issued a proclamation announcing a policy of requisitioning shipping to serve national requirements. At first they traded like any other charterers bargaining around the prevailing market rate but in October 1914, in an effort to simplify matters, they prepared a schedule of rates based on the average of previous months and printed them in the 'Blue Book'. At the time the 'Blue Book' rates were fair but they were not increased as the war proceeded despite the rapid rise in the rates in the free market, rates which reached seven times the 'Blue Book' figures. As a compensation the government departments were supposed to spread the requisitioning over the whole tramp fleet, but in practice many firms suffered unfairly, especially those with the modern, efficient ships. When challenged the government spokesman replied, "It must be clearly understood that in selecting vessels the Admiralty has to consider which are most suitable for the required service and available at the due dates. So far as considerations allow, a vessel belonging to an owner with a lower percentage in service is taken in preference to one belonging to an owner with a high percentage, but no uniform percentage is maintained, or could possibly be maintained without serious injury to naval or military services." The percentage of requisitioned vessels referred to is shown in the following table:

Owner	No. of vessels in fleet	No. of vessels on Admiralty service	Percentage requisitioned
E. Thomas Radcliffe & Co, Cardiff	25	12	48
W.J. Tatem Ltd, Cardiff	14	6	43
Maclay & McIntyre, Glasgow	29	16	55
Prince Line Ltd, Newcastle	39	8	21
Constantine & Pickering S.S. Co, Middlesbrough	17	10	59
Glover Bros, London	13	3	23
Farrar, Groves & Co, London	9	3	44
R.Ropner & Co, W. Hartlepool	43	16	37
W. & C.T. Jones S.S. Co, Cardiff	13	6	46
W. Runciman & Co, Newcastle	30	14	47
Sutherland S.S Co, Newcastle	11	4	36

The above was the situation in February 1916, but does not indicate how many ships had been taken over by other government departments. It has been stated that at one point during the war almost every British vessel over 500 grt. was on requisition.

Further losses were inflicted on the unfortunate tramp steamer owners, financial this time, when their vessels were stopped in the English Channel on their way to German ports. The steamers were diverted to English ports where they lay until the Prize Court passed judgement. The tramp owner lost his freight and lost valuable time until his particular case was heard.

It was not only Great Britain that was hit by the war. All over the world other countries were affected by the lack of British tonnage to uplift their products. In Argentina the grain lay at the docksides, unemployment rose and bread lines formed. In U.S.A. in the southern states, a depression hit the cotton trade. Sugar stacked up in Java, wheat in Australia, wool in New Zealand. Neutrals were also affected by a form of blackmail. Britain was the major coal supplier to the world. When a neutral wanted coal, Britain wanted something in return; the hire of the neutral's ships. Government controllers decided who carried what cargo between which ports.

Insurance played a large part in the shipping business and it had decisive effects on the availability of shipping. Shipping insurance covered almost every risk to be encountered at sea but excluded what was known as 'war risk'. It was many years since Great Britain had fought a war at sea and the submarines and surface raiders caused losses which came as a shock to the shipping world. Insurance companies could not work out rates or provide cover. As a result shipowners would not sail. Although war risk premiums were quickly issued they were so high that owners would not pay and ceased to trade. On July 28th 1914, 5/- per £100 was common for a voyage U.K. to U.S.A. In August 1914 the war risk raised this to £21 per £100. When the main raiders *Emden* and *Konigsberg* were put out of action, the first by her destruction in the Pacific, the latter when she was cut off in the Rufiji Delta in East Africa, insurance rates dropped. In January German raiders were out again in the South Atlantic and insurance rates rose again. Throughout 1916 U-boat sinkings pushed up the rates until by 1917 it was difficult to get insurance for shipping; there was almost a blockade. However, by May 1917 the sinkings were reduced easing the insurance situation. The answer lay in the Government assuming war risk insurance as it was beyond the capacity of the marine insurance market to provide. However, Lloyd's and the insurance companies continued to provide the channel for owners placing risks, passing premiums to the Government Department and collecting claims which they passed on to the assured.

The power of the submarine was demonstrated when the cruisers *Aboukir, Cressy* and *Hogue* were sunk on the 22nd of September 1914 within minutes of one another by a single small submarine, U9. Fearing for the vulnerability of the Fleet anchorages the Admiralty purchased 32 old vessels to be sunk as blockships in 1914 and 1915. Among them were vessels belonging to tramp steamer owners: *Almeria* 2418/88 (R.E. Morel, &

Co, Cardiff), *Chicklade* 2410/88 (M.H. Horsley, West Hartlepool), *Fernlands* 2042/85 (R. Hardy & Co, West Hartlepool), *Newbridge* (131) 3737/06 (J. Temperley & Co, London), *Rosewood* 1757/89 (Constantine & Pickering S.S. Co. Ltd, Middlesbrough).

Neutrals were affected in another way. To cut off the enemy's essential food and raw materials Britain established 'The Big Blockade', a ring of warships and armed merchant cruisers which lay across all the trade routes leading to Germany. Any neutral wishing to trade with Germany had to run this blockade and risk losing the cargo if it was deemed to be contraband. What was contraband was not always clear and neutral countries found it difficult to obtain insurances for their cargoes.

Losses during the war were heavy. They began when war was declared and all British ships in German ports were interned. In all about 87 British cargo steamers were held, together with sundry fishing boats and sailing ships. Among the vessels held were; *Bellailsa* 3797/96 (Bell Bros & Co, Glasgow), *Cogent* (131) 2051/83 (J. Westoll, Sunderland), *Dacre Hill* 2674/06 (W. Price & Co, Liverpool), *Fleetwing* 1351/07 (Witherington & Everett, Newcastle), *Garvel Park* 927/01 (J. & J. Denholm, Glasgow), *Leversons* 1774/09 (R. Gordon S.S. Co, London), *Lothian* 4959/02 (J. Warrack & Co, Leith), *Scarsdale* 2099/03 (Lucas & Co, Bristol), *Strathyre* (Burrell & Son, Glasgow), *West Quarter* 1548/10 (J. Ridley, Son & Tully, Newcastle)

That was on the minus side; on the plus side were the vessels seized by Great Britain and her allies. 144 in British ports, 12 in French ports, 30 in Russian ports and 59 in Italian ports.These vessels were put into service in this country under the management of well known shipowners such as Witherington & Everett and E.R. Newbigin of Newcastle. Losses due to enemy activity were alarming yet despite the proved effectiveness of the convoy system in the days of sail, it was not until 1917 that convoys were introduced. Anti-submarine defences were not very effective but by moving ships in groups the spread of shipping was reduced and the risk of sightings by the submarines was lessened. The reduction in sinkings was slow to become evident. On the 9th of January 1917 Germany announced a policy of unrestricted warfare against merchant shipping and the convoy system was put into operation.

February	86 ships sunk		August	84 ships sunk	
March	103	by submarine	September	68	by submarine
April	155		October	79	
May	106		November	56	
June	116		December	76	
July	88				

There was always a body of opinion that held that in the event of a submarine starting an attack, fast ships were less likely to be sunk by U-boats, an opinion which was only partially upheld by figures, which showed that to be reasonably certain of escape the steamer had to be really fast:

Percentage Sunk: 100 93 90 80 75 65 60 50 45 40 35 25 20 10
Speed: 5   6   7   8   9 10 11 12 13 14 15 16 17 18 knots.

An interesting feature of the First World War was the dazzle painting of merchant ships (62 and 144). The merchant ships had no defence against the submarine apart from an old gun mounted on the poop. Most of the tramp steamers were lucky if they could still manage a steady 8 kts. Once they had been sighted by a submarine and the submarine was able to manoeuvre into a good firing position the tramp was doomed.

The first proposal was to achieve invisibility by painting the vessel to blend with her background, but the background as seen from a submarine was the sky which could be blue, grey, dark or light. Secondly any colour used would have to tend towards a light shade which would soon be soiled by coaling, working cargo, rust streaks from the scuppers, scrapes from lying alongside a quay. More important than anything else, it was not possible to disguise the column of smoke rising from the funnel of a coal burning tramp bunkered with inferior coal. The Admiralty appointed the well known artist Norman Wilkinson to study the question of camouflage. His proposal was quite startling; no attempt should be made at camouflage, instead, bright contrasting colours should be used, applied in planned patterns to suit each type of vessel. He created what became known as 'dazzle painting'. The whole idea was to break up the outline of the hull in such a way as to confuse the enemy commander as to her true course and speed. A bow might be painted to look like a stern and vice versa. A false bow wave might be painted at each end of the hull, exaggerated to give an impression of speed. The mast might be set off the centreline so that the angle of approach would be misjudged.

131.

1914–18 WAR.

Newbridge 3737/06 of J. Temperley & Co, London was sunk in 1914 in the Rufiji River, East Africa during the *Koningsberg* action.

Cogent 2051/83, a well deck steamer managed by J. Westoll of Sunderland, was interned in Hamburg at the start of the first world war in 1914. She had been built by Short Bros, Sunderland and had the dimensions: 275.0' x 38.6' x 20.6'.

The spar deck steamer *River Clyde* 3913/05 on arrival at Alexandria from the Dardenelles after taking part in the Gallipoli landings. She was repaired and became the Spanish flag *Angela.*

Photos: I.W.Rooke collection.

Models of each type of ship were made and these were dazzle painted. The model was viewed through a periscope against different backgrounds, and the pattern would be altered until the best effect was obtained. It was claimed that while a U-boat could carry out a successful attack after sighting an unpainted vessel at 15,000 yards, she would have to, close to 5,000 yards if the vessel were dazzle painted in order to press home her attack.

In October the Admiralty decided to paint all merchant ships with dazzle schemes. No figures are available to prove the effectiveness of dazzle painting but it was acknowledged that "a far larger percentage of dazzle painted ships reached port safely compared with those painted light grey."

PANAMA CANAL. The opening of the Panama Canal in 1915 removed the necessity of making the long and hazardous voyage round Cape Horn when sailing from the Atlantic to the Pacific. The canal was 50 miles long and rose 87 feet above sea level. It was 500 feet wide and 45 to 85 feet deep. Comparable voyages were:

	Via Cape Horn	Via Panama Canal	Days saved by 10kt. Steamer
London to Valparaiso	8,777	7,360	6
London to Callao	10,013	6,190	16
London to Vancouver	14,348	8,810	23

During the building of the canal the Americans caused a great deal of concern by proposing preferential terms for American flag vessels, even to the extent of giving them free passage. However the other nations invoked an international agreement made in 1902 during the planning stage of the scheme in which "the canal was to be used on terms of entire equality". The Americans withdrew their proposal and tolls were levied equally on all comers. According to official figures the Panama Canal was not so busy as the Suez Canal:

Year:	1915	1925	1929	1935	1947
Number of Vessels:	1,058	4,392	6,289 (the peak figure).	5,180	4,260

1919. This was a boom year, yet it was not without its troubles. Congestion in the U.K. ports prevented shipowners from making full use of their vessels and in South Wales ports as many as 75 to 100 ships were to be seen waiting in the roadsteads for their turn to go under the coal tips. Even loading bunkers could entail a delay of 10 days before a berth under a tip was available. In Barry only 7,750,000 tons was loaded against 12,000,000 tons in 1913, and in Swansea only 1,750,000 tons against 4,500,000. In the second half of the year there were strikes on the railways, in the docks and in the mines. In the Bristol Channel 200 vessels lay waiting to load. In the U.S.A. there was also a coal strike and vessels which had left the U.K. with partially filled bunkers hoping to top up in the States were tied up in port. Many tramps were forced to go coastal to keep themselves in business.

Many ships were still operating under government orders and controls were holding down freight rates. As vessels were released they had to go in for long overdue refit leading to further loss of revenue. The secondhand market was affected by restrictions on the sales of vessels less than 15 years old. Looming over all this was the general concern of what would happen if America put on the market or into service the thousands of wartime built ships.

1920. Another boom was over. Rates fell as the year progressed. Tyne to the Mediterranean: January 65/-, July 47/6, Tyne to France: January 40/-, July 29/-. New orders for the shipyards were almost non-existent by July, a situation made worse by the fact that 301 ex-enemy ships were available for allotment including tramp steamers equivalent to 1,470,663 dwt. The price of secondhand tonnage plummeted. The export of coal was hampered by a miners' strike and restrictions on the export of coal imposed by the Coal Controller. There was an embargo on the export of cobbles, nuts, beans and peas (all types of coal). Collieries were given allocations for bunker and export coal. The number of ships laid up grew.

Britain had more ships than in 1913, but her imports were down by 10,500,000 tons. Despite the increase in the number of ships, her share of the world's tonnage had dropped: (1909 - 48%, 1914 - 44%, 1920 - 35%)

1921. The shipping slump showed some signs of slackening. A strike in the coalfields brought exports of coal to a halt and tramps were being used to carry coal from the U.S.A. to Britain and to all the countries abroad which before the war had been supplied on a regular basis with U.K. coal. To add insult to injury coal was being brought into South Wales ports. It was not just the strike; British coal now cost four to five times the pre-war price and few Continental consumers could afford to buy it so 2,500,000 dwt. of coal-carrying ships were laid up. Ship prices reached an all-time low:

		Waltham 3636/06	*Ridley* 3332/13
Purchased by the Craggs S.S. Co.	February 1920	£173,500	£171,000
Valued in prospectus	March 1920	£186,000	£185,000
Sold	January 1921	£ 50,000	£ 53,000

The Danube froze up on 11/12th December in the worst snowstorm for many years. When released on 2nd March 1922 many of the ships which had been caught in the ice drifted in the pack-ice and were damaged, among them *Butetown* 2525/06, Harrison, Sons & Co of Cardiff.

1922. There were moves by countries abroad which weighed against British shipping. France introduced a decree which ensured that most of their imports were carried by French ships. Portugal increased charges levied on British shipping using their ports. Further coal strikes brought exports of coal to a halt once more and again tramps were chartered to carry coal from America to Britain and also to Belgium, France and Germany, which in the past had received coal from the U.K. In 10 months up to October 3,433,000 tons of coal was imported against 151 tons in 1913. In the middle of the year the miners in America went on strike and British tramp steamers were chartered to carry coal to the U.S.A. Around 2,600,000 tons were transported. The ridiculous situation arose where steamers lay in the same docks, one unloading coal from America while the other loaded coal destined for U.S. ports, each fulfilling its own particular contract. A quick look at export figures showed a considerable drop in goods sent to our traditional markets: (Figures in millions of tons)

	France	Italy	Russia	S.America	Spain	Scandinavia	Holland	Belgium	Portugal
1912	12.78	9.65	6.00	6.91	3.65	9.90	2.02	2.03	1.36
1922	14.00	6.50	0.58	3.50	1.70	6.70	6.20	3.00	0.75

The Russians declared a twelve mile limit and laid mines outside their Black Sea ports with access only through swept channels.

1923. Some alarm was felt in shipping circles when it was reported that Turkey was laying mines outside Smyrna harbour. For some years there had been concern about the American mercantile fleet which had been swollen to over 2,000 foreign-going ships by the tremendous shipbuilding effort during the war. There had been fears about the effect of all that government subsidised and controlled shipping on the world market. However, the financial losses of state owned shipping were such that the Americans laid up hundreds of steamers to try to reduce the huge deficits. This year there was another example of the inter-action of various aspects of tramp shipping. The French occupied the Ruhr coal fields which created a shortage of coal in Germany. The demand pushed up freight rates drawing tonnage from other routes creating a scarcity of tonnage for the Mediterranean and South America. This, and improved freight rates, drew steamers from the pool of laid-up shipping. Even deep sea tramps found themselves taking coal in the short sea trades. Laid up ships: October 1921 (1296), October 1922 (456), October 1923 (395). In the autumn there was heavy chartering to load grain and flour from the Pacific coast of U.S.A. to Japan and China. The Russian grain harvest was poor and the tramps which had gone to the Black Sea to load had to turn back to load ore.

1924. A somewhat better year, with idle shipping dropping to 278 vessels in October, a drop partly due to extensive breaking up of elderly vessels. However there was no significant rise in freight rates. Strikes again caused trouble. Disruption of the railways delayed coal for shipment, there was a reduction in coal chartering and a congestion in loading ports saw up to 400 vessels idle and waiting. The transport workers struck and the London and Liverpool dockers refused to unload ships.

1925. Once again the tramp market looked as though it was on the up-turn and once again this proved to be a false hope. A demand for tramp tonnage to carry Australian wheat drew the big cargo carriers to the long distance voyages, but the demand in Europe for wheat was too low to sustain the business. The good 1924 European harvest had left countries with a stockpile sufficient for normal needs. The situation was somewhat alleviated by the Russian demand for grain, a result of a bad crop, which gave employment to the Baltic and Black Sea. The Canadian Government came up with a proposal to start a Dominion fleet of ten 10,000 dwt. cargo steamers, a move which worried the shipping interest in the U.K. The move came to nothing in the end. National shipping lines were notorious for running at a loss. The U.S.A. lost £34,000, France £3,500,000, Canada £6,225,000 and Brazil and Portugal also ran at a loss.

1926. Once again nature brought trouble for the insurance market. A hurricane struck the Southern States of America, a typhoon off Siberia caused a lot of damage to shipping while lesser storms created havoc at Pensacola and Mobile. Another coal strike in the U.K. brought the now inevitable import of foreign fuel, a situation which lasted for seven months:

	Imports – tons	Exports – tons
April	591	1,290,652
May	3,618	1,448,368
June	600,634	34,485
July	2,319,657	7,381
August	3,970,880	2,184
September	3,940,880	5,225
October	3,489,083	3,812
November	3,467,921	5,111

The effects of the strike were reflected in idle tonnage, the number of ships idle rising from 259 in January to 518 in July, falling to 311 in October.

1927. The grain harvest in the world again upset the workings of the tramp shipping companies. A poor harvest in Europe led to a demand for grain produced elsewhere, but the Argentine harvest was late owing to drought. An unprecedented slump in shipping values and the trade depression finally forced many shipowners to write down the value of their fleets.

1928. The production of grain in Russia was very low and she was in the market for the import of grain, a far cry from the 'good old days'. The shippers were willing to oblige but the problem was one of payment as Russia was not noted for prompt payment in cash. A good harvest in South America encouraged tramp shippers to charter for grain home, but the large number of ships offering for outward cargoes brought down the coal freights to such a level that many owners sent their steamers out in ballast rather than accept a freight which barely covered loading and discharging. Other steamers went to the Pacific coast of Canada in ballast to pick up grain which otherwise would have had to wait for opening of navigation on the St. Lawrence. The Chilean authorities took measures to encourage the export of nitrate and attracted a fair number of steamers to revive a trade which had been badly hit by synthetic products.

The secondhand market was still bad. The turret steamer *Gwynmead* 3825/06, Sutherland S.S. Co, had been built for £36,000. She was sold in 1920 for £140,000, in 1921 she changed hands for £23,000 and this year she was sold for only £10,350.

1929. The year started badly in South Wales where a heavy snowstorm followed by a severe frost brought the coal ports to a standstill. Coal froze in the wagons and had to be hacked out with pickaxes. Coal loading equipment was put out of commission. The impossibility of clearing trucks and returning them to the pithead brought many pits to a halt. Ships kept arriving until 89 vessels were waiting for space at the coal tips.

For the first six months the freight market was buoyant and for the last six months exactly the opposite. In the middle of the year labour trouble in South America created congestion in the ports with long delays in loading. Vessels missed their cancelling dates and they lost their cargo. Many vessels quit the River Plate in ballast to seek cargo in the U.S.A. and some even returned to the Danube ports. To crown it all there was a good harvest in Europe which reduced the demand for imported grain; however some tramps were hired at £35 to £40 a day to act as floating warehouses. A miners' strike in Australia resulted in a demand for U.K. coal but due to the length of the voyage there were a lot of cargo fires which hit the insurance market.

1930. This was one of the worst years to date. Another good harvest in Europe reduced the demand for imported grain and with many owners unwilling to lay up their vessels, too many tramps were seeking outward cargoes and too many were in Black Sea ports flooding the markets and forcing down the rates, and creating congestion. There was a poor harvest in the Plate area in the early part of the year and although there was a good maize crop later there was no market for it. There was little demand for tramps for the Far East as the liner traders were satisfying what little business there was. However some of the liner owners were laying up their own vessels and chartering tramps to do their work. A slight relief came when the Russians chartered vessels for

135.
Dumfries managed by Griffiths, Payne & Co, and *Northborough* of Humphries (Cardiff) Ltd, laid up in the River Torridge in the 1930s. See below.
Photo: Miss M. Love/
I.W.Rooke collection

the White Sea and Baltic trade, but here there was always the problem of payment and the fact that the vessels were used to undercut open market rates. As business got worse there was a knock-on effect. As tramps were laid up, the demand for bunker coal overseas dropped which in turn reduced the amount of coal being exported.

1931. A brighter note for British shipping was the time chartering of 22 steamers totalling 96,000 grt. by the Russian Government, including *Dumfries* 3650/01 (above) and *Oakfield* 3646/12, both owned by Griffiths, Payne & Co, Cardiff. Towards the end of the year there were signs of a revival in trade and a number of laid-up vessels were put back into service. Against this, the French authorities took steps to reduce the import of foreign coal. A Board of Trade committee was appointed to consider the economics involved in the disposal of old ships and their replacement by new. Their figures showed the comparative ages of British owned vessels:

Under 5 years old	4,581,614 grt.	22.5%
5 – 10 years old	9,531,697 grt.	46.9%
10 – 20 years old	2,998,185 grt.	14.8%
Over 21 years old	3,209,730 grt.	15.8%

1932. Market conditions were low enough to encourage shipowners to send their ships in ballast seeking cargo rather than incur port charges and costs of loading and unloading uneconomic cargo. Other shipowners maintained that it was better to lay up a vessel rather than to attempt to trade at unremunerative rates.

One of the leading British shipowners, E.H. Watts, concerned with the strength of foreign competition, investigated the actual extent of the problem and found the following percentage of various trades carried by British flag vessels:

Grain from South Russia:	October	1931	41 out of 87	47.12%
	November	1931	20 out of 69	28.90%
	December	1931	3 out of 21	14.20%

Grain from the Danube. Last quarter 1931, only 22 out of the 256 involved (8.59%)
Coal from South Wales to Mediterranean, last quarter 1931, 58 out of 230 (25.22%)
Grain from River Plate to all ports, last quarter 1931, 243 out of 455 (51.40%)
Grain from River Plate to U.K. only, last quarter 1931, 124 out of 170 (72.94%)
Coal from South Wales to River Plate, last quarter 1931, 56 out of 89 (65.17%)
Russian timber from the Baltic, last quarter 1931, 20 out of 75 (26.66%)

He also reviewed the laid-up shipping in the U.K. and found that the largest number of British ships laid up each year had been:

1928	1929	1930	1931	1932
125	82	287	496	456

Further figures published showed the decline in tramp shipping over the years. June 1933 compared to June 1913 showed a reduction of 50% in numbers and 33% in tonnage. There was enough improvement by the end of the year to bring some laid-up vessels back into serice and no less than 45 Cardiff managed 'tramp steamers were re-commissioned: 12 Hain S.S. Co steamers, 7 Sir William Reardon Smith, 7 Evan Thomas Radcliffe & Co, 4 John Cory & Sons, 3 Tatem S. N. Co, 2 Morel Ltd, and others.

1933. Another miserable year for the tramp steamer owner with freights dropping rapidly over the year. With under-utilisation and ballast voyaging one expert estimated that in 1933 space capable of carrying 22,000,000 tons of goods was not used. This did not even take into account laid-up tonnage. At long last the British tramp shipping industry got over the message that things were going so badly for them that if something was not done, the country would be left without a tramp fleet. A subsidy scheme was proposed to provide a payment of 10/- per grt. on ships in commission and 5/- per grt. for ships which were laid up for 30 days and longer (2 million tons). Some opponents of the scheme were against subsidising obsolete steamers and felt that the money would be better spent building 'economy steamers'. They produced the following argument to back their views:

Value		£75,000 new		£40,000 ten years old
Interest	5%	3,700		2,000
Depreciation	5%	3,700	10%	4,000
Coal for 200 days:	18 tons/day	3,600	30 tons/day	6,000
Repairs		1,000		1,500
Loss on freight, as new steamer could carry 300 tons extra on three voyages per annum:				2,400
		£12,000		£15,900

Thus a saving of £3,900 per annum could be achieved.

1934. The world-wide laid-up tonnage went down by about 30% helped to a large extent by the increased demand for ships for scrapping and to the improved prices being offered. As usual grain played a large part in tramp steamer activity. Plenty of grain from the River Plate, a poor harvest in America leaving little grain for export, while Canada with a good harvest demanded too high a price and attracted few buyers. With the short Baltic trading season, timber carriers were facing serious congestion in the U.K. ports of Bo'ness, Hull, Sunderland, West Hartlepool and London. Once more the proportion of the world tonnage of sea-going ships owned by Britain dropped:

1913	1929	1930	1931	1932	1933	1934
45.09	27.69	27.42	27.12	26.47	25.58	24.87 %

1935. The freight rate for the River Plate dropped to an uneconomic level from 16/6 to 12/- per ton and the International Shipping Conference, in response to appeals from shipowners, negotiated a minimum rate of 16/6 which just covered costs. A similar rate was established for the St. Lawrence at 1/6 per quarter against 1/3, and for Australia at 22/6 per ton against 19/3. This move encouraged shipowners to send their steamers out in ballast to the Plate, many without a homeward cargo fixed, flooding the market with excess tonnage. On 14.2.1935 there were 96 vessels on the way and arrived; unfixed. On 30.6.1935, 31 were committed to the River Plate unfixed but these were carrying outward cargo. This was the result of regulations restricting vessels from proceeding beyond Las Palmas in ballast if they were not fixed for a cargo from the River Plate. As a result of the River Plate scheme Britain's share of the trade went up from 41.5% to 49.9% in number of ships. The number of tramps laid up fell off, January (83), April (125), July (71) as a result of the minimum freight scheme.

SUBSIDIES and SCRAP & BUILD: The question of shipping subsidies was raised from time to time and, although these were fairly comon abroad, in Britain owners and govenment fought shy of making any decision. However, the slump of the early 1930s had depressed the earnings of the tramp companies to such an extent that it became obvious that something must be done or many companies would have to be wound up and their fleets dispersed. As mentioned earlier, in 1933 the committee of the Tramp Shipowners section of the Chamber of Shipping applied to the Government for a cash subsidy. As a result of discussions the British Shipping (Assistance) Act of 1935 was passed allocating £2,000,000 as a cash subsidy to help tramp steamer owners, but it contained a proviso that should freight rates exceed 92% of the 1929 level, the subsidy would be reduced by £250,000 for each 1% of excess. In 1935 237 companies applied for financial assistance. The largest individual grant was £76,780 for the Bank Line (A. Weir & Co of Glasgow), but the Ropner Group received a total of £118,285. Other large sums went to such well known companies as the Carlton S.S. Co Ltd of Newcastle (£42,714), R.S. Dalgliesh Ltd (£22,998) and Sir William Reardon Smith & Sons (£43,581). At the other end of the scale were small sums by today's standards, to F. Bowles & Sons of Cardiff (£12), Galleon Shipping Co of Newcastle (£25) and Stanhope Steamship Co of London (£341). In 1936 the number of companies applying for assistance had risen to

426. Again the 'big names' featured high on the list: A. Weir & Co (£65,967), Ropner Shipping Co (£47,741 plus £67,036 for the Pool Shipping Co), Hogarth (£45,817) and Reardon Smith (£39,212). Once again the host of small claims was made: the Cormack Steamship Co of Leith (£77), and the Westwick Steamship Co of Sunderland (£705). In 1935 the total paid out was £1,989,999.12.0d. while in 1936 the figure was £1,991,015.

Not only were the tramp steamer fleets in dire trouble but the British shipyards were in a sorry state with half the work force unemployed and annual production at a low of only about 200,000 tons. To assist the shipyards the 'Scrap and Build' scheme was introduced. Shipowners were to be encouraged to scrap obsolete vessels and to replace them with new ones built in British yards on the basis of two tons new for each ton scrapped. In return the Government offered low interest loans to meet the cost of the new vessels. At first it was stipulated that the old steamer had to be broken up in this country but as the prices offered by Continental shipbreakers were consistently higher than those offered in this country, this rule had to be abandoned to enable the scheme to work. The benefit of the scheme lay in the fact that a large proportion of the tramp shipping fleet was old and no longer economic to run, a high percentage were single decked and therefore did not attract charterers who wanted vessels to carry general goods, and more important, good designs were available for larger vessels with economic engines. (Consumptions were quoted at 17 tons per day against 25 tons per day for an old tramp steamer) and also higher operating speeds were being offered. As a result of 'Scrap and Build' 97 old vessels were scrapped and 50 new vessels launched, 27 of them steamships, 23 motorships, only two of the total were not specifically for tramp service. Of the 97 old ships broken up only 49 were of British register, the shipowners having had to purchase foreign flag tonnage in order to meet the requirements of the Act. 186,000 gross tons were built, 386,625 gross tons were scrapped. The 27 steamers built were:

Tramp steamers, 4,300 to 5,800 gross tons each	19
Tramp steamer, 2,700 gross tons	1
Cargo liner, 2,000 gross tons each	2
Tramp steamers for the Baltic trades, 1,175 to 1,550 gross tons	5

Forty were built in English shipyards (24 being constructed in Sunderland) and 10 in Scottish yards. The shipowners who took advantage of the 'Scrap and Build' scheme included Thomas Dunlop & Sons of Glasgow – 4, Joseph Constantine – 3, T.E. Evans & Co, London – 4, Springwell Shipping Co, London – 5, but in the main the applications were for single ships such as the *Dan-y-Bryn* 5117/39 (see below).

By 1939 orders for merchant vessels being placed with the shipyards were down once more as freight rates dropped after a temporary revival in 1937 and owners were not in a position to order new tonnage. As a result a new Shipping (Assistance) Bill was prepared in 1939 to help the shipping industry in general with operating subsidies for tramp owners and grants and loans to help purchase new vessels. The liner trades, which were suffering from competition with heavily subsidised foreign flag vessels were also to

137.

Dan-y-Bryn cost the Brynymore S.S. Co Ltd (Ambrose, Davies and Matthews, Swansea) a total of £123,000 of which £110,000 was the loan (see above). She was built by the Burntisland Shipbuilding Co Ltd, Burntisland in 1939. The photo shows her when owned by Jersey United Transports Ltd, Jersey.

Photo: I.W.Rooke collection

be given financial assistance. Although world war two broke out before the details of the Bill had been finalised and the Bill made law, the government honoured its promises and grants and loans were given out for the construction of 100 new vessels. As a result of these actions by the government the British merchant fleet included some modern useful vessels when the war began in September 1939 - unfortunately more than 50 of them were destroyed by enemy action.

1936. A better year for British tramp shipping. Europe imported more wheat and maize. A drought forced North America to buy maize from Argentina, though the late harvest in the Argentine caused alarm in January. There was a rise of tonnage on the move and a rise in freight rates. There was a brisk trade in scrap metal from the Northern Range of U.S.A. ports to Japan and the Continent. France bought huge quantities of rice from Saigon. By the end of the year British laid up tonnage had dropped to around 500,000 grt. compared with 3,250,000 grt. in 1932, part of the drop being due to the sale of ships abroad or for scrap. The situation in the shipyards was brighter with 1,000,000 grt. under construction as against 250,000 grt. in 1932. Other factors which helped the tramp companies were the war in Spain which held back Spanish shipping and the war in Abyssinia which took up Italian shipping. In addition, re-armament in Britain was calling for more raw materials.

SPANISH CIVIL WAR 1936-1939. During the Spanish Civil War the British and French governments declared a policy of non-intervention while the British merchant navy attempted to carry on normal trade with Spain. Naval vessels were despatched to protect British owned vessels in International waters but once inside the three mile limit they were on their own. Once they were within Spanish territorial waters they were liable to be fired on by warships or bombed by aircraft. Despite this a great number of British tramp steamers ran the blockade and many suffered damage. Some were captured, taken into ports, had their cargo confiscated and then released. The ships sunk included: *Thorpehaven* 3688/12 (Thameside Shipping Co, London), and *Thorpeness* 4798/14 (Westcliffe Shipping Co, London), both managed by P.B. Pandelis. Some of the damaged steamers were *Euphorbia* (139) 3380/24 (Stag Line, North Shields), *Hillfern* 1535/20 (Angel Son & Co, Cardiff), *Stancroft* 1407/08 (Stanhope S.S. Co, London), *Thurston* (139) 3077/18 (Murrell S.S. Co, West Hartlepool), and *Zelo* 2294/21 (Pelton S.S. Co, Newcastle).

A lot of questions were asked in the of Commons. Some M.P.s seemed to be more worried about foreign vessels transferring to the British flag in order to obtain naval protection than the fact that British ships were being attacked. During the middle six months of 1937 no less than 148 foreign owned vessels were transferred to the British register and another 51 had been granted temporary certificates. The largest number belonged to the Netherlands (45), U.S.A. (26) and France (19).

Another problem which was encountered was that a vessel which had traded with a port belonging to one combatant was not welcome in a port belonging to the opposing faction. *Willesden* (below) 4563/25, Watts, Watts & Co, London and *Hamsterley* 2160/25, Hartley S.S. Co, Newcastle both delivered cargo at Valencia and then proceeded to Huelva to pick up iron ore, but were ordered to leave the port empty as they had had

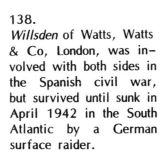

138.
Willsden of Watts, Watts & Co, London, was involved with both sides in the Spanish civil war, but survived until sunk in April 1942 in the South Atlantic by a German surface raider.

Photo: I.W.Rooke collection

dealings with the other side. One steamer, *Macgregor* 2498/19, Guardian Line Ltd, Cardiff had a narrow escape when she was leaving Santander with 1500 refugees on board. She was fired on by the cruiser *Almirante Cervera* but she kept going and managed to reach the three mile limit unscathed where she was taken under the protection of H.M.S. *Kempenfelt.*

1937. This was a much improved year for tramp steamer owners despite upsets to the normal flow of goods. Heavy shipment of grain once more led to the fixing of minimum rates to safeguard tramp owners. A poor harvest in North America left steamers sent there without their usual return cargo and many carried scrap as an alternative to grain. Increased industrial activity at home provided a boost to imports. Many Continental countries had by now become almost self-sufficient in coal and were importing very little of this commodity. Fighting in China was affecting trade into Shanghai and one of the tramp trades, timber from the Pacific Coast of North America to China had become impracticable. Freight rates rose sufficiently to cancel subsidy payments due for the third year under the British Shipping (Assistance) Act, 1935.

This year the price of second-hand tramp steamers rose to new levels:

	Year of Purchase	Minimum	Maximum
For a second-hand 7,500 dwt. steamer:	1900	£51,500	£60,750
(minimum and maximum prices)	1910	£36,500	£39,750
	1920	£105,000	£258,750
	1930	£49,750	£56,000
	1937	£90,000	£105,000

Although over the years Britain's share of the world's carrying trade had been dropping steadily, the share of her own import trade was still fairly respectable; Grain (67%), sugar (81%), oil seeds, nuts and kernels (67%), iron ore and scrap (40%), cotton (65%), wool (94%), timber (18%).

139.

SPANISH CIVIL WAR.

Thurston 3077/18 shown arriving at Preston with a timber cargo, was attacked and damaged while trading to Spain during the Spanish civil war when owned by the Murrell S.S. Co Ltd of West Hartlepool.

Stag Line's *Euphorbia* 3380/24 was also damaged while trading to Spain.

Photos: I.W.Rooke Collection

1938. After the upsurge in 1937 this proved to be a very disappointing year. A heavy frost at the end of 1937 affected the harvest in the Argentine, the grain available for export was small and only needed less than a third of the usual number of tramps for transport. Ships bound for the River Plate had to be diverted to look for cargoes in Chile, South Africa, Cuba, the Gulf, and the North Pacific. Of the tonnage which was chartered, the proportion of British tramps was smaller than usual. A better than normal harvest in Australia gave extra grain for shipment. However, grain shipments to the U.K. and Continent were down because of a bumper crop in the European countries. The British Government ordered 600,000 tons of grain from the Danube ports and much was carried on foreign bottoms until a public outcry forced them to charter British tonnage. There was little call for ships to carry iron ore and scrap as the industrial countries had built up good stocks the year before. In general our tramp steamers were having to make long voyages in ballast to pick up cargo. It was estimated that in 1938 only 37.5% of the tramp tonnage in the world sailed under the British flag.

1939. The year opened badly with a tremendous slump in grain prices. The Argentine government would not release grain and held on for higher prices. Fifty ships lay idle in the Plate awaiting cargo. Although some was released for sale to Spain to relieve hardship in the aftermath of the Civil War, most of it was carried by Greek tramp steamers, at low rates. Russia began to buy grain from Australia for shipment to Vladivostock and South Africa had surplus maize for export. Despite this relief the world's idle tonnage rose to 3,500,000 grt. by June. Early in the year Germany began to buy up second-hand shipping including 16 cargo carriers, among them the British flag tramp steamers *Dunstaffnage* 4525/22, Glen & Co, Glasgow, and *Essex Envoy* (below) 5210/22, Meldrum & Swinson, London.

Things became so bad that the tramp owners asked for a renewal of the subsidy scheme and a figure of £2,750,000 was agreed, to start on 1st January 1940, but on the outbreak of war this was withdrawn. Orders for new tramp vessels had reached rock bottom; 1936 (56), 1937 (18), 1938 (5). Foreign competition was killing the British tramp shipping industry with cheaper ships, lower manning levels, lower wages, government subsidies and trade protection. As the war threatened, the Admiralty closed the Mediterranean to British shipping and recalled British vessels trading in the Baltic. When the war broke out the Government introduced hire rates based on running costs, expenses plus reasonable profit. Charterparty T98A was on a 'bare boat' basis, while the Charterparty T99A left the owners responsible for running the vessel under Government orders. In 1940 the rates under T98A ranged from 2/9 per ton for a 4,500 dwt. vessel to 6/- for a 1,000 dwt. vessel. Under the T99A the corresponding rates were 8/3 and 18/6. During the Abyssinian War sanctions against Italy had resulted in an almost complete loss of trade which British shippers had not been able to win back.

WORLD WAR TWO: 1939-45. As Britain entered the 1930s an uneasy feeling pervaded Government circles that war was inevitable. As the first world war had demonstrated, almost disastrously, this country was absolutely dependent on its sea-borne trade for survival and investigating committees were set up to report the state of affairs and how they would be affected by war. The three main subjects for research were shipping, the ports, and the road and rail network for distributing the goods.

140.
Essex Envoy built as the *Therese Horn* at Danzig for A.C.Horn, Flensburg. Sold to German owners in 1939.

At the time British shipping was going through another slump with around 3,000,000 gross tons laid up, shipbuilding output stood at less than 1,000,000 tons per annum and the share of the world's merchant tonnage of ships of 100 grt. and over was only 25% against the 44% before world war one. In actual terms Britain's tonnage had dropped by only 8% but the total world tonnage had risen by 46%. The most disturbing feature was that nearly 44% of Britain's imports were carried by foreign flag vessels. Could these be relied on to continue trading with us in time of war? Britain's seagoing cargo tonnage was 13,000,000 grt. with another 1,000,000 grt. owned by Empire countries. The tonnage owned by friendly neutrals was estimated to be about 8,000,000 grt. In terms of carrying capacity this represented 19,000,000 deadweight tons of British and Empire shipping, backed up by 12,000,000 deadweight tons of neutral shipping. In peacetime this country was importing nearly 56,000,000 tons of merchandise, but in time of war what changes would have to be made in the pattern of imports? It was evident that, as in world war one, a large number of big liners and medium passenger carriers would be requisitioned as armed merchant cruisers and, although these did not carry large cargoes, they nevertheless represented a loss in carrying capacity.

When studying the ports of the United Kingdom it was realised that many of them were within range of German bombers and that they would probably have to be abandoned as working units. It was assumed that the use of ports from the Tyne round the coast to Southampton would be lost. Based on the figures available at the time this meant that 50% of the country's imports would have to be diverted, and so the loads on other ports would be doubled within weeks. This was a daunting prospect, but on investigation the position was found to be worse. Ports had a tendency to specialise in a given type of cargo. Grain which was sucked out of a steamer's hold was stored in silos fed by a maze of conveyor belts, ore which was lifted out with giant grabs was loaded via hoppers into waiting railway wagons. Meat had to be stored in refrigerated warehouses, timber required special handling and vast areas for storage. Ports exporting coal had staithes, loading chutes or wagon tippers. How could all this be handled in ports without the proper equipment? Not only that but increasing the number of ships using a port would inevitably create queues of vessels awaiting their turn at the quayside. This would affect the efficient use of the merchant navy's vessels, as had become very evident in the first world war. Then there was the question of distribution: whether or not the road and rail networks would cope with an increased volume of traffic taking material long distances from their new points of arrival. All iron ore delivered on the west coast would have to be carried to the industrial areas on the east coast. Grain would have to go to the densely populated areas in the south-east around London, and so the problem went on and magnified. In London and Hull much cargo was handled by the ship's derricks into barges and lighters alongside, considerably speeding up unloading. The same ship in a west coast port would take twice as long to discharge. General cargo arrived in small parcels which had to be laid out for identification and for Customs purposes, thus occupying much floor space. Since the hinterland at Liverpool absorbed the intake of that port almost 80% was taken inland by road and only 12% by rail, the remainder going by canal. Not a good pattern for a possible increased throughput.

The idea of the investigation was good but unfortunately there was little guidance from above, obtaining information was laborious if not impossible, and there was little or no discussion between the three groups, who were therefore unaware of the interaction of the various problems. As the years ticked away the committees began to arrive at their conclusions. British shipping should be capable of carrying imports of 48,000,000 tons per annum while the Government calculated a requirement of 47,000,000 tons. Apparently a satisfactory situation. On the port question it was estimated that the west coast ports could absorb 75% of the imports diverted from the east and south coasts. The railway system was very much under-utilised and was carrying only 17,000,000 tons of goods each year against a capacity of 75,000,000. On the face of it a satisfactory state of affairs, but it was evident that the groups had their doubts about the validity of the results and there were a lot of 'ifs' scattered throughout the reports. Some evidently remembered the chaotic situation with prevailed in the first world war.

1938 came and went and even in 1939 no information or advice was available on which to formulate plans. One thing was evident; London would be a prime target for German bombers and in London nearly 1,000,000 tons of goods were stored, this at least should be spread around. Then, at the last moment, the Ministry of Transport appointed groups responsible for the organising of port operations and the distribution network, not a perfect system, but at least a system. For the time being shipowners were left alone, but being only human, and needing a profit to survive, they went for the cargoes with the best freights. As in the first world war the Government had had to appoint a Shipping Controller with powers to direct the use of shipping, so in world war two the Ministry of War Transport was formed for the same purpose, with powers of requisition for essential purposes.

As soon as the war began in September 1939 the German attack on British shipping commenced with submarines, commerce raiders and aircraft sinking 150 ships totalling 800,000 grt. in the first nine months. Unexpectedly they did not bomb east coast ports at first. However there was a significant reduction in imports, nearly 50% in the first two months, due to the introduction of the convoy system, the withdrawal of neutral tonnage from the U.K. trade routes, and the temporary closing of the east coast ports. Despite strong pressure the essential reserves of material had not been built up and when the war broke out were still below the 1,000,000 ton marks, a shortage aggravated by the late home harvest and bad weather at sea delaying shipping. Stocks of iron ore and timber were also particularly low.

Shortages in British tonnage were made up by chartering foreign vessels. Considering vessels of 1,600 grt. and over, the use of foreign flag ships started at 400,000 grt. in 1940, rising to a peak of 7,000,000 tons in 1944. With the invasion of the Low Countries, Denmark and Norway, Germany captured 1,400,000 grt. of shipping while the services of the remaining 4,000,000 grt. which remained free was gladly accepted by Great Britain. Ships were bought, requisitioned and chartered and taken as prizes from an amazing variety of countries;

	1939/40		1940/41		1942		1943		1944		1945	
	No.	Losses	No.	Losses	No.	Losses	No.	Losses	No.	Losses	No.	Losses
Belgium	0	0	34	12	28	12	128	5	24	3	23	2
China	1	0	1	1	0	0	0	0	0	0	0	0
Denmark	4	0	43	15	30	13	30	4	30	1	26	4
Egypt	12	0	2	5	3	2	3	0	3	2	3	0
Estonia	0	0	3	0	3	0	3	0	2	1	2	0
Finland	0	0	4	1	4	3	4	0	2	2	2	0
France	1	0	59	20	49	13	59	9	43	20	35	8
Germany	11	0	10	10	12	2	12	0	11	1	11	0
Greece	36	1	156	58	127	51	108	24	97	6	95	2
Hungary	2	0	0	2	0	0	0	0	0	0	0	0
Italy	0	0	18	11	14	6	14	2	13	4	12	1
Latvia	0	0	2	1	1	1	1	0	1	0	1	0
Netherlands	0	1	147	48	139	48	124	23	157	7	133	1
Norway	13	0	180	59	162	40	143	19	153	9	141	4
Panama	0	0	21	4	20	5	20	0	18	2	18	2
Poland	3	1	13	2	16	0	19	0	18	1	18	0
Sweden	0	0	40	23	25	16	21	4	21	0	21	0
U.S.A.	15	0	73	29	42	31	31	11	26	5	26	0
Yugoslavia	1	0	34	10	24	14	21	4	22	3	23	0
TOTALS	99	3	840	311	698	257	640	106	641	67	590	24

Note: the number is the number of vessels in service on a given date and sometimes the losses which are for a whole year may exceed this. The losses total 5,600,000 deadweight tons of carrying capacity.

After the fall of France the Germans realised that there was no hope of Britain joining them against Russia and the onslaught on east coast ports began and all large tonnage shipping was barred, only coasting traffic being maintained against severe attacks by E-boats, U-boats, aircraft and the menace of the contact mine and the acoustic mine. The chaos in the west coast ports created delays which in turn led to a reduction in the utilitisation of shipping. Parcels of general cargo lay in warehouses awaiting an owner to claim and remove them. Government cargoes lay while officials decided where they should be sent. Awkward items lay until suitable transport could be found to take them away. It has been estimated that 10% more could have been imported if these delays had been ironed out in time. In 1941 Regional Port Directors were appointed with wide powers to operate the port facilities at maximum efficiency. For example, the Port Director for the Clyde collected barges and tugs from various parts of the country and introduced unloading over the side while at anchor at the Tail of the Bank, an innovation for the Clyde which relieved the congestion at the quaysides in Glasgow and Greenock, giving discharge rates of 760 tons per day against a normal 560 tons per day. Fortunately the air raids on the west coast ports, although intensive at the time, were not maintained. At Liverpool after one raid only 12 out of 130 berths were workable, but the port was reopened quickly and only a few thousand tons of imports were lost.

Another cause of lost carrying capacity was the ever mounting list of ships under repair and awaiting repair which at its worst represented over 10% of British controlled tonnage. Not only damage to ships by enemy action had to be attended to, but the blacking out of ships and reduction in navigational lights led to a rise in collisions and groundings. Over and above this was the problem of keeping in service the aged fleet of requisitioned foreign tonnage. However the need for standard tramps had been learned from the first world war and a steady stream of standard types (144, 145) were built both at home and overseas, see page 58.

A remarkable fact is that, despite the sinkings due to enemy action and the attendant loss of life, there was never any shortage of men to serve in the ships. Nearly 26,000 British seamen lost their lives in the 1,565 ships which were sunk, nearly half the number of men who formed their crews. It has been stated that there were approximately 145,000 British seamen serving at any one time during world war two. The loss of life was therefore about 18%, a higher percentage loss than any of the other fighting services.

PROBLEMS OVERSEAS: It was bad enough having to cope with these problems at home but once the war had spread to the Middle East and to the Far East further difficulties presented themselves. Harbours which had hitherto seen only occasional activity suddenly found themselves the centres of intense action. Freetown found itself a key convoy port, having to house, feed and water a population swollen by troops and naval personnel. Ships called there in large numbers, on one occasion 50 vessels entered the harbour in one day. When the war started in the Middle East, Alexandria, Port Said and Suez which in peacetime handled mainly passing traffic became the receiving ports for arms, equipment and supplies for the battle fronts. The laying of mines in the canal forced closure until they were swept, adding to the delay and chaos. As many as 117 ships were held up outside Suez while in the port unloading proceeded at a snail's pace: no fault of any one person, just the way things had developed.

Apart from military considerations immense quantities of civilian goods had been carried by British vessels in what were known as cross trades, i.e. cargoes carried between overseas countries. Coal for Egypt from Calcutta, grain and rice from Egypt to India and Ceylon, fertilisers (nitrate and phosphate) for Egypt from U.S.A. and South America, now that the European sources had been cut off. Withdrawal of British tramp steamers to serve the vital supply line to the British Isles meant that these cross trades more or less ceased. All during the war the threat of famine was ever present, only just kept at bay except in 1942 when a disastrous famine hit India. When Japan entered the war the sources of fertiliser, the islands in the Pacific, were lost and Australia had to be supplied from alternative areas. When Russia appealed to the West for arms and aid, a further strain was put on the British merchant shipping fleet as the notorious Arctic convoys got underway. Because of the attacks by German aircraft and submarines and the threat of surface attack the escorts for these convoys had to be out of proportion to the number of cargo ships in the group. As it happened most of the material bound for Russia came from America, carried by American vessels, and the number of British ships involved seldom exceeded six a month. Even this was a strain on Britain's resources as the ships had to be modified for the voyage with extra heating, strengthening against ice and heavy derricks to unload the vessels in the poorly equipped Russian ports. Also the supply of additional bunkers and provsions which the Russians could not, or would not, supply. A total of 216 British flag vessels sailed with cargo on the northern run to Russian ports.

MILITARY CONSIDERATIONS: The foregoing is a simplification of the highly complicated business of running the U.K. shipping industry during the war. However, every now and again, military operations placed a further strain on the already stretched resources of the Merchant Navy. The many needs of the Admiralty were met by requisitioning such ships as they required. Freighters to carry stores, colliers to supply coal to those units of the Fleet which still burned coal, vessels for conversion for service with the Combined Operation landings and finally in 1944 a large group of antiquated or

144. Top: *War Shamrock* 5174/17 was the first of the standard ships to be delivered in world war one. She was handed over by Harland & Wolff in August 1917. Middle: *Fort Vercheres,* on bare boat charter to the M.o.W.T and managed by the Hain S.S. Co, was completed in 1943 by United Shipyards, Montreal (424.5' x 57.2' x 34.9', 7,156 grt). She was built to a design based on the *Empire Liberty* and complemented the home production of 'Empire' ships such as *Empire Treasure,* completed in the same year by Lithgows Ltd, Port Glasgow. Note the full rig of derricks and paravane gear well seen in this picture of her trials on the Clyde.

Photos Top and Middle: W.Lind,
Bottom: Glasgow University.

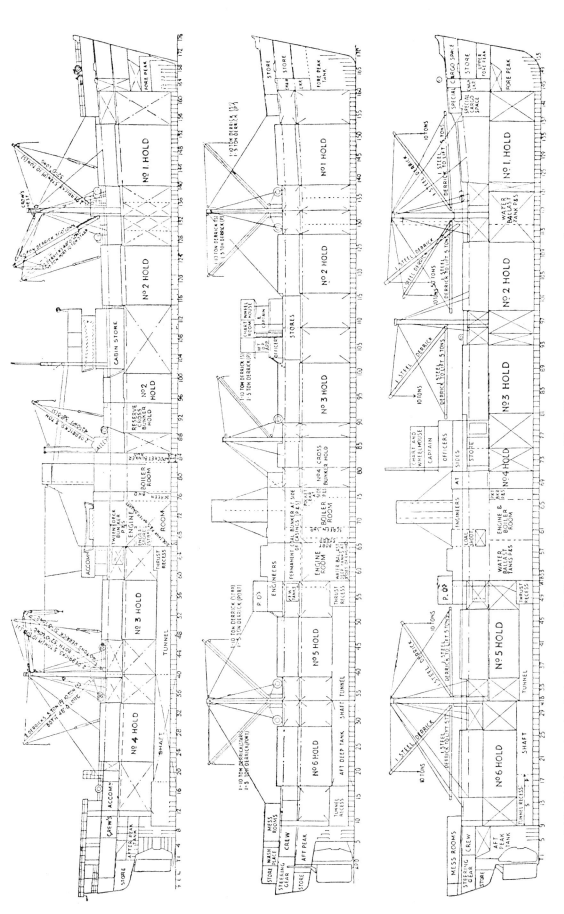

145. Various standard designs were built throughout the war. The 'Y' type (top), was among the first designs constructed followed by the 'B' type (centre and 98) designed for partial fabrication of which 41 were built. The 'A' type involving heavier prefabricated sections never got further than the drawing board. The 'C' type was also partially fabricated (65). They had a 'v' shaped transom stern and 17 of this type were built followed by 10 of the closely similar 'D' type with a slightly different poop.

Shipbuilding & Shipping Record, 1946

unserviceable vessels to be sunk as blockships to form a breakwater to protect the precious Mulberry Harbours constructed after the D-Day landings. They were mainly between 3,000 and 6,000 grt. and included such familiar names as:

Alynbank (147)	5157/25	M.o.W.T. (ex A. Weir, Glasgow).
Dover Hill	5815/18	Counties Ship Management Co, London
Flowergate	5156/11	C. Strubin & Co, London
Elswick Park	4188/20	Weidner, Hopkins & Co, Newcastle
Vera Radcliffe	5587/25	Evan Thomas Radcliffe & Co, Cardiff
Innerton (147)	5276/19	R. Chapman & Son, Newcastle
Maycrest	5923/13	Crest Shipping Co, London
Stanwell	5767/14	J.A. Billmeir & Co, London

During the first eight days of the Normandy invasion a large numer of merchant vessels were employed to carry essential supplies, and despite their size several deep-sea tramps, not in the hands of the Ministry of War Transport, were present, including some well-known names:

Baron Ruthven	3178/25	H. Hogarth & Sons, Glasgow
Bramhill	1834/23	Hudson S.S. Co, London
Demeterton	7345/44	R. Chapman & Sons, Newcastle
Gryfevale	4434/29	Andrew Crawford & Co, Glasgow.
Indian City	7079/44	Sir Wm.Reardon Smith & Sons, Cardiff
Langleecrag (147)	4909/29	Medomsley S.S. Co, Newcastle
Romney	5840/29	Bolton Steam Shipping Co, London.

1945. Now that the war was finished shipowners looked back over the six years of conflict and loss to find that about 75% of the pre-war tramps had been lost. In 1939 there were around 750 deep-sea tramps on the United Kingdom and Colonial registers. By the end of 1940, 179 had been sunk, followed by another 155 in 1941. 1942 saw the loss of 151 while the number dropped to 60 in 1943. By the end of the war a further 26 were lost bringing the total to 571. While many had been replaced it was estimated that only 350 tramps were left in private ownership by the end of the year.

1946. This was a reasonable year for the tramp shippers despite excessive delays in loading and unloading and high operating costs. One main hindrance to trade was the necessity to obtain official permits for voyages and these were frequently refused and the owner compelled by the Board of Trade to accept a directed freight. The coal miners in America went on strike and to obtain cargoes American owners turned to the grain trade, depriving British owners of one of their regular sources of income. To counter-balance there was a flood of goods from the U.S.A. to help rehabilitate Europe. The River Plate began to export heavily once more and took a lot of coal as the inward cargo. During the war the railways had been forced to burn maize as a fuel. The U.S.A. now had 51% of the world's tonnage including 2,000 vessels in their reserve fleet which were to be sold off.

1947. With home demand taking all the coal produced, outward cargoes of coal were unobtainable and tramps were forced to make long ballast voyages for their return cargo. Once again America was the all-important supplier of food and coal though Poland had also become a coal exporter. 600,000 tons of coal were shipped to the U.K. with British tonnage providing 50 vessels, America 9 and Canada 4 with another 6 from various other nations. The problem for Britain was that her ports were equipped for the export of coal and not for import. The result was that, while the continental ports could discharge 3,000 tons per day, British ports could only manage 1,000 tons per day. Grain from Australia also provided considerable business. India needed grain but it had to be bagged. As a result 60,000 tons of hessian had to be exported from India to the Argentine to make bags to hold the grain for shipment to India.

1948. Another satisfactory year as large numbers of vessels were required to carry rice from Egypt to India, coal from South Africa to India, grain from the Northern Range (U.S.A.), River Plate, Australia and the Black Sea. Japan required salt from the Mediterranean, coal from Calcutta, iron ore from Mormugao and potash from Stettin. Japan exported a considerable quantity of scrap metal. The American coal market was disappointing this year with strikes holding up production leaving little surplus for export, though good grain shipments helped compensate. There was surplus grain in the River Plate but with freights low and grain prices artificially high there were few takers. Many of the tramps carrying grain from Australia and the Black Sea had had to make their outward voyages in ballast.

147.

**TRAMPS AT THE
D–DAY LANDINGS,
1944.**

Alynbank 5157/25 was purchased from Bank Line by the Ministry of War Transport and sunk to make part of the breakwater for the Mulberry Harbours, (top). *Innerton* 3776/19 was also used in this way. *Innerton* was managed by R. Chapman & Son, Newcastle. A single deck steamer, she had been built by R. Ropner & Sons, Stockton. The photo shows her in pre–war days off Cape Town.

The shelter deck steamer *Langleecraig* 4901/29, took a more active part in the landings being one of the first tramps not in the hands of the Ministry of War Transport to arr–ive with vital supplies. She belonged to the Medomsley S.S. Co of Newcastle (F. Carrick & Co Ltd managers). She was one of the last ships built by Palmers yard and measured 416' x 55.8' x 25.2'.

Photos: I.W.Rooke collection.

1949. One of the main movements of cargo was Marshall Aid shipments for Europe, though the enforcement of the 50-50 rule was a nuisance. Some official control was still in force for certain voyages. There were a fair number of charters in cement, chalk, clay, and refined sugar, but coal was still to the fore, despite excessive prices. The Mediterranean and Black Sea were busy though freights were somewhat low. Ore from Bilbao was hit, freights dropping from 17/- to 10/6 per ton. Business was poor in the East with rates falling and shortage of water at Calcutta restricting the draught of vessels crossing the bar. There was a shortage of dollars which universally affected cargoes from the U.S.A. Few charters were settled for the Plate and liners took most of the grain cargoes. Liner traders chartered tramps as relief vessels for general cargo to Australia, but these were left without return cargo and had to seek cargo in India, thus depressing rates in those trades. Devaluation of the pound made British owners more competitive in the timber trades from the North American coasts. The Ministry of Transport was now permitting sale of ships over 15 years old.

1950. The tramping trades with India faced greatly reduced volume except in grain and flour from Australia, U.S.A. and the Plate. Kernels and manganese ores were offered as return cargo. Some of the tramp steamer owners had taken the opportunity of starting 'lines' on their own account instead of depending on time charters. There was a universal problem of delays in port, loading and unloading which was adversely affecting trade. Sugar and ore companies began to order specialist vessels for the carriage of their raw materials. The end of the year saw a sharp rise in tramp freight rates in response to a widespread demand for tonnage stimulated by outbreak of war in Korea. The United States Maritime Administration had been selling off war built ships and so far had disposed of 1,113 (218 of them to Britain).

1951. The boom in freight rates reached its peak in May. World-wide rearmament spurred on by the Korean war and stock-piling created a demand for boats which exceeded available shipping space and the United States began to release vessels from the moth-ball fleet to meet the world's needs. A big demand for grain pushed freights up, with a near famine in India needing heavy shipments from the U.S.A., from both the Gulf and the Pacific coast. As a result a shortage of shipping space was created in the ore and phosphate trades which pushed rates up: 46/6 for pyrites from Huelva rose to 75/-. Trade with South Africa was adversely affected by internal transport problems resulting in a drop in goods available for the tramp steamers. Time chartering was again 'lively' this year.

Shippers had a difficult time because of excessive demands on tonnage: 800,000 tons of grain to be shipped in an agreement between the U.K. and Russia. Up to 2,000,000 tons of coal to be shipped from the U.S.A. to the U.K. A demand for timber from the Pacific coast of North America called for ships to be sent in ballast from wherever they were available. American ships had to be chartered even though their rates were twice British rates.

1952. "The spectre of another shipping depression has haunted tramp owners throughout 1952". Throughout the world countries were trying to cut back on imports and many others were unable to offer return cargo, thus tramps were making frequent ballast voyages in search of homeward cargo. The general cargo trade slumped and with it the time charter of tramps. Freights fell; grain from India to the U.K. from 192/6 a ton to 165/-. U.S. coal fell from 79/6 to 24/- a ton. Late in the year another famine scare in the East created a demand for grain from Canada and the U.S.A. which pushed up rates from 75/- to 90/- a ton. For the first time since the war the River Plate was regaining its position as a grain exporter. It was difficult to keep old tramp steamers profitably employed and with the drop in requirements the U.S.A. returned some 500 ships to the moth-ball fleet.

1953. The North American grain markets were at a standstill but shipments of American coal continued to give employment. Imports of grain from other areas filled the silos and ships were held up waiting to unload. Some vessels were time chartered to act as floating granaries. The demand for grain was cut in the latter half of the year and tramps were deprived of one of their traditional cargoes. One of the major problems encountered was the lack of return cargoes which forced the tramps into carrying out frequent ballast voyages. Freights were down on 1952 and once more only modern tramping vessels were profitable. As a commentary on the state of the British tramp shipping industry, figures were quoted comparing pre-war with the present position in Cardiff, once the leading tramp steamer port. In 1938 there were 41 companies with 145 vessels totalling 528,847 grt, while at the end of 1952 only 23 companies remained with 63 ships totalling 268,301 grt.

1954. The U.K. was now exporting coal but at the same time was importing coal to keep the exports going; queer, but the tramp owners were not complaining. There was a drop in the domestic demand for coal in the U.S.A. and the Americans were selling their surplus coal at bargain prices. Britain's traditional role as a supplier of coal to Argentina was also threatened when Poland and Argentina began to exchange coal for grain. For the first half of the year there was little grain on the move but in the latter months Australia, U.S.A. and Canada had surplus grain available. As the year advanced the demand for tramp tonnage rose.

1955. This was generally a satisfactory year with good rates though inadequate handling facilities in ports and labour disputes slowed down turn-round in port. Ports in the U.K. were built for exporting coal not for import and it was not easy to unload the 10,000 dwt. Liberty type vessels. Delays in ports were also forcing liner companies into heavy chartering of tramp tonnage to avoid disruption of schedules. Experts calculated that fast merchantmen were losing as many as 3 to 4 voyages per year because of delays. Britain was now importing 12,000,000 tons of coal to meet the increasing home consumption and coal carriers were being chartered for years ahead - even as far as 1958. Most of the owners who obtained U.S. charters were content to send their vessels back in ballast for the next cargo. Good grain crops generally kept down the demand for grain, and in the East good crops of rice reduced the need for grain as a substitute. Specialised vessels were taking over the ore trade as they could make 20 voyages per annum against the 10 of the ordinary tramp.

1956. The Suez Canal was blocked as a result of the Anglo-French action against the Egyptian take-over and the enforced long haul round the Cape of Good Hope effectively reduced the tonnage to the Far East by a third. It was estimated that eventually the demand for U.S. coal for Europe would reach 50,000,000 tons per annum and many shippers were taking charters for up to 10 years to ensure availability of tonnage. Severe winter conditions affected European grain crops. Floods and bad weather in India and Pakistan ruined their grain economy. Even Russia was short of grain. This resulted in good competition for tramp tonnage. Ore shippers began to take out long term charters to make sure of capacity for their goods. Dock disputes throughout the world continued to force up running costs with delays in port while heavy taxation at home gave owners little incentive to build new ships.

1957. After the boom of 1956, 1957 was a poor year for the tramp owner. To safeguard against shortages due to the closure of the Suez Canal, European countries had built up their coal reserves. A mild winter left them with a large stockpile and a reduced demand for the tonnage which was on long term charter. Many ships were laid up but there would have been more had not Australia, which was suffering from drought, been unable to spare grain for India where there was near famine, creating a demand for grain from the west which provided much needed employment for the tramps.

1958. This year ended with about 5,500,000 gross tons of over capacity in the tramp market with a resultant drop in freight rates. Again one factor was a low demand in Europe for coal from the U.S.A. Oil tankers were being used for carrying grain for which there was a good market. War-built tonnage was proving more uneconomical to run and owners depended on higher rates than the market was offering. An interesting feature was the chartering of 140 ships by China for her coastal coal trade.

1959. Freight rates dropped even further this year. Nearly 3,500,000 gross tons of dry cargo shipping was laid up. India, Pakistan and Turkey bought a lot of war-built standard ships to create their own merchant fleets. Drought in Europe produced a demand for grain and again surplus tanker capacity took away much of the business from the tramps. Coal exports from the U.S.A. were down to half the 1956 figure. Many of the vessels involved in this trade had been specifically designed for the Trans-Atlantic coal trade. Experts predicted that from now on there would be a decline in tramp tonnage.

1960. A year of disappointment and frustration. An excess of tonnage meant that freight rates remained low. Grain demand in Europe was low and tramps were in competition with about 1,000,000 gross tons of tanker capacity which was regularly carrying grain. There was a welcome increase in the demand for ore and scrap metal.

1961. A fairly good year for the tramp owners helped by a demand from Japan for ore, scrap and grain. Even war-built ships could be operated at a profit. China and

Russia took 3 to 12 month charters on a large number of vessels. This year about 2,000,000 gross tons of tanker tonnage was engaged in the grain trade.

1962. A bad year for the tramp owners as freight rates dropped and running costs rose. Specialized bulk carriers were taking over the basic trades from the tramps which were forced to look for new outlets.

1963. A world-wide series of crop failures sparked off a heavy demand for grain shipments pushing rates up to levels which made any age of steamer profitable, lifting grain from the U.S.A., Canada, Argentina and Australia. A hard winter in Europe caused such a demand for oil that the tanker inroads into the grain trade virtually ceased.

1964. A fairly steady year without the usual wild fluctuations in freight rates. The older tramps were surviving because many ports could not accommodate bulk carriers. Although China was chartering heavily there were signs that she was building up her own national fleet. Large amounts of grain, coal, sugar, fertilizer and scrap were on the move but much of this was carried by specialised vessels. However, the River Plate trade was still reliant on 'Liberty' size vessels.

1965. A reasonably profitable year despite tankers encroaching once more into the grain trade.The Russians now had a fleet of their own, carrying large quantities of goods to meet their demands, but China was still chartering; 100 vessels this year. At least another 100 tramps were chartered to liner companies with a preference for large carriers (10,000-14,000 tons). 'Liberty' ships were still operating to the smaller ports despite higher insurance rates on them. About 100 were chartered to carry ore to Japan.

1966. Freight rates dropped again affected by a world recession and the number of bulk carriers in service carrying grain from the U.S.A. to Europe at low rates. Despite the experts who predicted the demise of the 'Liberty' ships they were still required to service the smaller ports. Ore imports to the U.K. were small but Japan again was taking large quantities mainly using 'Liberties', about 130 of them.

1967. The Israelis and the Arab States went to war and the Suez Canal was closed once more. This took most of the tankers out of the grain trade leaving the dry cargo tramps a free hand. With delays in port and interference with crews, charterers declined to enter into contracts with the Chinese. Freight rates remained stable and profits were moderate. Bulk carriers took more business away from smaller tramps.

About 100 years have passed since the 'Diary' started and we have seen how the pattern of prosperity and hardship was repeated over and over again. For years the experts had been predicting the demise of the tramp ship. In the case of the steam tramp their forecast had now come true. In 1937 the Shipping World Year Book listed the names of 102 British tramp shipping companies which owned fleets of 2 or more vessels. Following these names through the Shipowners' appendices of Lloyd's Register we can see how rapidly the number of companies and ships in the tramp shipping industry fell away. The figures illustrate also the demise of the steam tramp:

Year	Number of Companies	Number of Ships			
		steam	motor	bulk carrier	total
1937	102	715	77	–	792
1956	60	254	139	–	393
1966	45	20*	187	7	214
1973	30	3	110	23	136

* Of these only two were war-built. Bear in mind that these are not the total numbers of tramp ships in the British Mercantile Marine but only those managed by the companies in the original list, or those that were still in existence on the later dates.

The final few years of the 'Diary' saw the usual fluctuations of the freight rates as shown by the highest and lowest figures quoted below from the maritime press:

Rates per ton carried.	Highest	Lowest
Grain-River Plate to U.K.	188/6 (1956)	53/9 (1959)
Coal-Cardiff to Italy	46/- (1957)	17/6 (1960)
–Hampton Roads to U.K.	116/6 (1956)	16/- (1962)
Ore-Huelva to U.K.	64/- (1956)	28/- (1952)
–Marmagoa to Continent	193/- (1956)	24/8 (1966)
Timber-Canada to U.K.	510/- (1952)	165/-(1959) [Pit props per fathom].

In 1958 it was estimated that a 'Liberty' ship on the trans-Atlantic coal run to Europe could not operate profitably at rates below 40/- per ton. Bulk carriers needed about 25/- per ton to be profitable, and so the reign of the traditional steam tramp ended.

Index

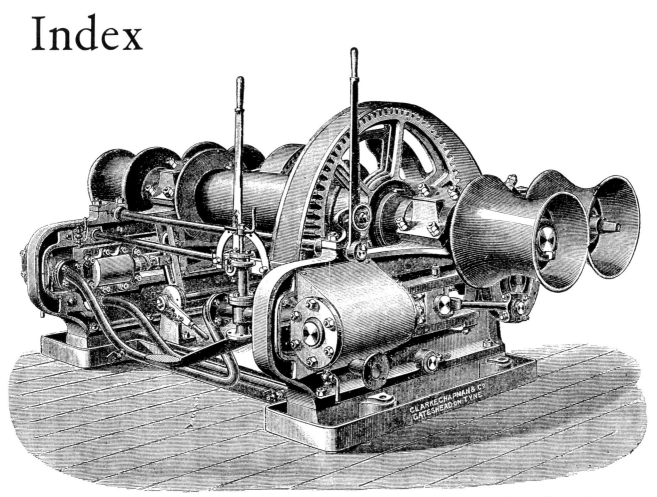

151. Horizontal steam cargo winch by Clarke, Chapman & Co of Gateshead, the leading suppliers of deck machinery. The twin cylinder design using Stephenson's link motion remained practically unchanged until the end of the steam era. Most offered two speeds via gears unlike Taylor's winch (5) which was single speed. Manufacturers recommended the horizontal type, but some early steam ship owners preferred to save deck space and use ones with the cylinders canted up (26). The Engineer 1882.

SHIPS

SHIPOWNERS & BUILDERS

CHARTER-PARTY.

London
~~LIVERPOOL,~~ *5 August* 1910.

IT is this day mutually agreed between *Messrs. The Helmsdale S. S. Co. Ld.*
of ~~Glasgow~~ Owners of the screw Steam Ship called the
"Devonshire" (of *3650* Tons gross Register, and
2336 Tons nett Register, horse power, provided with Steam Winches, Condenser, and Lloyd's Certificates
for Hull and Machinery, classed *100 A. 1.*, the Builders' Displacement Scale of which shows that on
23 feet *1* inches, Lloyd's Summer Draught, the deadweight capacity is *5880* Tons *for cargo & bunker coal*
capacity on ——— feet ——— inches is ———————Tons, inclusive of bunkers which have capacity to contain
about 28 ~~Tons of Coal,~~ her average speed *West Welsh* *being about nine* knots upon a
consumption of *1* Tons of ~~best~~ Coal per day, ~~which the Owners guarantee to maintain during the currency of~~
~~this Charter~~), and the *Liverpool Brazil and River Plate Steam Navigation*
Co. Ld. of Liverpool, Charterers, as follows, viz.:

1. The said Owners agree to let, and the said Charterers agree to hire the said Steam Ship for the term of *one*
round voyage ~~(or, in the Charterer's option, until the completion~~
~~of any voyage commenced at any time before, but not terminated until after the expiry of the said period),~~ commencing on
the *27th* day of *August* the then being placed at the disposal of the Charterers, in their loading
berth, in such Dock or at such Wharf or Place in *Tyne* or at other port in the United Kingdom ~~on the Continent~~
such readiness on the 20th August 1910
where she may always safely lie afloat, as the Charterers may direct, (failing which the Charterers shall have the option of
cancelling this Charter), she being tight, staunch, strong, and every way fitted for the service, having water ballast, steam
winches, and donkey boiler, with capacity to run all steam winches at one and the same time, with full complement of
officers, seamen, engineers and firemen for a vessel of her tonnage, her bottom newly painted, and her machinery in perfect
order ; to be employed in any lawful trades between *the United Kingdom &/or the Continent of Europe*
&/or South America &/or the United States in any order, with cargo or in ballast, and having liberty to
call at any port or ports for orders or cargo, or other purposes, as the Charterers or their Agents shall direct. The
Charterers shall have the option of employing the vessel in any other trade, they paying the extra insurance which the
Owners may thereby incur upon the Vessel. St. Vincent, Cape Verde Islands, shall be considered a port of call for
orders to proceed to the United States, or elsewhere.

2. The Owners shall provide and pay for all oils, paint and stores for the Vessel, and for all the provisions and wages,
and consular shipping and discharging fees, and all other charges appertaining to the Captain, Officers, Engineers,
Firemen, Crew and Riggers ; shall pay for the insurance on the Vessel, also for all engine-room stores ; shall provide and
pay for all the gear, tackle, slings, *up to three tons* blocks, rope, and appliances which the Charterers may require for loading and discharging
the cargo and coal, also lanterns for night work, and shall maintain the Vessel in a thoroughly efficient state in hull and
machinery for the service. The steamer shall not come on hire until she is fitted with the gear, tackle, rope, and
appliances above referred to, and if she be delivered to the Charterers on a Sunday or holiday, or later than 7 o'clock a.m.
on any other day, hire shall not be paid for that day, nor for the following day or days if not working days.

3. The Charterers shall provide and pay for Coals, Port Charges, Pilotages, Agencies, Commissions, and all other
charges not appertaining to the working or efficiency of the steamer.

4. The Charterers shall pay for the use and hire of the Vessel at the rate of £ *800* sterling
per calendar month, and at and after the same rate for any part of a month ; the hire to continue from the time specified
for *commencing* ~~terminating~~ the Charter until her delivery to the Owners (unless lost, the date of loss to be that upon which she is last
seen or heard of proceeding upon her voyage) at any port in the United Kingdom, or on the Continent of Europe, at the *Havre/Hamburg range*
Charterers' option ; payment whereof shall be made in Cash month by month on completion of each month's hire, the
account being made up voyage by voyage ; and in default of such payment or payments as herein are specified the Owners
shall have the right of withdrawing the Steamer from the service of the Charterers, without prejudice to any claim the
Owners may otherwise have on the Charterers in pursuance of this Charter. In computing the hire for part of a month
the days shall be taken as fractions of a month of thirty-one days. ~~The Charterers shall have liberty to commence a fresh~~
~~voyage, on the same terms as are herein specified, at any time before the conclusion of the period for which she is hereby~~
~~Chartered.~~

5. The cargo or cargoes shall be loaded and/or discharged in any dock, or at any wharf, place or anchorage, that the
Charterers or their Agents may direct, where the vessel can always safely lie afloat. ~~If the vessel be detained in her~~
~~loading and/or discharging or prevented from sailing by the strike or lock-out of workmen, lumpers, or coalheavers, by ice~~
~~or fog, taking in or discharging ballast or cargo, and if the Charterers or Shippers are prevented from having their goods~~
~~sent alongside the vessel by any of these causes, or in consequence of the navigation of the rivers or canals being impeded~~
~~by ice, fog or flood, the Charterers shall only pay half hire for the time lost.~~

6. The draught of water sanctioned by Lloyd's Committee for this vessel is—Summer, *23* feet *1*
inches, mean ; Winter, ——— feet ——— inches, mean, in salt water ; to which draughts the Owners
authorise the Charterers to load the vessel, ~~and upon which draughts they guarantee her to carry respectively~~
~~and~~ ——— ~~tons deadweight, all told.~~

7. The whole reach, burthen, and passenger accommodation of the ship shall be at the Charterers' disposal, reserving
only proper and sufficient space for ship's officers, crew, tackle, apparel, furniture, provisions, and stores. Cargo and/or
coals and/or cattle may be taken on deck and cargo carried in the peaks at the Charterers' risk, so far as the same do not
endanger the safety of the vessel. The Charterers shall have liberty to remove stanchions for the purposes of stowage,
replacing them at their expense.

8. The expense of loading and discharging shall be borne by the Charterers, but the loading, stowage, and
discharging shall be under the control of the Master, and the owners shall be responsible for the same. Ballast and
dunnage as required shall be found by the Charterers.